HEROES
WITHOUT
GLORY
Some Goodmen
of the Old West

for his pen, and the result is a most remarkable and entertaining portrait gallery.

Jack Schaefer, author of many note-
worthy stories and novels about the West,
was borr in Cleveland, Ohio, in 1907, and
studied ᵗ Oberlin College and Columbia
University. A journalist by profession, he
has worked as a reporter for the United
Press, an editorial page writer for the
Norfolk *Virginian-Pilot* and the Baltimore
Sun, and as editor for the New Haven
Journal-Courier. His first book, *Shane*,
which appeared in 1949, is now used in
many school literature courses. Among his
latest works are *Company of Cowards*
(1957), *The Kean Land and Other Stories*
(1959), and *Monte Walsh* (1963). He and
his wife Louise live in the midst of vast
range spreads in New Mexico, within driving distance of Santa Fe and Los Alamos.

Also by Jack Schaefer

HEROES WITHOUT GLORY

——◦✦◦——

Some Goodmen
of the Old West

——◦✦◦——

Jack Schaefer

HOUGHTON MIFFLIN COMPANY BOSTON

The Riverside Press Cambridge

1965

Contents

Introduction

THE cult of the old-time western badmen flourishes like the green bay tree. Some natural perversity in too many an otherwise amiable human animal aims his morbid interest at the outlaw, the renegade, the killer — particularly when the unpleasant aspects of such are adorned with big hats and an assortment of Colt and Winchester period hardware and their equally unpleasant roles are played out against a backdrop of the great open spaces. Then comes a feeling of guilt, of shame at this interest in the asinine and the despicable, which is often translated into an effort to gild the stinkweed.

The gilders — sentimentalizers, glamorizers — had their heyday in the latter decades of the last century and the early decades of the present century. The more shameless and flamboyant among them infested the *Police Gazette* and the dime novel. Others of them published in seemingly respectable hard-cover form. They splattered the gilt so effectively that whole batches of onetime schoolboys who hid forbidden writings behind geogra-

phies still cherish notions of the badmen that bear about
as much relation to reality as a snowball does to the few
drops of water it makes when melted. Their descendants
are still with us, still publishing. No longer quite so
effectively.

They are outnumbered nowadays by the debunkers,
the sober serious scholars who publish sober serious works
dedicated to the quaint new thesis that perhaps the badmen really were bad. And overrated. Much paper and
much ink is used to demonstrate that this badman and
that badman did not kill quite as many people (even
with Indians and Mexicans included) as the glamorizers
claimed they did, that they were not as debonair and gallant and courageous as the sentimentalizers painted them,
that most of them were, in simple fact, rather stupid,
often drunken parasites on the rest of society who attracted interest merely because of the violence and gunpowder associated with them.

No doubt that is a salutary reaction. But it is still an
example of devotion to the badmen, only in a temporarily
reversed direction. The number of writers and readers
worshiping the badmen, from the one perspective or the
other, and the amount of research and publishing lavished on them are downright startling. Books about the
West, primarily nonfiction, have increased rapidly in re-
cent years. The names which occur and recur most frequently, in titles and in subject matter, are those of the
badmen. About ten years ago, for a single small example,
a reputable state university press launched a Western
Frontier Library, a series of reprints of western books
regarded by the editors as worth preservation and reissue.
The first four, the entire output of the project for its first
two years, were books about badmen. More of the same

have since been liberally scattered through the later additions to the list. The cult flourishes, unwithered and unpruned.

The ardent cultist who turns up a new item about a badman acts as if he has found a nugget of pure gold and rushes immediately into print. One item justifies an article; two or three a complete book. The scope of the continuing movement is suggested by three current books sometimes found side by side on bookstore shelves. The first is devoted entirely to a bibliography of the multitudinous writings about a single badman, Billy the Kid. The second represents the debunkers; methodically and with scholarly precision it punctures most of the myths about that same Billy. The third is a package of contemporary gilt, a fictional essay depicting what a noble soul the buck-toothed Billy might have become if Pat Garrett had not shot him and he had lived on under a new name to let the essential sweetness and light of his character and disposition flower in new fields.

There can be no valid complaint. In this era of the affluent society and the new leisure, people need activities to fend off boredom and fill in time. One puzzles over double-acrostics, another is a do-it-yourself home carpenter, yet another collects stamps. The badman cultist pores over old papers trying to determine whether this or that gunman or bank robber was left- or right-handed, had a mole on his chin or his nose, stood here or stood there at such-and-such a moment, and really shot so-and-so in a daring head-on long-walk duel or did so with buckshot in the back from behind the bulwark of a rain barrel. It is a good substitute for playing bridge or staring at a television screen. The sole trouble is that it seems plain silly.

It is silly because the badmen of the old West, those

with careers of sufficient length or sufficient events to give
real substance and of sufficient flavor to give some basis
for legend, were so few and far between that both glamorizers and sober chroniclers have to keep reworking the
same long-since-stale material — and in so doing give a
lopsided view of the period and place they are discussing.
It is silly because writing and reading about the badmen
so soon becomes monotonous, is invariably limited, repe-
titious. Bank robberies, holdups, horse-stealings, gun-
fights, getaways — occasionally a hanging. Then what?
Simply more of the same. Differences in details, but the
same patterns constantly repeated.

It becomes even sillier when the discovery is made, the
discovery the gilders dodge and the debunkers are too
busy debunking to pursue, that the badmen not only
were pikers, amateurs, often bunglers, in the very things
for which they supposedly arouse interest — but were
outnumbered and outclassed right across the board in
skill at gunplay, in courage and hardihood and endurance, in gallantry of action, in flavor of personality, in
saltiness of character, in excitement and variety of adventures.

Outclassed. Right across the board. By the goodmen.

Not the good men, who alas have the habit of being
dull. The goodmen, as opposed to the badmen. Independent individuals who broke outside the mold of routine
living as definitely as ever did the badmen and did this
in infinitely more varied and more admirable ways. Men
who left records of achievement or attempts at achievement beyond that of relieving other humans of money
and/or lives and need no dubious aura of outlawry to
make them worth remembrance. Men who played out
their roles on the side, not necessarily of the law because

the law was often a nasty muddle in the old West, but of
clean consciences and a reasonable respect for the rights
and persons of their fellow men. The authentic annals
of the West are full of them.

Shucks, the average sweat-soaked flea-ridden cowhand
bringing a trail herd up to a rail head or the northern
ranges had more straight courage, the steady enduring
brand, faced obstacles and danger and death more often
and more gallantly than any badman on record — and
did this day after day without fuss or feathers as part of
his job. The best that can be said for the badmen is that
a few of them were fair cowhands — before they went
bad.

Look further into that epic migration, the opening of
the West, one of the great movements of human history,
the coming of a new people into a new region, colliding
with new conditions and with the native peoples — at
the wide variety of them and the vast sweep of their activities, the multiple varied ways in which they wrung
some meaning for their lives out of the harsh facts of
existence — and the badmen fade away, almost out of
sight, few and isolated clinical cases of regional hoodlum-
ism that merit at most only brief tiny-print footnotes as
insignificant curiosities.

Outclassed. By the goodmen. Five, ten, twenty, thirty
to one.

They came from everywhere, the goodmen. Western
goodmen in that each, in his own way, took on some imprint of the raw rough violent geography of the West and
the raw rough violent conditions of the opening and settling years of the West and each, again in his own way,
left some mark, whether of success or failure, upon his

time and place. Some of them were born in the West, part of it, so to speak, by natural inheritance. More, many more, inevitably in the very nature of the movement, came from elsewhere, from the eastern states, from Europe, from far places around the world. They spilled out over a continental expanse that dwarfed all previous experience. They confronted a new environment of a kind to bring out their qualities, throw these into sharp relief. They were as varied, in ancestry, in background, in education, in appearance, in activities, as the vast land they strode, but they had two things in common. One was courage, consistent, lifelong, unquestioning and unquestioned, not always and perhaps not even often that of the flamboyant powder-burning kind but that of the head uplifted, the eyes forward, of resiliency in the spirit, of the unflinching uncringing response in the face of whatever confronted them. And the other was a sure instinct, beyond law, sometimes cutting across law, for decency and honesty and carrying-your-own-weight in the world.

Not all of them stayed in the West. Some left for one reason and another. But the imprint was on them. A surprising number of those who did leave always wanted to return, intended to return. A few died trying to return. The imprint was on them. They had been branded for life. Whether they stayed or whether they left, whether their careers were suddenly short or stubbornly long, they were western goodmen. They belong to the American West.

True enough, it is sometimes difficult to sort them out. Borderline cases occur in which a shift of perspective can bounce a man from one category to the other. In the

opening and settling years the West was not so much lawless in the sense of laws being violated as simply lacking
in law — and then, when getting some, suffering from
the attempted application of laws framed in the East or
based on experience in the East which did not make
sense under western conditions. A revealing history of
the area could be written solely in terms of eastern-bred
land laws and concepts of water rights finally being hammered into some semblance of agreement with western
geography. Think of the Homestead Act, based on the
true-in-the-East notion that a family could make a living
on 160 acres of land — land which, in much of the arid
West, could barely support a lean coyote, a few jackrab-
bits, a sidewinder or two, and a family of horned toads
to the whole section.

Again, at times, there was too much law, too many sets
of it not jibing with each other: local law vs. territorial
law, town law vs. county law, early state law vs. federal
law. Instances can be found of a marshal and his deputies
opposing a sheriff and his deputies, each group regarding
the other as lawless, both ready to pull guns on each
other. Drawing a straight line down through such a situation is a tough proposition.

Yet again, a man might be rated by his own contempo-
raries both a badman and a goodman. A warrant might
be out for his arrest in one town at the very time he was
serving, and ably, as a peace officer in another town . . .
And who was and who was not a rustler in the wild and
hairy days when the big herds running loose and unbranded and past counting in Texas after the marketless
years of the Civil War were being shunted north and the
cattle empire was taking the territories and, a little later,

when snatching cow critters back and forth across the Rio Grande was an American and a Mexican pastime akin to the coup-counting horse-takings of the Plains Indians in their prime? Many a rancher who got his own start by cavalier treatment of all stray calves within reach of his rope would be the one to howl louder than his neighbors when some enterprising cowboy tried to follow his example.

Then, too, there is the problem of viewpoint, so readily deflected by loyalty to or sympathy with one side or the other in a given set of circumstances. It is easy to forget that, in those confused and confusing times, in such things as feuds between townsmen and rangemen, ranchers and nesters, cattlemen and sheepmen, fencemen and wire cutters, gringos and greasers, there might have been a goodman or two on each side of any particular conflict. This is emphatically true in regard to the Indian Wars, to the larger conflict of two ways of life, the white and the red, disputing the half of a continent. There were goodmen of both colors and the fact that they faced each other, weapons in hands, intent on each other's lives, does not in itself swing the balance either way. In this respect each man is an island unto himself. He is a separate individual to be assessed as such, in terms of his own individual background and situation. Motives and character, the manner of life in everyday affairs and in the long run of living, the choices made at the crucial moments, the habitual attitude toward existence — these are the determining factors whatever the accidents of birth and race and circumstance.

There is only one honest approach: to shake eastern notions out of your head, take the mixed-up, scrambling, lusty, dusty, deadly, dirty, superb old west on its own

terms, tot up the known whole of a man's career, and try
to arrive at an impartial opinion. And even so, borderline cases remain.

There was nothing borderline, not after they hit their
strides, about the badmen favored by the cultists: the
Billy the Kids, the Jameses, the Daltons, the Doolins, the
Wes Hardins, the Youngers, the Clay Allisons, the Kid
Currys, the Butch Cassidys, the Muriettas, the Henry
Plummers, the Black Jacks of numerous surnames. And
there was nothing borderline about the goodmen discussed in this book. They were goodmen all and others
like them turn up by the dozens when you start looking
for them. Not surprising. The American West would not
have been explored, opened, exploited, settled in just a
few generations if goodmen had not been plentiful.

Those discussed here are only a corporal's guard, a
handful selected almost at random as reasonably diver-
sified representatives of their breed. The big historic
names, which really belong in another category, and the
relatively few goodmen (like Jim Bridger and Kit Carson
and Wyatt Earp and old Hugh Glass and pretty-boy
Custer) who have been popularized and even glamorized
almost to match the badmen, are not included. They
have had their share of attention, some of them more
than merited. The attempt here is simply to suggest the
kind of men waiting for the kind of treatment, the attention and the research, that has been and still is being
lavished on the badmen and to indicate something of the
diversity and wide-ranging interest they can offer the
student of western history.

They are the men who set the real flavor of the old
West. Some of them with guns hotter-barreled and more

deadly than those of the badmen. More of them in quieter more enduring ways as varied as human activities and aspirations anywhere in the world.

One day back in the trail-driving years three strange apparitions appeared in a wagon at the Red Fork Ranch stopping-place on the old Chisholm Trail. Three Englishmen clad in knickerbockers, golf stockings, low boots, wool shirts and caps. They carted an amazing amount of luggage. Their leader gave his name as Wilson. *Burke's Peerage* would have revealed that he was Sir Raymond Robert Tyrwhitt-Wilson, 4th Baronet of Stanley Hall, Bridgenorth, England. He and companions had been seeing the rest of the world and now the United States and they wanted to stay a while and observe the cattle country.

They were something weird and wonderful in that cowboy land. Their costumes were startling enough. But they refused to ride, except in the wagon — and that in a region where men rode, even in town, just to cross the street. These men walked, long walks before breakfast, then all the way to whatever they wanted to watch that day. They had a positive mania for bathing. And they did not talk straight lingo; they used "langwidge."

When they were ready to depart eastward by train they went into the town of Caldwell a day early to see the cowboy in that environment. They saw him, numbers of him, assembled for the sport of seeing them, escorting their wagon into town to the accompaniment of wild cavortings on horseback and much usage of ammunition. A reception committee, constantly growing, continued to escort them everywhere about town, particularly into saloons where somehow the drinks were invariably on the visitors. They were told endless tall tales, some of which they actually believed, in particular the one about snipe hunting. Inevitably a snipe hunt was organized. Towards evening they were escorted in the wagon far out of town, down the Trail, over Bluff Creek. They were handed game bags to fill and stationed well apart in the dropping darkness and told to wait while the mounted escorts would round up the delectable snipe and drive them towards their shotguns.

Along about the time the uproarious cowboys had absorbed all they could at the Caldwell bars to which they had promptly adjourned (with the wagon), Lord Wilson and companions realized what had happened. They managed to locate each other in the dark and started tramping towards town. On the way they talked over their experiences with these uncouth and almost incomprehensible Americans and arrived at an approximation of the truth. These cow-country cavorters regarded them as fair game, easy marks, probably as soft-skinned faint-hearted lily-livered sissified dudes. Well, maybe they were dudes — in the local terms. But not precisely that kind of dudes. Striding along in the dark, damp from wading across Bluff Creek, Sir Robert Wilson made the simple elemental decision, claiming the privilege as leader of the party, that he would not leave until he had talked to these blasted Americans in the one "langwidge" they seemed to understand.

It was morning when they reached town. They went straight to the building that passed for a hotel and to their room. Sir Robert Wilson unpacked his favorite rifle, loaded it carefully, and strode out into the middle of the dusty main street. He shed his British dignity and began to shout. He informed the town of just what he thought of it and everyone currently in it. He surprised himself inventing epithets and insulting comments. He invited anyone who disliked his remarks to come out and settle the argument with gunpowder. He was heard very well but no one accepted the invitation. He invited all within hearing to come at him en masse. No response. He threw down his rifle and invited them to come try it with fists. Still no response.

How could there be any response? There were men keeping quietly out of sight up and down that street who would have cheerfully stepped out if for no other reason than to see if this dude really knew how to handle the fancy gun in his hands. There were men who would have joyfully tied into him with their fists just to work up an appetite for lunch. But they were plumb ashamed of themselves. They had made the mistake of misjudging a man on the basis of silly clothes and polite manners. They had let him reach again and again into his pocket without returning the compliment. They had this coming. The more vigorously he denounced them in choice new phrases in that cultured voice, the better they liked it and the prouder they were of him. They would have ripped the hide off anyone who tried to interfere with that rooster making his play out there in the middle of the street. They waited until he had blown off enough steam and retired to the hotel. Then a delegation called on him to apologize and to suggest a new round of the saloons with hands going into American pockets. When he and his companions boarded the train they had one of the heartiest send-offs of a lifetime.

Those hard-bitten trail men knew. They knew that knickerbockered gamecock had the makings. Let him stay around a while in that wide open country and have the wind and the dust soak in some and learn to fork a horse, western style, and he would make a goodman with the best of them. In the sayings of a land where a man's life often depended on the caliber of the man siding him, he'd do to ride the river with, he'd do to take along.

HEROES
WITHOUT
GLORY
Some Goodmen
of the Old West

James Capen Adams

OCTOBER 20, 1807 — OCTOBER 25, 1860

NEW ENGLAND produced him, this James Capen Adams, but the West gave him the scope he needed.

He came of an honest family, respected by its neighbors, which had been New England, solid Yankee, for generations. He was born not far out of Boston itself, in the little town of Medway; raised there and raised regionally right, with some years of stern copybook schooling then apprenticeship to a respectable trade, shoemaking. He grew up to have the wiry body, all bone and sinew, and the strong features with prominent nose and sharp eyes so common to that hard-scrabble stony land. Even the surname, the Adams, was exactly right, as New England as Thanksgiving and hard cider.

But the Capen slipped in there somehow, something offbeat, suggesting he might break out of the mold and cut a few capers all his own.

He tried, once, in his youth. He made shoes, good dependable New England shoes, until he was twenty-one,

his own man, then promptly threw aside his pegging awl
and hired out as an animal trapper with a show
company. For several years he hunted through upper
New England, trapping for skins and trapping alive the
wilder animals that could still be found there, foxes and
wildcats and a stray wolf and even an occasional panther. He found this a much more congenial occupation
than making shoes. Then he made the mistake of trying
to discipline a backsliding once-supposedly-tamed Bengal
tiger for his employers and was so severely mauled that
for months it was doubtful he would survive. For a long
time thereafter he could barely hobble around. Eventually he could take care of himself again — by sitting at
a bench and making shoes.

Shoes he made for the next fifteen years. He sat at his
bench and stitched and hammered and thought long
thoughts and his body knit back into tough durable
shape. He made good shoes. He acquired his own shop in
Boston, a wife and a daughter, and considerable savings.

Fifteen years. He was past forty now. A proper New
Englander, properly industrious, successful, plying his
trade. The nonsense had been clawed out of him by fate
in the form of a Bengal tiger. Not quite. He took a flyer
in the western market, put most of his savings into a shipment of boots and shoes and sent this to the frontier
outfitting outpost of St. Louis — just in time for the entire shipment to be destroyed in a big fire there.

No more of that. He was through with shoes and shoemaking. He threw aside his pegging awl for the second
and final time. He left his wife and daughter settled in
Boston and went west with the first gold rush, a '49er,
overland, by the southern route through the Southwest
to California. He tried mining, tried trading, tried ranch-

ing. He made money and he lost money. In three years he failed three times, dropping from prosperity to poverty through speculations of his own and through the villainy of other men.

No more of that either. In the summer of 1852 he took stock of himself and his situation. He was disgusted with the world in general and dissatisfied with himself in particular. Deliberately he turned his back upon the society of his fellows and determined to make the wilderness his home and wild beasts his companions. He was doing, in his own way, in the western style, what another New Englander named Henry David Thoreau had done back in Massachusetts by Walden Pond only a few years before.

James Capen Adams, accent on the Capen, onetime shoemaker and shopkeeper, forty-five years of age, headed into one of the then wildest sections of the Sierra Nevada in a wagon drawn by two oxen. He had a few tools, a few blankets, some extra clothing. He had an old Kentucky rifle that threw thirty balls to the pound of lead, a Tennessee rifle that threw sixty, a Colt revolving pistol, and a pair of bowie knives. He had enough.

He picked a small upland valley about forty miles northwest of Yosemite and made friends with the Indians thereabouts. He shot game for them and they helped him build a shelter and make hay for his oxen and taught him to tan deerskins. From these, with the skill born of his trade, he made what would be his invariable costume the rest of his life — fringed buckskin jacket and pantaloons and moccasins. He had a full beard now, graying fast, and he usually wore a round cap made of untanned deerskin, lined with rabbit fur, and with a dangling fox-tail ornament.

When the cold came, the Indians left for the lower levels and he stayed in his upland valley, alone and content. He did not see another human being all that fall and winter. What he did see, among other wild-beast companions, was the monarch of the mountains, the great grizzly bear.

The California grizzly was numerous then, not even started toward the swift extinction of later decades. And this was almost untouched wilderness. He saw grizzlies, many of them in the fall, a rare few in the winter, many again in the early spring. There was respect on both sides. Between them, the bears and the man, they observed a sort of truce. He kept out of their way and they in turn did not bother him.

He stayed in his log shelter during the bad weather and tramped long miles through his wilderness during good weather and shot small game for his meat and always he watched and studied his wild-beast companions, particularly the great grizzlies. He became rich in knowledge of them and their ways.

For a fall and a winter and on into the spring James Capen Adams lived alone in his upland valley of the Sierras, content with himself and happy as a king.

No man can ever quite escape his background. Adams wore western buckskins — but beneath them was New England woolen underwear.

He went into the western mountains disgusted with the world and dissatisfied with himself and he found contentment and happiness there. But with the first hints of warm weather came the itch of that underwear, the nag of his ingrained New England conscience. There was no *purpose* to his mountain life — none that the dour puritanical tradition of New England would recognize. He was not *doing anything* in the accepted meaning of the phrase. He was not engaged in a gainful occupation, making money, plying a trade.

Then New England itself came to visit him in the person of his brother William.

This brother William had traveled to California not long after brother James. Being an industrious man not given to speculations and the long chance and trust in his fellows, he had acquired a fortune in the northern gold camps. Ready to return home with it as a proper seafaring or land-faring New Englander should, he had by mere accident heard of brother James's failures and present whereabouts. He wanted to take brother James back home, set him up in the shoemaking business again, make a respectable New Englander of him once more.

No. Brother James was in no mind to leave his mountains.

Practical men, these Adams brothers, able to face facts and make a decision. Brother James had another trade, one practiced briefly before a Bengal tiger mauled him. They hit upon an ingenious partnership plan and in proper New England style drew up contract articles and signed them. Brother James would become a professional hunter for skins and furs and a trapper of wild animals alive and would ship them to Boston. Brother William would dispose of them to museums and animal shows and menageries.

Brother William departed eastward. He had done his duty, had recalled brother James at least partway to respectability, to plying a trade.

And all unknowing had pointed him toward becoming Grizzly Adams.

*

All the man's life to date had been a waiting and a preparation for his new career. A new-old trade cut to his individual last. A business purpose to provide a justification for wilderness wandering and whole vast areas of the still wild west in which to wander. It was as if energies and capabilities long pent in him were suddenly released to be spent swiftly in a few brief years.

He had heard tales of the rugged wilderness of the northwest territories. Very well, the first expedition would be to that region. Within a few days he had gone down from his mountain fastness close enough to civilization to exchange his oxen for two mules, purchase a supply of ammunition and other necessaries, and hire three men — two young Sierra Indians, Tuolumne and Stanislaus, and a young Texan named William Sykesey.

They traveled north. They traveled on foot, leading the mules packed, but they traveled light and they traveled fast. James Capen Adams, onetime shoemaker in far-off Boston, buckskinned now with fox-tail ornament of his cap bouncing, strode in the lead and the freshness of spring was fresher to him than ever before and now and again he paused to look out over the clean unspoiled magnificence of the mountains and feel himself a part of the glory of creation.

The three young men with him were lucky. They had a superb leader for such an expedition, an almost unique combination of mountain man to match Bill Williams or Jim Bridger and of practical ingenious New England craftsman and trader. A man honest and straightforward always, absolutely fearless but rarely reckless, ready to confront any emergency in simple resolute manner. A man who demanded exact obedience from them and repaid them (beyond fair wages) with steady consideration for their safety and welfare. A man with the sense and the decency to establish prompt friendly relations with each Indian tribe whose territory they entered and to barter fairly for any assistance needed. A man, too, able to enliven long hard hours of labor with flashes of humor — and to see a joke on himself as readily as on anyone else.

He led them north through upper California, across what is now Oregon, into the Big Bend country of what is now Washington. Again he picked a high upland valley and established summer headquarters for hunts all through the area around.

There had been adventures along the way. This man Adams was deliberately seeking them. His truce with the great grizzlies was ended. As a professional hunter now, plying his trade, he felt it a point of honor to give battle at every encounter. The most memorable of this first expedition, not so much in violence of action as in later consequences, occurred soon after establishment of the summer camp.

Adams had found the den of an old dam with two yearling cubs. He lay in wait by a path they used, both old single-shot muzzle-loading rifles by his side. When the big grizzly was within close range he fired a ball from the Kentucky into her breast. She fell — and almost instantly recovered and rushed at him. He leaped up, the Tennessee in his hands, and waited until she was almost upon him, then fired through her open mouth into the brain.

That was one of the few times he did not have to finish the job in a death grapple, bowie knife in hand.

The dam was dead. There remained the two cubs. He tried to catch them alive with a rope he had with him.

They dodged for a while, then turned on him in such vigorous and effective attack that he had to scramble up a small tree. They tried to climb after him and he had to pound at them with his feet to keep them down. For some lively moments they kept him busy — but not too busy to fail to appreciate the ludicrous figure he, the mighty bear hunter, made clinging to a swaying small tree while two yearling cubs snapped at his heels. When they finally withdrew, he was more than ever determined to capture them.

That proved to be quite a proposition. The cubs refused to leave the vicinity but were so desperate and agile that Adams and his men spent several futile days trying to catch them on foot. He called on the local Indians and bartered for some horses. Mounted on one of these, with whirling lasso, he chased one of the cubs and at last had it. A vigorous healthy female. Meanwhile the other men managed to run down the second cub. A male. They brought it in so trussed and bound and wound with rope that Adams could not help laughing and joshed them unmercifully about it.

He now had two yearling grizzly cubs. The male was a morose, stupid, intractable animal. The female positively delighted him. He thought her the prettiest little animal in all the country. He pondered appropriate names. And had one. Lady Washington.

This was the start of a strange and enduring friendship between man and bear. Beginning, as such relationships can, with downright battles — as in the chasing of him up that tree. She was already more than a year old with formidable teeth and claws. He kept her, his usual custom with captured animals, fastened to a tree with a chain. Cudgel in hand, stern but kindly, he began to try to tame her. She gave him many a tough tussle, but he felt she was worth the trouble.

Piles of skins and furs grew about the camp and the menagerie of animals increased. A busy man, this Adams, doing more than his share of the work to make certain it was done right, leading in every hunt, some of them far afield, devising methods for trapping and securing the animals — and meanwhile studying them, working with them, striving to gentle them for easier handling. And spending as much time as he could spare in tussles with Lady Washington.

He planned to ship from Portland. A long trek across rugged country and dangerous rivers. By now, in early autumn, his party had grown. Two more white men, fair hunters, had temporarily enlisted with him and he had recruited six more Indians from a local tribe. He needed them, all of them. That stubborn persistent journey across that wilderness was an epic in itself.

A strange assemblage coming down out of the northern mountains with the long-bearded buckskinned Adams in command. A cavalcade in the lead. Five horses packed with buffalo robes, four with bearskins, two with antelope skins, one with fox and other small animal skins, seven with dried meat, one with pack boxes holding two small bear cubs, two with boxes containing wolves, tagged by one of the mules with foxes and fishers in baskets and the other piled high with tools and blankets and camp luggage.

Enough right there to catch any eye, especially with all the horses, besides the seven used solely for that purpose, draped with strings of dried meat. But following was the real sight — a train of animals driven along in a small herd.

Was there ever another herd like this to come down out of mountains to a riverport? Driven as a herd? Six bears, four wolves, four deer, four antelope, two elk, and an Indian dog!

It took considerable doing and long fast marches, but they reached Portland in time for the sailing of the bark *Mary Ann,* bound for Boston. All of the skins and furs and all of the captured animals (except Lady Washington) were quickly put aboard with most of the dried meat to be fed them on the long voyage. In due time brother William would dispose of them, plus some unidentified "curiosities," to good advantage. Meantime brother James drew on brother William's credit, paid off Sykesey and the two other white men, made proper presents to the northern Indians, and in company with faithful Tuolumne and Stanislaus headed southward for his winter camp near Yosemite.

Once again James Capen Adams stayed through the high-country winter in his mountain fastness, content with himself and happy as a king.

Not alone this time. Tuolumne and Stanislaus were with him. And Lady Washington. And a scrubby dog given him by an Indian chief named Kennasket up in the Big Bend country.

And even in winter now he plied his trade. He fashioned snowshoes and went hunting when the weather permitted, sometimes with one of the Indians as companion, sometimes alone. No. Never quite alone. Always Lady Washington was with him. She would follow along now like a huge dog, led on a light chain. He had already taught her to carry a pack on her back. Now he rigged a harness and taught her to draw a sled. She was slow at learning this, but once she had it she worked with a will, hauling game back to camp for him.

One night he and Stanislaus and the Lady were caught out in a bad storm and made a quick camp around a roaring fire. The men had one blanket each. In the small hours Adams woke and saw Stanislaus shivering under the one blanket. He made the Indian take his blanket too, then he coaxed the Lady to lie down as close to the fire as she would come and he lay down himself snuggled against her shaggy coat between her and the fire. She made no objection and he soon fell asleep. He woke again later at movement beside him. The Lady was rising to her feet. She retired to nearby bushes for a few minutes then came back and licked his hand and lay down beside him in the same position as before. James Capen Adams, a grizzly for a bedfellow, slept warm and comfortable the rest of that bitter cold night — and through many another like it.

In the spring a Mr. Solon of Sonora, who had been hearing tales of an Old Bruin, a Grizzly Adams, living up in the mountains, appeared and proposed a hunt together in the valley of the Yosemite. Adams agreed to a month's expedition. Stanislaus stayed at the winter camp — captured animals were there to be watched and fed — and Tuolumne went along. And, of course, Lady Washington. And a greyhound bitch Adams acquired while preparing for this jaunt.

It was a fair hunt, reasonably profitable, though Mr. Solon proved to be something of a foolish amateur and Adams had to save him from a panther and do crude but effective doctoring. No matter. He was hunting through the most magnificent section of the whole of the Sierras, feeling himself again a part of the wild wide free glory of creation, and that in itself would have been compensation enough.

A fair hunt. And, of course, grizzly adventures as before. The man against the monarchs of the mountains. That point of honor with him. To give battle at every encounter. Again the most memorable had important later consequences.

Again he had found the den of a grizzly dam. From the tracks he knew this would be one of the biggest bears in his experience. He was convinced she was holed up in the den, probably with a cub or cubs. He left his companions, including the Lady, at their temporary camp and laid siege to the den alone. For a night and a day and another night and another day, hidden in juniper bushes about a hundred yards away, he lay in waiting. Twice he discharged his Kentucky and the first time evoked an answering growl and the second time a sight of her head and front paws. But she did not come out.

He decided he was too far away for an effective assault and crept around and up the hillside and took a position about forty yards above and behind the den. Now in the third night, tired from the long vigil, he fell asleep — and was suddenly awakened in terror at the close scream of a panther. What an old fool he was, he told himself, to tremble at the cry of a sneaky cowardly brute while waiting for combat with the mightiest of them all. Wide awake again, he waited on.

The first light of morning and still the bear had not shown. He stuck small leafy branches in his cap to mask his face and crouched low in bushes and let loose one of the high piercing yells with which he sometimes started grizzlies to their feet for a good shot. That turned the trick. The great grizzly dam rushed out of the den, larger, more formidable even than he had expected, and rose on her hind feet, looking about. She failed to see him and sank down on her haunches, back to him. He gave a low whistle and she rose again, turning toward him, and he fired. She staggered and fell, biting at the ground, and he knew she had a mortal wound. After the long waiting he could wait no longer and he leaped down toward her, pistol in one hand, knife in the other. She sprang up and plunged toward him. Thick brush between slowed her and he fired the six shots in his pistol and the last hit her under an ear and stunned her for a moment. Instantly he was on her, driving the knife into her side. As she tried to struggle up again, he drew the knife across her throat.

Old Bruin, Grizzly Adams, three thousand miles away from his Boston shoemaker's bench, looked down at the dead grizzly and felt like Alexander flushed with another victory.

The dam was dead. There remained the possibility of cubs. He reloaded his guns, let the rifle lie just inside the entrance, and with a small torch of pine splinters in one hand and the pistol in the other crept forward. A tunnel about six feet in, then a rounded chamber in which he could rise to his knees. Nothing there, except a carpet of leaves and grass. No. He heard a rustling in the leaves. Bending down, he found two tiny cubs, so young their eyes were still closed. Two males.

Back at camp with his prizes, he faced a new problem. Feeding them. The greyhound bitch had recently surprised everyone by giving birth to a litter of pups. He disposed of all but one of these and gave her the cubs to suckle. He had a way with animals. She accepted them for him.

In a matter of days the lone pup and the two cubs were tumbling about together. Adams presented one of the cubs to Mr. Solon, who named it General Jackson. A great name, in its way, admitted Adams. But he had a greater for his cub. Benjamin Franklin.

The hunt with Solon was merely a spring interlude. Grizzly Adams had ambitious plans for the summer — an expedition to the Rocky Mountains. Four men again: himself and the faithful Tuolumne and Stanislaus, who said simply that wherever he led they would follow, and a young Mississippian named Gray. Four draft animals: two oxen to pull a wagon and two mules to carry packs. And five animals of another kind: Lady Washington, now nearly grown and easily carrying a two-hundred-pound pack on her back, and little Ben Franklin and the Indian dog and the greyhound bitch and her lone pup named Rambler who was rapidly becoming the boon companion of his foster-brother Ben. All other animals accumulated at the winter camp were taken down to a ranch near Stockton and left to await shipment to Boston.

Another epic journey. Up and over the Sierras with the passes still choked with snow. Adams recruited a whole clan of Digger Indians, men and women and children, to help on this stretch. At times they had to carve a passageway out of huge snowbanks and along steep hillsides and once, in a particularly narrow cleft, had to pack everything through on the mules and Lady Washington and their own backs and take the wagon apart to reassemble it on beyond. But by shooting enough game to keep all bellies full and rationing out whisky and dis-

tributing tobacco, Adams kept everyone in good spirits
and they made it up and over. Safely started down the
eastern slopes, they halted for a hunt and a feast and an
evening of shouting and dancing about a big fire. Gray
delighted the Indians with a Mississippi hoedown.
Adams himself tried kicking up his heels — but when he
saw the others, all of them, rolling on the ground in
laughter, he retired to a quiet seat and his old pipe and
concluded that his dancing days were over.

An epic journey. On through the Walker River country and the Humboldt Mountains, the original party aug-
mented by two of the Digger Indians who too would now
follow Adams anywhere. Day after day through an almost virgin wilderness, seeing no other human beings,
stopping occasionally to hunt and once to acquire some
panther cubs by invading a den. On across the barren
desert of the Great Basin where little Ben's feet became
sore and Adams made him leather moccasins which he
wore with seeming pride. A brief stop at the new settlement of Salt Lake City, where Adams decided it was foolish to pay attention to what the Mormons said and
preached and wise to see what they did and what they
were doing was admirable. Then on deep into the Rockies from the west for months of hunting and trapping.

And, always of course, more grizzly adventures. That
point of honor. The Rocky Mountain grizzly, was
Adams's verdict, was a match for the California in courage and character, but not in size and strength.

One night, there in the Rocky Mountain camp, a male
grizzly approached and paid court to Lady Washington.
Adams gave order there should be no attempt to shoot
him. Two nights more he came, a perfect gentleman, at-

tentive to his lady and disturbing no one and nothing else. The result of that, in due time, would be another cub christened Fremont.

Near the end of the summer Gray decided to continue on eastward, to return to his native Mississippi. After proper division of the hunting spoils, he departed and Adams in turn started his own long journey back to his permanent camp. An aging ex-shoemaker, white-bearded now, and four young Indians, two Sierra and two Digger, taking quantities of skins and furs and tamed wild animals and caged wild animals out of the Rockies, across the Great Basin, up and over the Sierras. They did it, quietly and stubbornly, almost as a matter of course. They arrived at the permanent camp near Yosemite to find it completely destroyed by a forest fire that had swept through the area.

They had stout hearts and willing hands. They built a new shelter and laid in hay for the winter. The two Diggers departed to rejoin their people with presents enough to set them up as rich men of their tribe. Tuolumne and Stanislaus stayed on.

Along came a letter from brother William, who was temporarily in San Francisco. Some grizzly bears were wanted by a zoo in Lima, Peru. Adams had two at the ranch near Stockton and he promptly trapped another and took it on down. He carted all three into Stockton, along with other animals, to be freighted to San Francisco. Crowds swarmed around him, fascinated by his costume and the contents of his cages. People poked sticks at the bears to arouse them. One man ventured too close and lost a pawful of meat. He drew a pistol, intent on revenge. Adams drew his own and informed the man that the bear's action was just and justifiable and that he,

Old Bruin, would stand by his bear to the last wag of his eyelids. The man cursed and ranted and Adams ranted right back, as dangerous as one of his grizzlies. The crowd cheered for him — and the man slipped away.

Old Bruin, Grizzly Adams, chuckled at the spectacle he had made of himself — and stood treat at a nearby bar for the whole crowd.

Once again he was wintering in his high upland valley with the faithful two and a growing menagerie. And one day he saw tracks, grizzly tracks, and was astounded at their size. The next day, by cautious maneuvering, he caught a glimpse of the bear itself. It looked to him like a moving mountain. He had to have that one — alive.

Days were spent in studying its trails, learning its habits. A week's labor was needed, all three men working, oxen dragging logs, to build a trap that might hold such a monster. Then came days and nights of waiting, Adams and Tuolumne concealed close by with no fire or food that might betray their presence. During the third night they heard a mighty roaring echoing through the mountains. The bear was in the trap — and busy ripping it apart. Quickly they built a big fire beside it to daunt him and worked the rest of the night buttressing it with additional timbers. For the next week, day and night, Adams stood guard, using iron rods and firebrands to keep that monster from breaking out. It was more than a month before he felt it safe to try to transfer that moving mountain to a special cage he had prepared. The transfer took several days and was accomplished only when Adams managed to get a heavy chain passed through the cage and into the trap and around the bear's neck and a team of oxen hauled him, inch by inch, into the cage.

There was only one adequate name. Samson. The largest and the finest specimen of the California grizzly ever captured. He was weighed once, on a hay scale, and tipped it at over fifteen hundred pounds. In later years artists sketched him and he became the trademark, the symbol, of the California magazine, the *Overland Monthly*. His likeness still rules his native mountains — on the California state flag.

Now a change was coming over Grizzly Adams. Age and the effects of his tremendous exertions and of the innumerable injuries suffered in hand-to-claw battles with grizzlies were slowing him down. He was developing a new attitude toward his wild-beast companions of the wilderness. He no longer considered it quite such a point of honor to give battle, was more interested in capturing them and not for shipment to brother William but for his own private menagerie. And he was no longer so averse to the society of his fellow men.

Perhaps that was because he had won an almost unique identity for himself, a reputation, a fame, and these could best be enjoyed in the presence of others. But it was also and more directly a result of his wilderness life and his own habit of long thoughts and quiet reflections in the quiet of his wilderness. Communion with the great enduring grandeur of his mountains had given him a serenity and a security within himself. And his intimate acquaintance with Indians had altered his outlook on humanity.

He was too much a white man of his time, and a New Englander to boot, not to look down upon Indians, not to feel superior to them. But he was shrewd enough to realize that this superiority was primarily a matter of

viewpoint, was only in what he called the advancements
of civilization, not in intrinsic quality and character. Tuolumne and Stanislaus had taught him this, and old chief
Kennasket, and even the lowly Diggers, and others he
had known along the far ways. He reflected that they too
had been created by the same Providence which had
created him and no doubt for a purpose which they too,
in their way, fulfilled. He had learned that it was the
part of wisdom not to try to change them, not to rail and
complain that they were not what they were not, but to
take them as they were — and to make the best of them.
And that, he came to understand, was the fundamental
lesson of life and a lesson to be applied to all men everywhere.

Then, too, it was becoming difficult to take adequate
care of his growing menagerie up there in his high
valley. And more people were constantly coming into the
general area and it was being hunted out anyway.

He moved his camp down to the Merced River and a
little later, along with his entire collection of animals, to
Corral Hollow, a narrow steep-sided valley that opened
out into the San Joaquin plains. Much closer to advancing civilization. In fact, a wagon road from San Francisco
to San Joaquin passed right through the valley.

Tuolumne and Stanislaus helped with the moving and
saw him well established in his new headquarters. But
they were restless there. They had been away from their
own people for a long time. They left, intending to return to him sometime later. He never saw them again.
Too much happened too quickly.

He hunted some in the neighborhood of Corral Hollow. Then he made a trip back up to his old camp to

gather a few things left there and could not resist one last
hunt in his old haunts. This was only a quick trip and
Lady Washington, now a great full-grown grizzly, was
not with him. But Ben Franklin, about half grown now,
and Rambler the greyhound were. They enjoyed roaming free so much, tagging after him when he strode
afield, that he had let them come along.

He was not as alert as he used to be, not so constantly
on the watch. That point of honor no longer nagged
him. Suddenly a big grizzly with three cubs jumped him
from a thicket of chaparral, struck the rifle from his
hands, and threw him to the ground. She was on him,
biting and clawing, when Ben and Rambler burst out of
the bushes and leaped to attack her, Rambler wisely
snapping at her rear while half-grown Ben went straight
for her throat. She ignored the dog as a mere minor nuisance and turned on Ben. He was far outmatched but he
kept her busy while Adams scrambled up and retrieved
his old Kentucky. He fired the single shot and plunged
into the fight with his knife. It was soon over and then,
only then, did little Ben, head and throat badly torn,
blood streaming from him, run yelping for the security
of the camp.

For the rest of his life Grizzly Adams never mentioned
Ben without an accompanying adjective — noble Ben.

Now that the battle was over, he realized that he too
was badly wounded. On one of his first Sierra hunts a
grizzly had ripped his whole scalp almost off and injured
the bone. This grizzly had torn open the same old wound
and he had other serious gashes about the neck. The big
dam had even punctured the bone of his upper forehead.
He made it back to camp and dressed Ben's wounds before he dressed his own. It was a week before they were

able to travel, slowly, back down to Corral Hollow. Ben's wounds left permanent scars and his own the same, including a depression about the size of a silver dollar in his forehead where skin closed over crushed bone.

That was in the spring of 1855. He was approaching fifty now, white beard and the effects of his rugged life making him look even older, but he kept right on. By early summer he seemed to be fully recovered and he hunted southward down the east side of the inner Coast Range to Tulare Lake and spent several weeks in that marshy region. He hired assistants as he needed them — but never found a one to match Tuolumne or Stanislaus. He followed the new gold rush into Kern County, supplying meat to the mining camps and trading in pelts and adding to his menagerie. Always Lady Washington and noble Ben and Ben's companion, Rambler, were with him, the two bears padding along beside him, needing no chains, no leashes. Ben was growing fast, attaining considerable size, and he gallantly collected more scars fighting in defense of Adams and the Lady. Together they hunted on through the Tejon Pass area and at last, with quite a collection of caged captives of many species, they headed northward up the west side of the range, bound for Corral Hollow.

Now a serious bout with fever did what neither age nor any aroused grizzly had been able to do, really slowed Old Bruin down. What with him could be called slowing down. He had crammed into only a few years more hunting than most sportsmen do into a lifetime. Hunting of a kind to chill the nerves of modern hunters who operate with modern equipment and long-range high-powered precision arms. All of his was close-range,

much of it knife-to-claw. He had captured alive more
grizzlies than any other man ever had or would — and
along with them just about every kind of animal in the
West. He would still hunt and trap some, make a few
forays into the mountains when there were calls for his
rifles and knife or he heard of an animal worth trapping.
But these would be brief excursions, only a few days
each, and not far afield. He was ready for a new career, a
new trade. One that would still make wild beasts his companions. One suggested by the interest he and his animals had aroused that day in Stockton.

James Capen Adams, Grizzly Adams, finished his regular, his full-time hunting career in proper style. He and
noble Ben and Rambler answered a plea from Spanish
ranchers in the foothills, caught a big outlaw grizzly in
the very act of outlawry, killing calves in a corral, and
after a hard-fought battle stretched it out for skinning. A
few weeks later Adams and his animals were giving exhibitions in the town of San Jose. On to Santa Clara.
And so at last to San Francisco to establish the Mountaineer Museum, soon moved to a better building on Clay
Street and renamed the Pacific Museum.

They were all there with him, all his animals: noble
Ben now full grown to eight hundred pounds and more,
and faithful Lady Washington, and her onetime cub Fremont on his way to becoming a thousand-pound adult,
and Funny Joe the comedian grizzly, and mighty Samson
shaking the whole building when he rattled his cage, and
many and many another big grizzly, and black and cin-
namon bears, and panthers and wolves and foxes and
wildcats and elk and deer and innumerable small ani-

mals. Exactly what the first advertisement said: "The Largest Collection of Wild Animals Ever Exhibited on the West Coast."

The museum attracted much attention and newspaper comment — but not nearly as much as Adams himself, bearded and buckskinned, strolling along city streets with the Lady and noble Ben beside him — huge, formidable, yet docile and obedient to his commands, indifferent to the shouts of startled people and the yipping of stray dogs. There, in San Francisco, a future historian named Theodore Hittell, then a newspaper reporter, became a close friend of Adams and rode on Ben's back and wrote articles about the man and his grizzlies and spent long afternoons through many months making notes as the man told him, in simple factual straightforward manner, of his experiences in the mountains. And there, in San Francisco, when Ben died of some internal disorder for which no remedy could be found, the *Evening Bulletin* printed a long account of the "Death of a Distinguished Native Californian."

He was a good showman, this Grizzly Adams. He worked as hard at this trade as ever he had at shoemaking or at hunting, training his animals, putting them through stunts, giving exhibitions, taking again at times almost as much punishment as in the hunting. It was Fremont who gave him the most trouble. Fremont, whom he had had from birth, in a way even from conception, and whom he stubbornly insisted on trying to tame to the same docility as his mother. It was Fremont who gave him many a bad clout on the head, adding to the old serious wounds before being subdued enough for show purposes.

He was a good showman all right. But he was no better a businessman than in his earlier California days. The big grizzlies were always the major attractions and perhaps could have carried the museum by themselves. But he continually added other attractions, often at considerable expense, even sea animals which had to be kept in large tanks. The old speculating habit was still with him. In 1859, not long after he had borrowed heavily to add a second story to the museum for a waxworks exhibit and compounded this by adding an amphitheater and circus ring for equestrian acts, he was in so deep that an attachment was levied against the whole establishment.

He lost the property but somehow managed to keep most of the menagerie. Particularly the big bears. And once again he started on a long expedition into the teeth of adversity. Early in 1860 he and his animals were aboard the *Golden Fleece* bound for New York.

A rough passage, particularly around Cape Horn. Taking care of his animals, keeping them under control during winter storms at sea, he again took fearful punishment. The old head wounds were reopened, the skull bones shattered more.

He arrived in New York with no connections, no advance preparations. But within a few days he was a partner at the American Museum with Phineas T. Barnum himself. The master showman was astounded at this apparition out of the far West, was convinced at once that the man was as much a show as his beasts, then was appalled when Adams removed the old deerskin cap and showed the head wounds. This man should have been dead long ago. He had the very vitality of one of his grizzlies. Barnum was astounded again when Adams, calm and matter-of-fact, told him:

Yes, that will fix me out . . . I'm a used-up man . . .
However, I am good for a few months yet, and by that
time I hope we shall gain enough to make my old
woman comfortable, for I have been absent from her
for some years.

His old woman came down from Massachusetts to be
with him and nurse him. Barnum's doctor was certain he
would not live more than a few weeks at the most. Barnum was certain that all that kept him from being on
his deathbed right then was his indomitable will.

Whatever it was, he was the feature of the parade opening the California Menagerie at the American Museum.
Down Broadway and up the Bowery the parade went,
Adams in the lead on a platform wagon with three great
grizzlies, two held by chains while he was mounted on
the other which was held by no fastening whatever.

Yes, it was Lady Washington there on the wagon with
him, bearing him proudly on her back. Later she went
for a stroll or two with him along New York streets.
Newspapers took the opportunity to whoop things up for
the establishment of the first Zoological Gardens in Central Park.

And every day for the next six weeks, to the amaze-
ment of Barnum and the doctor, Old Bruin was in the
ring, performing with his bears.

The doctor, certain now that this battered old grizzly
of a man could live only a few days more, insisted he
should sell out and settle his affairs. Adams promptly
named a very good price, which Barnum, dumfounded
at this man and perhaps for the one time in his career,
accepted without quibbling. Then Adams as promptly
talked Barnum, who could hardly believe what he was

hearing, into agreeing to pay a good salary and expenses for a ten-week tour of New England plus a very nice bonus if he lasted the full ten weeks.

Of course he lasted. He was in constant increasing pain and becoming steadily weaker. But he lasted. He was Grizzly Adams.

Far west in San Francisco a young reporter was writing a book, the adventures of a onetime Massachusetts shoemaker as told to him by the man himself. He was copying from his notes what the man had said at the end of his reminiscences:

I have looked on death in many forms, and trust that I can meet it whenever it comes with a stout heart and steady nerves.

Far east in the small town of Neponset near Boston, where his wife and daughter now lived with solid bank accounts in their names, Grizzly Adams was meeting death. A clergyman was there, supposedly offering solace, asking repentance for an unchurchly life. Old Bruin set him aback.

I have attended preaching every day, Sundays and all, for the last six years. Sometimes an old grizzly gave me the sermon, sometimes it was a panther; often it was the thunder and lightning, the tempest, or the hurricane on the peaks of the Sierra Nevada, or in the gorges of the Rocky Mountains; but whatever preached to me, it always taught me the majesty of the Creator, and revealed to me the undying and unchanging love of our kind Father in heaven.

The preacher departed. There was quiet in the house at Neponset. In a closet hung a fine new buckskin hunting suit, a copy of the old, which Barnum, always the businessman, had had made for Adams's successor in the animal exhibitions. It had been made during the last tour when Barnum was convinced that Adams could not last. Adams had asked to be allowed to use it and Barnum had agreed that Adams could keep it until "he had done with it."

Grizzly Adams, lying on his deathbed, called to his old woman. Raised himself a bit and told her he wanted to be laid out in that fine new suit of skins. His last words were: "Won't Barnum open his eyes when he finds I have humbugged him by being buried in his new hunting suit."

He sank back on the bed and met death.

George Augustus Frederick Ruxton

JULY 24, 1821—AUGUST 29, 1848

LIFE moved fast for George Ruxton.

He was the third of the six sons of an Irish father and a Scottish mother and that interesting amalgam of blood lines in him was given an all-around British tempering by birth and raising and education in England. The father was an army surgeon who came from an ancient Irish family with estates on the River Dee and a long roster of soldier-adventurers. The mother came from an equally ancient Scottish family which was actively interested in the famed East India Company.

Out of six sons of such a union one at least was certain to kick over the traces and go adventuring. George was the one. He himself readily admitted that he had vagabond inclinations and a wayward disposition and was afflicted with pride and determined self-will. His mother was inclined to be overly indulgent. His father might have been able to keep him in leash until he attained his majority; but when he was only eight or nine years old,

his father died and there was no more real restraint upon
him.

Except that inherent in him. He was born a gentleman and no matter how far and exotic and adverse his
adventures and in what strange guise he might appear, a
gentleman he would always be.

He had some years of sound British schooling. His
masters would not have called him studious, quite the
contrary, and he was regularly involved in one kind of
scrape after another. But he had a quick mind and considerable natural ability and he emerged from those relatively few years, almost despite himself, with a surprisingly good education. Then, a few days before his four-
teenth birthday, he was enrolled at the Royal Military
Academy at Sandhurst.

He entered with a mind filled with tales of ancestral
derring-do in the military line, determined to make a
good showing. Three days were enough to alter his attitude. He found he had nothing but contempt for the system in vogue at Sandhurst — based, in his opinion, on
the silly expectation that boys should be men and men
be boys. He spent most of his time there, when not
confined to the "black hole," ignoring classes and playing cricket and snaring rabbits and wandering the countryside. The academy stood him, off and on, for about
two years, then expelled him.

What next? He was sixteen years old, handsome,
erect, well built, sturdy — though he liked to complain
that his legs were too short. In the neighborhood of the
academy he had known and heard exciting tales from a
retired sergeant (currently keeping bees) who had recently been a volunteer fighter in the Carlist civil war in
Spain, where the Pretender, Don Carlos, was still trying

to wrest the throne from the regency of little nine-year-old Queen Isabella II. What better arena for a young would-be adventurer wanting to flesh his sword? He made preparations to depart.

At the start he was not even certain which side he would join in the civil war. He was seeking adventure, not a cause. But he was a true Briton and a true romantic of his time. It was inevitable he would fight for legitimacy and the child-queen.

He sailed from England and landed at Havre, intending to proceed overland to Spain. That would give him a chance to see something of France on the way. It did. He spent time and money in Paris and Bordeaux and Bayonne. At least he was working southward, down toward the Spanish border. Then the thinning of his purse spurred him on.

He crossed the border below Bayonne, bound for San Sebastian in Spain. When he had shown his passport and stepped onto Spanish soil, he was still boy enough to throw his cap in the air and cheer for romance and adventure — and already experienced traveler enough to apply a bit of British money in the right place to have the contraband British goods he was taking with him passed through customs without inspection.

At San Sebastian he passed several days savoring the old city, listening to the civil war arguments of people in the inns, and outfitting himself in proper cavalier style — with a horse and a mule and a servant. He made his decision, never really in doubt, to head inland, into the province of Navarre, and join either the French or the British Legion fighting there in the service of the Spanish queen.

There was a little problem of mountains in the way,

the Pyrenees. The best route would be to continue along the coast to Bilbao and strike inland up one of the river valleys. But the boat he expected to take to Bilbao was held up for days by bad weather and he was too impatient to wait longer. He turned about and with reluctant servant tagging backtracked to Bayonne, struck inland from there and headed for the Spanish border again and the Urdos pass over the mountains. This was midwinter of 1837 and the pass was certain to be packed with snow, and bitter weather was almost equally certain and he was frequently urged to wait for more favorable conditions. He had plenty of that determined self-will. More accurately, simple stubbornness, plain obstinacy. He pushed right on.

During that mountain-crossing he met and survived just about everything the winter elements could throw at him, had a fascinating encounter with a bear which his servant insisted was the devil himself, and was marooned for a night and a day and a night by a terrific storm in the crude crowded foul-smelling hovel of some mountaineers. And during that mountain-crossing he made discoveries about himself that would shape his life: that he could thrive on adversity and extract satisfaction from it; that the great outdoors was the one true temple in which he could worship; that he, to the manor born and raised, could get along well and find companionship with the strange eccentric beings in the shape of men who dwell in far out-of-the-way places of the world.

Young George Ruxton, all of sixteen years old, found the forces of the queen in Navarre and was given a commission as Cornet of Lancers in the British Auxiliary

Legion attached to the regular Spanish division commanded by General Diego León. He served with some distinction for eighteen months or more. After one particular battle General León himself paid him special honor and he was awarded, in the name of the little queen, the Cross of the First Class of the National Military Order of San Fernando which carried with it the title of knight. More important and more practical for the future, he became thoroughly acquainted with the Spanish language.

After the successful conclusion of the loyalist campaign in the summer of 1839, he returned to England, a military veteran and a decorated one before his eighteenth birthday. Almost immediately his own government gave him a commission, a lieutenancy in the 89th Foot Regiment — better known later as the Royal Irish Fusiliers. He had neatly bypassed Sandhurst and won a British commission in his own way. His own queen, Victoria, was "pleased" to issue an order granting him royal permission to wear his Spanish Cross in her service.

Most of his regiment was overseas at the time, in the West Indies, and for months he had nothing but home garrison duty, in England and then in Ireland. Once again he spent much of his time wandering the countryside, only now he was developing an intense interest in hunting. He was filling his mind too with thoughts of a new kind of derring-do from the Leatherstocking tales of James Fenimore Cooper. Dogs and guns were his constant companions. He was not above poaching when that was the only way to obtain game.

In the summer of 1840 luck played right to his inclination. He was ordered to join his regiment — which had been transferred to Canada. Not only to Canada, but to

the frontier post of Amherstburg on the Detroit River.
Not much was happening there, not in a military way.
The War of 1812, which had volleyed through the region, was long over and even the brief Canadian uprising of 1837 was already tucked into history. But right at
hand was the great North Woods where Indians still
roamed and hunting could have the Leatherstocking
tang. He made more than the most of the opportunity.

Hunting, as often as possible, as far afield as possible,
was his major, certainly his only memorable, occupation
during his military service in Canada. He obtained a
leave of absence and went home to England for a few
months — and on the way back to the post improved his
time on board ship popping at whales and sharks. As
with so many Europeans of that age of imperial explo-
ration and conquest and colonization, hunting was a
positive obsession with him. The world, they and he
seemed to think, had been created as an arena for sportsmen. Animals existed for the sole purpose of providing
targets.

Military service, routine and desultory, interfered
with hunting. Army life was dull. Soon after his return
to the post in the fall of 1843 he put in a request for
permission to sell his commission and retire. Under pressure from friends and superiors — he was regarded as
one of the best of the younger officers — he tried to with-
draw the request. Too late. It had already been granted.

Not too late in a larger sense. He had been freed for
more adventures.

The first of these was a winter hunt deep into the
North Woods with a Chippewa Indian friend named
Peshwego and several other Indians. It started well and

they were snug in a winter camp far into the woods. Then trouble came in the form of a prolonged spell of bitter cold weather with no snow. Few animals were out and moving and the few that were could not be tracked. The food at the camp dwindled and the hunters were close to starving. The Indians decided that somehow they had offended the Great Spirit and this was a warning to abandon the hunt. They started back and he went part of the way with them. Then that determined self-will, that stubbornness, asserted itself again. He faced about and returned to the camp alone. He managed to survive and he stayed out there alone, for weeks, in mid-winter, using the camp as headquarters for side jaunts, and he had enough adventures to last even him for a while.

It was spring now, the spring of 1844, and he went home to England. A small place and a dull place now to him, that tight little island. In a short while he was heading down through Europe again, looking up old friends in Spain, crossing to North Africa, to Morocco and Algeria, where the French were fighting the Arabs. He knocked about some and made a trip into the interior with a camel caravan. Though he heartily disliked the caravan owner and did not get very far, he saw enough to fire him with enthusiasm for African explorations. By the end of the year he had returned to England, made fresh preparations, and was bound by boat down along the west coast of Africa.

An ambitious project for the period. Nothing less than an attempt to cross South Africa paralleling the Tropic of Capricorn from Walvis Bay on the west coast to Mozambique on the east.

Obstacles, nothing but obstacles. The only maps available he found to be all wrong. The traders and missionaries on the coast, satisfied with their sinecures, had no desire to have the interior explored and its capabilities known. They refused assistance, gave deliberately wrong information, turned the native chieftains against him. He and a companion tried to make their own unaided way — and came close to death in the effort. He did manage to make a few short trips inland and to become acquainted with another kind of strange out-of-the-way beings, the coastal Bushmen.

He returned to England in disgust, read a paper on the Bushmen before the Ethnological Society, and tried to get the government to back him for another African attempt. His proposal was referred to the Royal Geographical Society, which approved it enthusiastically. It was sent to the Colonial Office, where it became entangled in bureaucratic red tape. Delays. Delays. More delays. He was not one to stomach delays. He turned away from Africa and faced westward again, westward across the Atlantic.

George Ruxton, British gentleman of Irish-Scottish ancestry, Spanish knight, soldier, hunter, adventurer, approaching his twenty-fifth birthday, sniffed war again. Where wars were, things happened. He was through with soldiering, but he liked to be where things were happening and in far places. There had been war in Spain and he had gone to Spain. There had been war in North Africa and he had gone to North Africa. There was war now between Mexico and the United States. In the summer of 1846 he landed at Veracruz in southern Mexico. He had in mind an overland journey of 2000 and more miles following the Camino Real, the Royal

Road of the Spanish conquistadores, from Veracruz to Santa Fe and Taos in far New Mexico.

He was not merely a romantic adventurer now. He carried credentials from the British government which certified that he represented British diplomatic and commercial interests. The government hoped, that is, that he might be able to straighten out some of the tangled problem of British overland trade into Mexico by way of the Santa Fe Trail which was blocked now by the war. And he might, of course, pick up valuable military data on the way. A helpful role for him, to be an accredited observer from a neutral nation in the midst of the confusions and ready suspicions rocking Mexico at the time and the mutual hatreds between the Mexicans and Americans he would encounter. But he did not take the role too seriously. Playing it gave him credentials, smoothed his way into Mexico, enabled him to travel where he pleased. His major purposes were purely personal: to wander again in a far strange place where things were happening, to see new sights and meet and know new peoples — and to hunt in a rugged new wilderness. Perhaps, too, he would write about his experiences. He had long had the notebook habit and back home in England were experimental manuscripts about his previous adventures.

Veracruz to Jalapa to Pueblo and on to Mexico City. Impressed with the strange beauty of the land — and disgusted with the people. His knowledge of Spanish was a definite asset. He dressed as a Mexican and explored the cities and listened to talk in the inns and attended the theater and a bullfight and discovered one thing Mexican for which he had nothing but praise — pulque, that

38 HEROES WITHOUT GLORY

powerful liquor made from the maguey plant which he rated the drink of thirsty angels. But everywhere laziness and laxness and rudeness and inefficiency and dirt. Particularly dirt. Mexico, he decided, was the headquarters of dirt. He was right ready to travel on northward.

Before leaving the capital he found there a Yankee who was making a fortune, despite the war or perhaps because of it, trading in horseflesh. He bought two horses, one of them the Panchito that would carry him 3000 miles and more during the next months. Finding a servant presented a more difficult problem. None wanted to head northward toward the land of wild beasts and robbers and wild Indians and even wilder Texans and kindred Americans and other unknown horrors. At last he found one who would go as far as Durango. He found too a young Spaniard who was interested in mines in the north country and agreed to travel with him. Other travelers, now and again, would be with him along the way.

Mexico City to Querétaro to Celaya to Silao. More impressed with the strange rugged beauty of the land — and more disgusted with most of the people. The further northward he went, the more he was an object of curiosity to the "provincials," who crowded around to examine him in detail and to admire the guns he had brought from England, his pistols and double rifle and the double-barreled carbine his servant carried. There at Silao he bought a pair of "California" mules, whose endurance and ability to get along on the coarsest food continually astonished him. Both were soon devoted to Panchito and needed no lead ropes. He could ride along without looking back, confident they would be tagging close behind. One of them proved to be a fine hunting

mule. An ugly, misshapen brute, but he could fire at anything from her back without her even twitching an ear
and he could leave her ground-reined for hours and return to find her patiently waiting.

Silao to Villa de León to Zacatecas and Fresnillo in the
heart of a valuable mining district. More impressed than
ever with the lonely forbidding ruggedness of the land
where the only travelers met were mule-train drivers —
and still disgusted with most of the native people. At
Fresnillo he found a brief, welcome change. He stayed at
the hacienda of the mines with the administrator, an edu-
cated American, and with the other officials, most of them
from Spain, and spent a few days in their company being
initiated into the mysteries of Mexican mining.

Fresnillo to Zaina to Sombrerete to Durango, through
wild and almost uninhabited country with long stretches
of volcanic badlands and no travelers met anywhere between the few towns. He had come to what was considered the last real outpost of civilized Mexico. Tales of
Indian depredations raced through Durango. Ahead was
the land of the Apaches, always hostile. The even-more-
dreaded Comanches, emboldened by the confusions
brought by the war, were raiding all through the area.
No man in his right mind, said the townspeople, would
venture on northward except in company with a large
well-armed party.

George Ruxton, of vagabond inclinations and wayward disposition and afflicted with determined self-will,
reacted in character. He adopted a fixed rule for himself,
never to stop on account of Indians. He pushed right on.
And as if some protective providence recognized and
approved the man's invincible stubbornness, he rode
through the Apache and the Comanche country un-

harmed. He came on places where raiders had struck just a day or two, even just a few hours, before his arrival. He left places which were visited with death and destruction only a short time after his departure. He helped bury victims. He organized and led a volunteer posse trying to save others. Always he rode unharmed.

Durango to Mapimí to Chihuahua, through a ravaged land where the only secure stopping places were far-scattered walled haciendas — and these several days' travel apart with welcome and entrance sometimes denied. At Mapimí his servant, enticed thus far only by extra wages, refused to go farther and his job was taken by a little Irishman who had been long in Mexico and had no fear of anything Mexican or Indian. At Mapimí, too, all of Ruxton's baggage and equipment and some three thousand dollars in money were stolen. The prefect of the town was profusely indignant. Theft from an American could be condoned, perhaps praised. Not theft from an Englishman. Not from this Englishman, who traveled with impressive credentials and a carte blanche from the governor of the province stating he could go where he pleased. The culprits were found. Ingenious tortures extracted from them knowledge of the hiding places of the plunder, almost piece by piece. Ruxton tried to stop the brutal proceedings. The prefect was immovable. Everything must be returned — and was.

From Chihuahua to El Paso he had an escort of a few ragged half-starved Mexican dragoons, pressed on him by the local authorities. These were simply a nuisance. They devoured everything available, including the provisions he carried for his own use. The party had to make forced marches through barren wastes where there was neither water nor wood. They were halted near a tiny village by a hurricane which made traveling impossible. They had not had a good meal in days and nothing at all for twenty-four hours. Ruxton determined on a feast. He set everyone to foraging and eventually had some beef and enough other necessaries for an ample succulent stew. This simmered over a fire in a big earthenware pot. He made everyone wait until it was properly and completely cooked. The little Irishman stepped forward to lift the pot from the fire. The bottom fell out. Ay de mi! Another day without a meal. Such was traveling in such a country.

He and escort came into El Paso across desert land with the trail marked by the skeletons and rotting carcasses of oxen and mules and horses. George Ruxton had reached what would soon be American soil.

Santa Fe, occupied by the Americans, was still far to the north. He left El Paso with another escort, fifteen ragged troopers who, he reflected, were such broken-down misfits with such rusty old weapons that they would have broken the heart of Sir John Falstaff. They would be no use at all in case of an Indian attack. He tried to dodge the honor, but the authorities regarded this as British modesty. He led off and the motley crew followed.

Northward he went along the Rio Grande to the start of the dreaded Jornada del Muerto, the journey of the dead man, nearly one hundred miles of waterless desert behind the bleak mountains which prevented passage along the river. Here, to his relief, the troopers suddenly discovered that their horses were too exhausted to continue. They started back toward El Paso. He and the little Irishman and a Mexican attendant he had hired rode on. They crossed the desert, seeing fresh Indian sign but unmolested, in twenty hours. They rested and moved on to the deserted hacienda of Valverde on the east bank of the river. They had reached the limit of territory still held by the Mexicans. Only a few miles beyond was the encampment of the First Missouri Mounted Volunteers under Colonel Alexander W. Doniphan, who would soon be leading them southward on a campaign to take Chihuahua. Backed up behind the encampment were many wagon trains belonging to traders waiting for the chance to continue southward, as they had long done before the war, to the markets on in Mexico.

There at Valverde the Mexican attendant, probably frightened at proximity to those legendary monsters, Americans, simply deserted, disappeared. The little Irishman collected his wages and departed southward. It was late November now and the weather was chill and his health was none of the best and he preferred a warmer climate. Ruxton shifted for himself — he was an old hand at it — and let his animals rest and meanwhile took care of a few official duties.

Not far from his own camp was that of young Lieutenant J. W. Abert of the United States Topographical Engineers, who was conducting a survey of New Mexico. He and officers at the main encampment were curious about the presence of this handsome, splendidly mustached, obviously capable and somewhat reserved young Englishman in New Mexico at this particular time. They could have demanded that he explain himself. They did not need to. Ruxton strolled into Abert's camp, greeted the young engineer and several officers there, and handed over certain documents. One was from the British government requesting all American officers to "extend every

facility to English traders on their route to Chihuahua."
Others were from Mexican officials offering assurances
that all traders, regardless of nationality, even Americans, would be permitted to carry on trade as usual
(Mexico needed the customs duties) provided they came
with Mexican drivers.

George Ruxton had completed his official mission, his
convenient excuse for a two-thousand-mile jaunt through
a strange land. In itself it was of little or no historical
importance. The same documents could easily have been
handled (no doubt similar ones were) through regular
diplomatic channels. His own government had merely
done him the favor of helping him on his travels by giving him official status. He in turn had done a favor for the
Mexican authorities through whose territory he had
been passing. He was on his way now to something of
more enduring significance than the delivering of a few
documents and the observance of military activities. He
had come at last to a land he would make, in his own
way and in an incredibly short span of time, completely
and forever his.

While camped there at Valverde he first experienced
friendship with a new breed of strange eccentric beings
in the shape of men with whom he would find the finest
companionship of his varied career. He went hunting
with a French Canadian and an American, free trappers
both, old mountain men.

He rode north with Lieutenant Abert's party, to Socorro, to Albuquerque, to Bernalillo. Here, on these
final stretches of the Camino Real, he caught his first
glimpses of his true goal, the distant Rocky Mountains,
the snow-topped peaks of the Sangre de Cristo range. He

reached Santa Fe late in December and was not impressed — except unfavorably. The old capital with its
adobe structures reminded him of a dilapidated brick
kiln, of a prairie-dog town. His opinion of Mexicans in
general was unchanged, though he was beginning to believe that the women came closer to being human than
did the men. At least he was impartial. He regarded the
several thousand Americans who had swarmed into Santa
Fe with the military occupation as even dirtier and row-
dier than the Mexicans. It seemed to him that every
other house sold liquor and was continually disgorging
drunken men who staggered about through dirt and
filth.

But he had only to raise his eyes and there, then as
now, behind the town rose the great clean beckoning
magnificence of the mountains, rolling on northward
into what is now Colorado, the mighty Rockies, the backbone of the American West.

Mountains — and the mountain men!

He rode north through bitter weather to Taos and
stopped at the home of an American, Stephen Luis Lee,
acting sheriff of the settlement. He stayed a few days and
sampled the liquid dynamite known as Taos lightning
and one evening, at a wild fandango, when racial animosities took fire, he helped a group of husky gringos clear
the hall of a swarm of knife-wielding greasers. He talked
about town of crossing the Sangre de Cristos and wintering on the other side. Lee was astonished and tried to
persuade him to stay in Taos until spring. Didn't he know
that the mountains were already in the grip of a particularly hard winter and passage would be all but impossible? Even the few mountain men in town at the time
warned against the attempt. But that familiar stubborn-

ness asserted itself. He shed his British clothes and adopted the buckskin garb of a mountain man. He found a half-breed Pueblo Indian who agreed to act as guide and rode on. Northward to Arroyo Hondo and to Rio Colorado, last and northernmost of the Mexican settlements.

And again that protective providence rode with him. He was battling snow and ice and intense cold and suffering such things as a frozen foot which forced him to stop for a few days. But back in Taos, just two days after his departure, the brief Taos Rebellion against the American occupation broke out and Stephen Lee's house was one of those attacked and Lee and all other "foreigners" in the town (except Lee's brother who escaped with the aid of a priest) were killed. Again, only three days after he left the home of Simeon Turley in Arroyo Hondo, the rebellion reached there and with the same results.

He knew nothing at the time of these happenings behind him. He and his Indian guide were facing the great wall of mountains beyond Rio Colorado, striking into one of the highest and wildest regions of the whole of the American West.

They followed as best they could an old trail used by the Ute Indians when crossing from the upper reaches of the Rio Grande to the eastern slopes of the mountains on their annual buffalo hunts. The cold was worse than the worst he had known even in Canada. Fierce storms halted them, forcing them to spend long dark hours crouched as much as possible out of the winds without the solace of a fire. It took them half a day to travel less than four miles through one small valley. The snow was drifted so deep, fifteen feet and more in unsuspected hollows, that they had to dismount and beat out a path for

the horses and mules with their own bodies. In the dark
of night, after one of the most difficult days, when at last
they had found a somewhat sheltered place to camp, one
of the mules slipped its pack around under its belly and
bolted in fright, kicking and scattering the contents of
the pack through the winter wilderness. It was the pack
that contained their provisions. They would have to de-
pend upon hunting for most of their food. But game
seemed to be nonexistent and on the rare occasions they
sighted any they were usually so benumbed as to be unable to handle their guns. Gaunt, hungry, half frozen, falling into snow-clogged ravines and wearily working out,
they battled on. Not until they had fought their way
across the whole wide-spreading range and were dropping down the eastern slopes to Greenhorn Creek did
they see another human being.

What they saw on a bluff overlooking the creek
seemed a positive metropolis. Three Indian lodges and
one adobe house. A party of French Canadian hunters
and their Assiniboin and Sioux squaws gave them a
proper welcome. George Ruxton, in well-worn buckskins
and moccasins and soft-fur turban, indistinguishable
now from the mountain men except for the clipped precision of his speech and a somewhat reserved manner and
an insistence on shaving as regularly as possible with due
respect for a splendid mustache, had won his way into
the heart of his promised land.

This was the twilight of the great days of the free trappers, the mountain men. Beaver skins were no longer
much in demand. Cheaper substitutes had been found in
the skins of the fur seal and the nutria. In the eastern

cities and far-off London and Paris high silk hats were
replacing the once popular beaver toppers. The price
of pelts had dropped until trapping was no longer
profitable, not even bringing enough for a short spree
after a long trip. Unwilling to give up their wild free
independent ways, the mountain men were camping in
the valleys all through the area. There was still plenty of
game in the mountain parks and advancing civilization
was still well to the eastward across the plains. They
could live by hunting — and hope for a revival of the
beaver market.

A group of them, Indian traders, trappers, hunters,
were wintering at the Pueblo (site of the present town
of Pueblo) on the Arkansas River. The Pueblo itself was
a square adobe fort enclosing a series of small shelters or
huts. Ruxton arrived there from the Greenhorn late in
January and was heartily welcomed into the lodge of one
John Hawkins. He had found his winter headquarters.

The Pueblo had long been a meeting place for the
mountain men. They came and they went, out of the
mountains rising immediately to the west and into them
again. They squatted on the ground around good fires
and told tales of their experiences, true tales because always there were others who knew to check them, and
they talked of the comrades of the great years who had
left their bones across half a continent. And George Ruxton, accepted in the ready friendship of men, many of
them too from far places, who could recognize despite all
superficial differences one of their own breed, squatted
with them and cut slices of meat with his knife from the
big chunks roasting over the fires and wiped his greasy
hands on his buckskins and listened through the lazy
loafing hours. In imagination he strode with them most

of the mountains of the West and absorbed the wisdom
of the wilderness. Perhaps he told a tale or two in his
turn. From his own long back-trail there were a few
worth the telling.

On through the winter and into the spring he made
the Pueblo his headquarters, savoring the wild free life
of the mountain men. He hunted like the others when
meat was needed, the staple of the Pueblo diet, and
proved that his fine British guns were as deadly as any of
their favorite long rifles. No longer did he regard wild
animals as automatic targets for a sportsman's pleasure.
They were food. Food that should not be wasted. He became proud that he, too, killed only when meat was
needed. He hunted with companions and he hunted
alone. He had his brushes with Indians and he held to
his fixed rule and again he rode unharmed. He was
caught in a mountain hailstorm that almost finished him.
He learned what it was to flee for days from a raging
forest fire.

Panchito and the mules were still with him, went
everywhere with him. He camped deep in the mountains, in the Bayou Salado, the South Park of today, and
found it a hunter's paradise. He camped all along the
upper reaches of the Arkansas and at Fisher's Hole. He
camped for days alone far up the Front Range in the
shadow of Pike's Peak and he felt the sinews of mind and
body expanding in response to the grandeur all about
him and he knew that the happiest moments of his life
were being spent in the wilderness of the American
West.

And always, often and often, at the Pueblo and at
campsites and in chance encounters along the trails,

there was the companionship around good fires and the strong flavorous talk of the men of the mountains.

Time was running out. He was expected back home in England. In late spring he left with a party of trappers headed for the States and during the next weeks added to his experiences that of wagon-train travel across the plains. They followed down the Arkansas to Bent's Fort and beyond, then struck up through what is now Kansas to Fort Leavenworth on the Missouri. There he found a kind master for Panchito and sold the mules to the fort commissary on the assurance they would have plenty of good food. He was amused when several dragoons, regarding the weather-worn dirty-buckskinned whole of him, debated whether he was an Indian, then proud when they decided he was a "white trapper," a "regular mountain boy."

The rest of the way was relatively easy, in supposed civilized comfort. By steamboat down the Missouri to St. Louis. Up the Mississippi and the Peoria to Chicago. Around by the lakes to Buffalo. By train to Albany. Then down the Hudson to New York and a good ship called the *New World* bound for Liverpool.

But accepting the ways of civilization again was not easy. His body rebelled at soft beds after the sturdy comfort of sleeping on hard ground. His head protested at a stiff stylish hat after the warm comfort of a fur turban. His feet resented boots after the flexible freedom of moccasins. Struggling into such things as braces and waistcoats and fashionable gloves was a series of miseries. Chairs were a positive nuisance; he caught himself frequently in the act of bending to squat on the floor. Forks

seemed unnecessary and ridiculous implements when
fingers and a knife were adequate eating tools. George
Ruxton had a new attitude not only toward hunting but
toward many of the fripperies of social custom.

He was back in England by the middle of August,
1847, and set to work to fend off restlessness by keeping
busy with his pen. All the notes and memoranda he had
made on his jaunt up through Mexico, along with manuscripts and documents on the history of New Mexico and
its Indians he had collected, had been lost during the
trip across the plains in the difficult passage of the flood-
ing Pawnee Fork of the Arkansas. But he did have what
he called his "rough notebook" and a good memory. Before the end of the year *Adventures in Mexico and the
Rocky Mountains* had appeared in both a two-volume
paperback edition and regular book form.

A good book, well received, crisp and vital and alive.
And along with it, written for magazine publication, an
article on "The Texan Ranger," another about "The
Battle of Buena Vista," and another developing the
theory that the Aztecs of Mexico had migrated southward out of New Mexico and were related to the Pueblo
tribes. Quite a satisfactory batch of writing to come in
such a short time from a new young writer only a few
months past his twenty-sixth birthday.

But George Augustus Frederick Ruxton was not
satisfied. He kept remembering the taste of buffalo hump
roasted over an open fire and the fierce free winds that
blew through the American West and those strange eccentric beings in the shape of men who strode the American mountains as other men strode city streets.

During the first months of 1848 he wrote *Life in the*

Far West. Fictional in form with even a thread of romance — yet no fiction in it. Disconnected incidents brought together to make a continuous narrative and characters sometimes placed where perhaps they had not been at the time — but every incident authentic and every character real. Not an incident he had not heard recounted by men who took part in it or had been close enough to it to know the straight of it. Not a character whose name cannot be found in the historical records of the West — except for the two whose names he changed, La Bonté and the other Killbuck. He was paying his tribute to the mountain men in a form he hoped would hold interest — and his tribute to the truth about them.

The manuscript was finished and in the hands of the editors of *Blackwood's Edinburgh Magazine* where it would appear anonymously in serial form during the latter half of the year. Early the next year it would be published in book form. Meanwhile he was restless again and discontented and his health seemed to be failing. While staying at the Pueblo he had been thrown from the bare back of a mule. He had landed on a sharp picket pin of an Indian lodge and had injured his spine. That had not bothered him much then, but it was beginning to bother him now. Inactivity irked him. He felt that if only he were out and doing again he would be himself once more. He tried to organize a yacht voyage to Borneo. He tried again to interest the British government in his plan to explore central Africa. He considered a proposition from the Aborigines Protection Society that he go to Canada to work with the Indians there.

Those were halfhearted notions, the result of restlessness. Then, with growing conviction, he knew what it was he needed, what it was he wanted. A far land had put its mark upon him and had made him its own. He was an alien now in the land of his birth. Across the thousands of miles he could still sniff the wild free breezes of the Rockies. Echoing the men of his book, he put it straight in a letter to a friend. He was "half froze for buffler meat and mountain doin's."

He booked passage to New York with an itinerary all planned. Albany, Buffalo, Chicago, St. Louis, Fort Leavenworth. The Santa Fe Trail to the Arkansas and up the river into the mountains, to the Bayou Salado. Winter there and in the spring across the mountains to see what might be doing in the neighborhood of Great Salt Lake.

He reached St. Louis in the middle of August, 1848, and checked into the Planter's House. There he would stay for a few days while outfitting for the trip across the plains. He was one month past his twenty-seventh birthday and the whole of the West lay before him.

Epidemic dysentery was raging in the town. The disease took him and two weeks later he died.

Years passed and the little cemetery in which he was buried was abandoned. The stone that had marked his grave had long since disappeared. His remains, with those of others, were removed to another cemetery and interred again, unnamed and unmarked. And that means nothing.

He needs no marker, no monument. Because his book, *Life in the Far West*, his book lives. The first and still the finest about the American mountain men, full of their weird and wonderful lingo and their epic doings, crackling with life and vitality and exuberance on every page, the major source book for all later writers. That crossbred Irish-Scottish Englishman met and knew and talked long hours with more of the mountain men out of their great days than any other man who would ever write about them. Briefly but thoroughly he lived their life with them. With his vagabond inclinations and his wayward disposition and his determined self-will he was the one man of those who knew them who could and did write about them, in that pious Victorian era addicted to stilted styles and the glossing-over of the unpleasant, with courage and honesty and simple unblinking acceptance of all aspects of them, the crude and bloody and brutal along with the fine and decent and admirable.

That second cemetery to which his remains were removed has in its turn been abandoned. A tall building stands on the site. Modern machinery, digging for the foundation, has ripped into the ground, scattering the dirt and the dust.

Winds blow westward from St. Louis out across the Mississippi and the Missouri. His dust is dust of the American West.

John A. Thompson

APRIL 30, 1827 — MAY 15, 1876

I N 1837 the good ship *Engiheden,* two months on the way, brought into New York harbor ninety-some Norwegian immigrants under the leadership of one Kleng Peerson who was making a business of organizing and establishing Norwegian settlements in the United States. On the roster this time was a ten-year-old boy named Jon Torsteinson Rui and with him were his mother, his stepfather Thom Thomson, his older brother Torstein, and his younger half-sister Tina.

The whole group stayed together and went on to Buffalo and then by boat again along the Great Lakes to Chicago and there some remained and the rest continued on in wagons provided by Kleng Peerson to a small settlement on the Fox River in western Illinois. The Thomson family went with them and moved into a small cabin that had been abandoned by previous settlers. They had been able to bring very little with them. Almost all their money had gone for the passage. Their major reliance

was the strength of big Thom Thomson and the willing
help of the two stepsons, Torstein and Jon.

*See him there, Jon Torsteinson Rui, ten years old,
blond as the blondest of his people, hair and eyebrows
the pale washed gold of the lightest corn tassel, fair of
skin, eyes a clear light blue, almost as tall already as his
four-years-older brother, shoulders already broader and
broadening, a stalwart young Viking from a far northland, faithfully doing the chores assigned him about a
small cabin on the flat Illinois prairie — and dreaming
of the great craggy mountains and the frozen winter
magnificence of his homeland.*

It was in some respects a typical frontier family, for
quite a spell always settling and never settled. Stepfather
Thom Thomson could adapt his name to the new world
as Thomas Thompson but not himself as easily to the
new land. He too missed the mountains. But he knew
that mountain land was poor land and he had left Norway because it was almost all mountains and therefore
poor, offering scant opportunity. He would forget the
mountains if he could find what he had come to America
to find, good farmland. But with so much land open to
settlers in this new country, might there not always be
better land just beyond the horizon? The climate in this
part of Illinois seemed to be unhealthy. Cholera hit the
settlement and graves had to be dug. After his own work
of the days he worked on into the nights to pay for a
wagon of his own and a team of oxen to pull it. When he
had these, he moved his family to another Peerson settlement in northeastern Missouri. Two years at the first
place in Illinois. Four at this one in Missouri. Then he
moved again, northward into Iowa to yet another Peerson colony. Two years and he moved again, back in-

to Illinois. He was tired of moving. Here he stayed.

There were more children in the family now, little ones not old enough to help with the work. Torstein was married and had left to find his own place in Wisconsin. Jon was the mainstay worker alongside Thomas Thompson.

Six years Jon stayed here in Illinois and plowed and harvested and brought in the winter wood alongside his stepfather, that big fine man who had taken a fatherless family unto himself and had treated the two sons of another as if they were his own. Jon's strength grew and in time surpassed even that of big Thomas Thompson. That strength was needed while the little ones in their turn were growing. But often in the evenings he sat on the doorstep and looked westward where, so tales told, were mountains to match and outmatch those back across the Atlantic and the North Sea. He was a slow reader and he read slowly through everything he could find about the West, about the mighty Rockies that struck north and south like the great spine of the continent, and beyond them the sheer steep uprise of the high Sierras. Reports came of gold in California, in the mountains, and the urge to go in search of it was an ache in him. But he had a debt to pay to a big fine man who was no longer as young as he used to be. Jon stayed, pouring his young strength into the plow furrows and into the long hard days of the harvesting, faithful and cheerful always, and only the faraway look often in his pale blue eyes told what was in his mind. In the early summer of 1851, with the plowing done and the crops in, it was his mother, speaking for herself and for her understanding husband, who told him that the debt which was no debt but a free giving of himself was long since paid, that he had done more than his part, that if ever he were to do it he should leave now and follow his own dream westward.

See him now, Jon Torsteinson Rui, still using that name given by his blood-father, twenty-four years old, six feet in his socks, shoulders broad as a weighing beam, body in proportion, one hundred eighty pounds of strong bone and sinewy muscle, able to outwrestle and outlift and outwork any man he had ever met, erect in the saddle on a good horse, a rifle in the saddle scabbard, a pistol in his belt, riding straight into the American West.

To St. Joseph on the Missouri he rode, where the wagon trains formed for the long journey northwestward into the Oregon country. Out along the Oregon Trail he rode, sometimes jogging for a few days with a wagon train, giving of the young strength that flowed inexhaustible in him to help dig out bogged wagons and repair broken wheels and heave against backboards in the fording of rocky streams, sometimes simply pushing on alone. Westward he rode across the plains of Nebraska with the vast rolling sealike land rising, always rising, and his heart rising with it and at last leaping in the fierce joy of the wanderer who sees his homeland again when he saw, far ahead in Wyoming distance, what had seemed a great bank of clouds sharpen in outline and emerge as the front line of the Rockies, the Medicine Bow range.

Mountains, yes. But when he reached them they were not mountains to match his remembrance. He did not know it at the time, but in following the Oregon Trail he was taking the low route through the Rockies. To the north or to the south of the trail he might have found mountains to satisfy and to hold him. Gold in them too as a few more years would show. He rode on and when he had crossed the continental divide, hardly aware he had done so, he left the Oregon Trail and swung south-westward into Utah and to the Mormon settlement that would be Salt Lake City, following the trail beat out by the '49ers.

It was midsummer now and the heat lay thick and heavy over the Great Basin between the Rockies and the Sierras. Ahead of him were the Great Salt Lake Desert and seemingly endless miles of sun-baked land and the sunken inferno of the Carson Sink. He rode on. The way was marked with the rotting bodies and the picked-bare skeletons of horses and mules and oxen and with aban-doned wagons and the piled stones and wooden crosses of graves. He rode on, day after day, and his fair skin was burned and whipped into western toughness, and he rode on and far ahead beyond and above the desert haze, striking across the whole western horizon, rose the great wall of the Sierras, sudden and superb in their swift up-sweep of two miles and more in height out of the Nevada desert, dark blue in distance against the pale blue of the sky that was the same pale clean blue of his eyes, and white-tipped in the topmost reaches with the eternal snows.

He rode to a place called Mormon Station on the Car-son River and dismounted and stood with head raised, looking upward into the heights of his mountains. Across fourteen years and thousands of miles of ocean and the soul-stretching distances of the New World he had come home again.

The gold diggings were on the other side of the Sierras. Better get across before winter sets in, he was told. He did. In the easy shifting partnerships of the

time he tried placer mining at Hangtown (now Placerville) and at camps with such names as Coon Hollow
and Kelsey's Diggings. It was hard rough work and that
was nothing to the strength that was in him. But there
was little profit. Only a lucky few out of the hundreds at
any camp ever hit it rich. He was not one of them. Most
men found that most of what gold they did manage to
grub out of the sands and gravels barely covered the high
cost of food and other supplies and what was left was just
about enough to keep them going. He was one of those.
The gold fever was not strong in him anyway. That had
been little more than an excuse to find and be near his
mountains. He took what gold he had been able to
scratch together and made a payment on a piece of land
on Putah Creek in the Sacramento Valley.

He was a farmer again and in a small way a rancher. It
was a living, but not much more. The land was fertile
enough. There was water enough — at the wrong time.
In spring the streams flooded from the melting snows in
the mountains. In summer, in the growing season, they
were dry or mere thin trickles and there was no rain. Irrigation would be the answer, the holding of the spring
flood water in reservoirs for release during the summer.
He knew that and talked of it with other men in the
valley, but there were not enough of them yet and not
enough with foresight enough to do much about it.
Meanwhile there were the mountains.

He was a friendly outgoing man though not much of a
talker and he was well liked by his scattered neighbors
though they did think him a bit strange. A big healthy
man like that — and not given to cards or liquor or
women or any of the usual pleasure pursuits of the rest
of them. He was a good man with a gun, could drop a

running deer with the best of them, and obviously he
could be a mighty man with his fists. But he was never
mixed up in any of the frequent shooting affrays or the
riotous brawls of the area. A few men jeered at him and
called him "Holy John." That soon died away. In the
west of those days a man could be as strange as suited
him as long as he did not step on other people's toes too
hard — especially a man so plainly able to take care of
himself in any kind of trouble and so willing to help
others with theirs. But he *was* a mite peculiar. When his
neighbors were relaxing from hard work or just blowing
off steam at saloons and dance-halls, sometimes even
when for his own good he ought to be working at home,
he would be off in the mountains, usually alone and
afoot. They told friendly tales about him. He really liked
to be up there in the snows. He actually enjoyed battling
a blizzard. He could sleep comfortably only when curled
up in a snowdrift. Maybe he was part grizzly bear.

They speculated too about him. What was he doing
up there? Hunting? Looking for gold?

He was doing both at times, not very actively, not car-
ing much whether he killed a deer except when he
needed meat, not particularly interested in trying to follow any gold scent to its source. Such things again were
mere excuses. He strode the high places for the simple
joy of the striding, of matching his strength against the
strength of the mountains. He was not yet directly aware
of it, but he was seeking his own way to the full release
of the ancestral Viking song in his blood.

For all his lonely mountaineering, he was a staunch
family man. He wrote regularly to his mother and stepfather in Illinois and to his brother in Wisconsin and

they wrote to him. He kept up with their doings and the progress of the littler ones. But letters were a long time going and coming. The only fairly certain method of mail delivery to California was by boat from the east coast all the long slow route down and around South America. Even this was not certain. There would be references in letters at last received to others that had never arrived.

Major George Chorpenning had the government contract for overland mail delivery to and from central California. That is, for attempts at overland delivery. He and a partner named Woodward made a start in 1851, dispatching a mule train carrying mail from Sacramento up and over the Sierras and to Salt Lake City. That was in May with the high passes already well cleared of snow and even so the train took many weeks on the way. Service continued at intervals through the summer. In the fall partner Woodward started with another train of mail carriers — and what happened to him and them was not known until late spring when the bodies were found. They had been delayed for weeks by the drifts already piling into the passes and after finally getting through had been killed by Indians out on the desert beyond.

In February of 1852 Chorpenning dispatched another party, five men with ten horses and mules. Fifty-three days later, on foot, they staggered into Salt Lake City. Not a one of them would ever try that again. Even in April another mail party took forty-seven days to get through.

The experience of that winter was enough. For the next few years there were no more attempts to take mail over the mountains during the winter months. Chorpenning shifted to a route far southward through Arizona and New Mexico. It was a long slow uncertain route and two or three mail deliveries through a whole winter were all that could be expected. At least it was some semblance of service for the people of central California on the western side of the Sierras. But the people of the settlements on the other, the eastern side, where the mountains dropped down into Nevada, were completely shut off. For five months or more out of each twelve they could neither receive nor send mail.

In the winter of 1855–56 Chorpenning tried again. There was no difficulty getting mail to Hangtown-become-Placerville at the western base of the mountains. There would not be too much difficulty distributing it to the settlements on the other side from Carson City at the eastern base of the mountains. Placerville to Carson City — such a seeming small gap on a map. Only ninety miles in distance as a condor might fly. But all of it through steep snow-choked frozen wilderness up and over the Sierras with landmarks lost in drifts and the passes and sudden canyons packed with snow forty and more feet deep and fierce blinding storms occurring almost daily.

Chorpenning published an appeal in the two Sacramento weekly newspapers calling for men willing to attempt the trip on snowshoes. The winter was just beginning. The real snows were yet to come. Three or four men in turn accepted the challenge. Each in turn started — and gave up and came back.

Jon Rui was snug in his cabin on Putah Creek. Already he had enough oak wood cut from the slopes behind his cabin to last him through the winter. There was no snow yet in the valley, but he knew it was piling ever deeper far up there in his mountains. As always when the chill winds began to sweep down from the heights, he was restless and dissatisfied with himself and what he had done and was doing. His mountains, building their winter strength up where the tall peaks climbed, were calling to him.

A rider stopped by his cabin, bringing two items, a letter and a copy of the Sacramento *Transcript*. The letter had been months on the way. It was from his stepfather in Illinois. The first line told him that his mother had died of the influenza.

Months ago that was. Months ago his mother had been in her last illness and he had not known. She had died asking if there was any letter from her Jon.

Ah, those damnable mails that took so long on the way and so often did not get through!

For a long time he stared at the letter and the newspaper on the rough table before him. Gradually his eyes focused on two lines of bold-faced type in the paper heading an appeal:

PEOPLE LOST TO THE WORLD
UNCLE SAM NEEDS A MAIL CARRIER.

In his slow careful way he read the piece through, once, twice. Yes. If the mail situation was bad for him and his neighbors on this side of the mountains, it was worse, much worse, for those on the other side.

Placerville to Carson City. He knew the country between. No man knew it better. Rugged wearing country even in summer, wicked in winter. Two years ago he had guided a merchant and his son over it and that was in

March with the snow going and clear weather all the way and even so he had been forced to fashion crude mallets so they could hammer out paths for the mules through innumerable great drifts and the trip had taken ten hard days with the merchant and his son exhausted at the end and vowing never to try anything like that again.

Placerville to Carson City. In midwinter? Even on snowshoes? Impossible. Those webbed frames, something like oversize tennis rackets, would sustain a man on the deep snow all right. He had a pair hanging on his cabin wall and had used them often. But they were good only for relatively short distances and over relatively level terrain. They were not for the steep slopes and the brush-clogged hillsides and the dizzying heights. And they made slow going. A man carrying mail could not also carry much food or such things as blankets. He would have to move fast, make time. It was impossible. No man could do it.

Impossible? What was it his mother used to tell him when she knew he was bored with the daily round of farm life and she wanted to cheer him? That perhaps he would be one who some day would do what no other man could do.

He stared long at the paper and memories stirred in his mind, memories out of his early boyhood in a far northland, memories of men skimming over the great snows that mantled that mountainous land, skimming on twin runners, one strapped to each foot, runners long and thin and curled up at the front ends. Not Canadian snowshoes like those hanging on his cabin wall. Norwegian snowshoes! Skis, they had called them!

He took a pencil and tried to make sketches. It would not be as easy as it looked. He strode outside and selected two good pieces of oak wood and went to work on them. Day after day he worked with his few tools, and under his hands something new to the new world and to the western mountains came into being. Two of them. Ten feet long they were and four inches wide and nearly an inch thick and they curved up on the front ends with small carved figures there as was right for the prows of these small Viking ships that would be launched onto the snows of the Sierras. Straps were fastened firmly to go over his boot toes and little wooden crosspieces behind to hold his heels. The undersides were whittled and scraped and sanded as smooth as he could make them. And as he worked, he worried that perhaps it would not be right, at least the postal people might not think it right, for American mail to be carried by a man with a strange-looking foreign name. He would take another. The Jon his father had given him, only spelled now with an "h" added, and the surname to show tribute to the stepfather who had raised him. To balance it out a middle initial. John A. Thompson.

He wrapped his Norwegian snowshoes in canvas and swung up on his horse and rode to Placerville. In Snyder's General Store he weighed his runners on the scale there. Twenty-five pounds. Heavy. Heavier than he had thought. There was no time to work more on these or to make others. People on the other side of the mountains were waiting for mail from the outside world. And there was still much to do. He went into the hills behind the town where the snow was piling toward winter depth and went to work again.

Work it was. There was no one to tell him, no one to show him. There was only an occasional onlooker to jeer and call his runners "snow skates." He had to learn by doing. He stumbled, he staggered, he floundered, he fell, often and often. He crashed into trees and into rocks jutting above the snow. When that happened, he twisted and flung his body to take the shock and save his runners from being snapped and broken. Bruised and battered, he kept on, day after day. And he learned. By harsh trial and error he mastered those long ungainly runners. He kept on until they were like wings added to his feet and he was skimming on the downgrades like the men of his onetime homeland. And he was right. Those long, only seeming ungainly runners could be used on the steep upslopes too. By throwing them out wide he could work steadily upward, leaving tracks like slant slashes or disjointed V's in the snow. On the even steeper slopes he could climb in long zigzags athwart the slant like cutbacks in a mountain trail.

Two weeks and he felt he was ready. He went to the Placerville post office and spoke to a clerk who thought he was joking but did take the word to another man in the back room. It was Major Chorpenning himself who came out, hurried and excited. He was not interested in names and how they looked or sounded. He would have taken this man, any man, under any name or circumstances. Mail for the Carson Valley had been piling up for months. After the formality of official enrollment, there was one question.

"Can you start in the morning?"

"I can."

See him now, John A. Thompson, early in January of 1857, twenty-nine years old, wearing no overcoat that could clog his movements, carrying no blanket that would add weight, sixty pounds of mail on his back, twenty-five pounds of Norwegian snowshoes on his feet, some jerked beef and a few hard biscuits in a pocket, some matches wrapped in oilcloth in another, alone all alone in the upper reaches of the high Sierras with the zero winds whipping at him and the snow packed fifty and more feet deep into the sudden treacherous gulches and canyons, working upward always upward toward the final crests, matching his strength against the winter strength of his mountains!

This was the harder part of the trip, climbing the western slopes. One after another the ridges rose ahead of him to be surmounted toward the tall peaks. But he was right. Norwegian snowshoes could do it. Norwegian snowshoes — and a man out of Norway with the blood of Vikings in him.

After the slow toiling ascent of each new ridge there was the sweeping release and partial rest of skimming into the high valley or over the benchland beyond before striking into the steep upward climb again. He was following in general the Carson Emigrant Road used by the westward migrations in summer. But with wings on his feet he could take shortcuts where the road had to follow a twisting tortuous course. The snow itself was a help. Packed into the gulches and fissures in the rock, it enabled him to skim over places that would have been impassable in summer.

Overconfident in his new prowess, he became careless. A deep narrow chasm blocked his way and he could hear water roiling over rocks far below. To climb on, seeking to head it, would take him miles out of the way. Ah, there was a snowbridge spanning it, ten feet thick and seeming solid. He started across and was out in the middle when there were cracklings behind him. The bridge was breaking loose from the rock wall. He scrambled forward as the bridge sagged and broke beneath him and he plunged forward, grasping at the cliff edge on the other side. One hand closed on a tough pine root and he hung there dangling into the chasm as the fragments of the bridge fell to the rocks far below.

Tough pine root! tough and stubborn as all things had to be to survive in the high Sierras! Stout strength built up through the years in the wide shoulders and thick-thewed arm of John A. Thompson! With the awkward weight of mail and snowshoes dragging at him he drew himself up and lay panting on the cold snow-dusted rock. That had been a foolish chance for a man to take and for a man carrying precious mail to people lost to the world. No more mistakes of that kind.

He went on. His back muscles ached from the unaccustomed load they held. His leg muscles ached from the hours of constant climbing. But somehow the aches were sweet and satisfying because the strength to take them and to make nothing of them and to keep going steadily on was there too. This job he was doing, striking straight into the heart of the white frozen magnificence of these mountains that resembled those rimming the horizon of his early boyhood — this challenge to all there was in him, he knew now, was what he had come west to find.

Twenty-five miles he made that first day. He snugged down for rest in the almost bare hollow in the lee of a big stump. He whittled some shavings from the old wood and lit these with one of his matches. As the fire took hold, eating into the stump, he scooped out a hollow in the drift facing the fire and lined it with boughs pulled from a nearby pine. He chewed on the jerked beef and hard biscuits. He slept and wind whistled overhead

and snow fell and closed over the opening of his hollow
and he slept warm and snug inside and in the morning he
broke out and shook himself like a shaggy bear and fastened the mailbag to his back again and the runners to
his boots and was into the long climb once more.

This was the country of Steven's Peak and Red Lake
Peak and the high frozen glory of Lake Tahoe and the
somber dread of Summit Valley where only a few years
before the Donner Party had been caught by these snows
of winter and forty of them had died in slow horror before help came. The great white silence was broken only
by the whistling of the winds and the occasional shatter-
ing roar of a snowslide in the distance. Nothing else human moved in the great white wilderness.

All day he worked his way upward. He was above timberline now where there was no protection from the
whipping winds and in late afternoon snow began again,
the tiny-flaked flinty snow of the upper altitudes, and it
thickened and was driven so by the wind that he could
scarcely see a few feet ahead. No crawling into a snow
hole in weather like this. He could be so buried that he
would never emerge alive. He found a flat ledge kept
bare by the wind and there he stopped. He crouched
low, chewing on what was left of the jerked beef, and
when the cold sank in deep, he would rise and move
about on the rock ledge and dance to a tune of his own
making to send the blood flowing strong again through
his body.

Alone in the dark of winter night in the heart of the
high Sierras, he jigged to the beat of the Viking song in
his blood and the spirits of Viking ancestors jigged there
with him.

In the first faint light of dawn the snow had slackened

some and he went on, still climbing. All that day he climbed, into the teeth of the storm, and the aches in his back muscles and in his leg muscles were constant and deepening, but the strength to make nothing of them was there too. That night he snugged down again in a snow hole.

In the morning he went on, still climbing, and the storm had worn itself out and the sun shone, brilliant on the fresh snow, almost blinding him, and he pulled his hat brim low and went on and in the afternoon topped out and saw below him Hope Valley with the beginnings of the West Carson River a frozen gleam running through it.

Hope Valley. Rightly named. There were mountains beyond it — but not mountains like those behind him. He had reached the crest of his trip. It would be mostly downgrade now and the wings on his feet would give him speed.

The afternoon of the next day, the fourth out of Placerville, he was skimming down the steep slopes from Genoa Peak to that same Mormon Station to which he had come from the east five years before, known now as the little town of Genoa.

Someone saw him coming and began shouting. Everyone in the small settlement was out, watching, when he banked in a big curve and coasted in among them. They stared in wonder at the strange things strapped to his feet. They stared at him as at a man suddenly dropped out of nowhere. But what was that he was unfastening from his shoulders? It looked like one of those black leather bags the Chorpenning line used.

Good God in heaven! Mail!

His back was thumped, his arm pumped; if he had let

them, the women would have kissed his hand. And who
was it who had brought something more precious this
time of year than nuggets of gold?

"John A. Thompson of Putah Creek."

No, no. Nothing that plain and prosaic. Was there no
better name to ring in countless tales on through the
years and his mountains?

Yes!

Snowshoe Thompson of the high Sierras!

Genoa's mail left at Genoa. A swift run on to Carson
City. He was there that night. In the morning he was
strapping on his Norwegian snowshoes again and asking
about return mail for the Sacramento Valley.

There was plenty of it. It had been coming in periodi-
cally from Salt Lake City and piling up here too for
months. With eighty pounds or more on his back he
started the return trip.

He knew what he could do now. No bothering to follow even in a general way any trail worked out in the
warm weather for earthbound creatures like mules and
horses and stumble-footed men. With the strength that
was in him and with those wings on his feet he was free
of the whole of his mountains, could strike out straight
into them anywhere as a condor might fly. On the evening of the second day he was zooming down the western
slopes and to Placerville. Two days for that return trip.
Six days in all for the round trip.

"Settle your bets, gentlemen! Pay up smiling, all you
who scoffed and said no man could do it!"

And through the rest of that winter and on through
the following winters the mail went through, both ways,
a round trip every two weeks, on the broad back of Snow-

shoe Thompson. Regular as clockwork. Three days for the eastward jump with its longer steeper climbs, two days for the return. Sometimes in good weather, just to see if he could do it, he cut the round trip down to four days. Sometimes, when the mail was plentiful, he slipped in extra trips.

Not just Placerville to Carson City and Carson City to Placerville. Side jaunts too on the way to any tiny settlement or lonely cabin anywhere in the whole vast expanse which would otherwise receive no mail until the late spring thaw. Wherever there was mail to be delivered in or about his mountains, Snowshoe Thompson delivered it. Sometimes without even making a stop. He might come swooping down one side of a high hidden valley, gobbling the miles at gathering speed, and toss a packet of mail to thump against a cabin door and keep right on for the momentum of his flying rush to carry him up and over the other side of the valley with cheers from the cabin's inhabitants following him on the wind of his own swift passage.

Weather meant nothing to that man. When the time set for his departure came he departed, heading if need be into a mountain blizzard, kept warm by his own astounding exertions as he fought his lone way up the snow-packed ridges. Day and night became the same to him, often the night better for traveling because there would be a better crust on the snows. He rested when he felt a need to rest and when he woke went on, into sunlight or starlight or storm the same. He had learned his techniques on that first trip, how to snug down by a burning stump, how to outlast the worst blinding blizzard by jigging on the high rock. In time he had a few more or less regular stopping places to be used when his route led past them. One was a small cave up near the topmost peaks which he had lined with springy pine boughs.

Frequently he varied his routes, exploring his mountains as he went over them. Let them try to trick him with great shifting drifts and wind-whirled snow hiding and distorting landmarks. He could strike out anywhere into them and drive direct where he wanted to go, guided by an unfailing sense of direction and a shrewd racial knowledge of mountain country. Snowshoe Thompson get lost? All he had to do anytime, alone in his winter wilderness, was study the trees, the prevailing wind, the rock configurations, the mountain formations, if at night the stars, and he could line straight to his goal. "I was never lost — I can't be lost," he said in his simple straightforward way, simply stating a fact. He tapped his forehead with a finger. "There's something in here which keeps me right."

Something was in there, true enough, which kept him "right" in more than merely directional ways.

They were sure of that, the men he rescued from their own foolishness in his mountains. Not a winter went by that he did not once or twice or more times come on exhausted travelers who had lost their way and wandered for days in the deepening snows. He guided them, led them, if necessary carried them, to the nearest settlements. There would be little time for gratitude. The moment he was sure they were in safe hands, he would wave one of his own — and be on his way again with the mail.

Once he was lost — for a time. He was hit by snow blindness. Four days he groped his way along a ridge top which was not the ridge top he thought it was. But he was Snowshoe Thompson. Somehow he found his bearings. He was stumbling from tree to tree straight toward a tiny settlement when woodcutters, coming out from it, saw him and led him in. The mail pack was still on his back. After a rest and partial restoration of sight, seeing dimly through slitted eyes, he was on his way again.

Chorpenning was having financial troubles. He had overextended his operations. He was having trouble collecting from the government far away in Washington, which was too busy with other matters to pay much attention to California. He could not pay. Not now anyway. Perhaps later. Snowshoe kept right on delivering the mail. He was not doing this just for pay in money. He was doing it for the look on the faces of the people in the lonely places when he brought them letters they would not have received without long months of more waiting. He was doing it because it satisfied an urge in him. It gave a meaning, a purpose, an excuse, for the use to full final extent of the seemingly inexhaustible power that pulsed in his big broad-beamed body.

But he was a poor man. He had need for the pay that was not being paid. No matter. He could get along by doing more. He carried more than mail. He carried medicines and lightweight supplies and tools and samples of ore for assays and small parts for mining machinery — and the people for whom he carried these things gladly paid. Only he himself really knew the total weight of some of the loads he carried over his mountains strapped in a huge hump up behind those broad shoulders.

He was the man who carried over the mountains to Sacramento the samples of the strange "blue stuff" that assayed out more than $2000 to the ton in gold and silver and started the rush to the Comstock Lode. He was the man who carried over the mountains the type and the first press, part by part, for Genoa's *Territorial Enterprise* (later moved to Virginia City) which was soon one of the famous papers of the West and published the first writings of a young man who used the name of Mark Twain. And when the *Enterprise* was publishing, he was the man who carried copies of it back over the mountains to the settlements on the other side.

One man — and for months each year a veritable lifeline for many men. And for women and children. They adored him. He was their contact with the outside world. Under the influence of such friendship and adoration his spirit expanded. He had found his niche, his function. He was doing what no other man could do, would even attempt to do. He became more talkative, even gay and joking. Along with the mail and newspapers and word of the outside world, he brought personal good will and cheer and zest for life.

Just a big not-too-bright Norsky, said a few jealous grumblers. Only a mailman after all.

No!

Snowshoe Thompson of the high Sierras!

Just by being himself he had started something. It was amazing how many people were fashioning Norwegian snowshoes and tumbling into snowbanks in the foothills on both sides of the mountains. He encouraged them all he could. He made better runners for himself (seven and a half feet long and much lighter and slimmer toward the rear and gently widening toward the front) and he made many pairs for others and would take no money for them. He never wearied of coaching anyone who asked for it. What he liked best was to make small runners for small children and to teach them and to watch them skim over the snows.

There were men who, when they felt up to it, would start out on a mail trip with him on their own Norwegian snowshoes and accompany him for a while. But when he headed into the real mountains, into the climbs toward the tall peaks, they would return and he would go on alone. No one else cared to try what was only routine for Snowshoe Thompson.

He had sold his farm on Putah Creek and established a small ranch on the other side of the mountains, in Diamond Valley about thirty miles south of Carson City, not far from Genoa. Naturally skiing (they called it skiing now) was popular in that area. Everyone, women and children too, seemed to be imitating Snowshoe Thompson. The men formed a skiing club, the Alpine, and gathered often for runs on the slopes of Genoa Mountain. Soon there were good skiers among them. But not another one like Snowshoe. He would go to the very tip of the peak and come sweeping down mile after mile, unchecked, unbraked, at forty to fifty miles an hour, his balancing pole held crosswise in front of him, threading at astonishing speed between the trees, swooping close around the bare rock formations, thrusting up, leaping out into open air from terrace after terrace and landing and zooming on. Once they measured one of his prodigious leaps. One hundred and eighty feet! It would be more than sixty years before any American skier would surpass that — and then only on a carefully prepared slide with an artificial upward takeoff

and on the best scientifically made skis well doped with
the latest scientific preparation for maximum efficiency.

It was the second winter of his mail-carrying for
Chorpenning. It was late in December, the 23rd. A
heavy load of Christmas mail for the Carson valley was
on his back. He was two days out of Placerville and far
up among the peaks just coasting down into high Lake
Valley where he would spend the night in a deserted
cabin that was used in summer as a trading post by two
men named Sisson and Hawley. He had been pushing
hard with no previous rest on the way, to get through in
time for the holiday. Tomorrow's run would bring him
into Carson City for Christmas Eve.

Good. The snow was not particularly deep in the valley
and the cabin was not almost buried as these mountain
ones often were in winter. He chuckled to himself, remembering the time he had tried to get into one by slid-
ing down the chimney. That was the closest squeak he
ever had. He had become stuck partway down. Stuck
fast. Only his tremendous strength had pulled him out
and then only after a long struggle.

He went around by the door and took off his skis and
rapped them against the cabin wall to clear them of
snow. He jumped, startled, at a sound from inside — a
hoarse voice faintly calling. He hurried in — and found
James Sisson on the floor, back propped against a wall,
legs stretched out in front of him. Both feet were frozen
hard, swollen painfully against the heavy boots encasing
them.

A tough man, too, that Sisson. He had been spending
the winter near Placerville and two weeks before had

started over the mountains on snowshoes for the Carson valley. He was well up into the heights on the evening of the second day when he was caught in a bad storm. He had staggered about for hours with his feet slowly freezing and at last had made it to the cabin. But by then he could barely stumble along — and the cabin had been virtually stripped, perhaps by wandering Indians weeks before, of everything in it. The matches he carried with him were wet and useless. Four days he had been there, able only to haul himself about with his hands, before he found a few dry matches in some straw in a corner. There was no firewood. What fire he could make from a broken chair and the scant debris in the cabin had meant little and for only a little time. Twelve days he had been there now and the only food a bit of dirty flour he had scraped from the floor where it had been spilled sometime in the past. He had tried to cut off his boots with a pocketknife and had failed. Both legs were cold blue now up to the knees. Gangrene was setting in.

Snowshoe Thompson had arrived just in time. Sisson was weak and feverish and close to hysteria. But he was a mountain man. He was still trying to do what he could. He was sharpening an old ax — getting ready to try to amputate his own feet.

There was another use for that ax now. Snowshoe stepped out of the cabin and swung it with the strength of those shoulders behind it into a dead tree. In a matter of minutes he had a good fire blazing in the fireplace and was stacking wood beside it. Gently he slashed at Sisson's boots with his own knife until he had them off, easing some the constant pain that Sisson was taking without complaint. He handed Sisson the bit of food that remained in one of his pockets and stepped to the door. "I'll be back," he said and was outside strapping on his skis.

It was a fast run he made that night, down the western slopes of his mountains. All caution thrown to the winds that whipped around him, he raced through the starlit dark, driving for speed, speed, speed, down the sharp descents, crashing through brush, taking jumps he would have dodged on an ordinary run, once leaping straight out from a fifty-foot cliff. In early morning he swept into Genoa.

Let someone else take the mail on to Carson City. There was other work for Snowshoe Thompson to do.

Dr. Daggett could not come. He was hurrying off on an emergency call to tend the victims of a bad accident in Gold Canyon. But other men could and would. Five of them, two on skis, three on Canadian snowshoes, started out with Snowshoe leading the way. It was late dark of Christmas Eve when they reached the cabin in Lake Valley. They did what more they could for Sisson and set to work to make a good-sized sled. Snowshoe Thompson, who had had no rest for three days now and the nights between, swayed a bit as he worked. Get some sleep, the others insisted. He lay down on the floor and slept. He did not know it then, but that sleep and a few hours more snatched during the next night would save Sisson's life.

In the gray of dawn, Christmas Day, they left the cabin, Sisson bundled on the makeshift sled. Two feet of fresh snow had fallen during the night. Sisson was a big man and his weight on the weight of the clumsy sled made it sink deep in the soft new snow. It was slow going even on the downgrades, almost impossible on the up, even with the other men pulling and the great shoulders of Snowshoe Thompson heaving behind. They were only halfway down to Genoa when night came and with it more snow, blinding snow whipped by the winds. They huddled by a fire under semi-protecting trees, waiting out the dark and the worst of the storm, getting only a few fitful hours of sleep in turns in the bitter cold, and at dawn were moving again. The snow decreased as they reached the lower levels and they could move faster. Along in the afternoon they staggered into Genoa.

A quick examination of Sisson by Dr. Daggett and the verdict was plain. Both legs must be amputated at the knee. But Dr. Daggett would not operate without chloroform and he was out of chloroform.

It would be dangerous to operate without an anesthetic. The patient was so weak that the shock might kill him. Against that could be set the inescapable fact that death would be certain unless an operation were performed. Even so, Dr. Daggett was adamant. He would not operate without chloroform.

Where was the nearest supply house where chloroform could be obtained? At Sacramento on the other side of the mountains.

On the other side of the mountains!

All right. Who was it the people of the Sierras depended upon to bring them such things?

Five days and the nights between had passed since Snowshoe Thompson had left Placerville. In all that time the hours of rest he had had from exertions beyond the capabilities of most men could be counted on the fingers of his two hands. He looked up at his mountains

marching in their cold serene indifference across the western horizon. He bent down to strap on again his Norwegian snowshoes.

*See him now, Snowshoe Thompson of the high Sierras,
thirty years old, just a big broad-shouldered not-too-
bright Norsky, just an unpaid country mailman, alone in
the great white frozen magnificence of his mountains,
slugging his way up the steep slopes with urgency in
every slap of his skis on the fresh soft unpacked clogging
snow, hurtling at express train speed on the downslopes,
driving as straight as his unerring instinct could take
him in disregard of all obstacles, leaping out from ledges
into unknown landfalls below, making it up and over
and down in a night and a day. See him on the immediate unrested return trip, hammering up the longer
steeper grades of the western slopes, eyes deep-sunk in
their sockets, color all but washed by weariness out of
them, the flesh of his face drawn and tight with the bones
seeming to start through the skin, great shoulders sagging
but still swinging into every steady stride, unflagging will
lashing flagging muscles to the last full limit of effort,
pitting his strength against the winter strength of his
mountains — and winning in another night and a day!*

Winning what? The life of James Sisson. The operation was successful and Sisson survived and moved away
to settle in the gentler East of the Atlantic coast.

But losing too, as flesh and bone must ultimately always lose against the eternal rock. The unparalleled
strain of those two swift mountain crossings, coming
hard after the instant previous exertions, had sunk deep
into him, had penetrated to the very base of his being.
He seemed to recover quickly and he was Snowshoe

Thompson still, the iron man of the mountains, scattering epic tales on through the years as another man might scatter seeds. But far inside him was an ache that never quite ceased and at times would rise and then wane and never quite ceased. He rarely spoke of it, never mentioned it except to those few closest to him. But it was there and it grew with the years.

The Pony Express came, to Carson City and over the mountains to Sacramento, and Snowshoe Thompson cheered as heartily as anyone. It was exciting and romantic and fine — for summer mail service. In the winter, when the snow took the mountains, the mail went on his broad back as it had for four winters now. And when the Piute Indians, aroused by the Pony Express and what it symbolized, attacked one of the stations and then led the avenging volunteers into an ambush and bitterly defeated them by Pyramid Lake, Snowshoe Thompson was in the midst of that fighting — and he was the one who took the word of the defeat over the mountains to Sacramento and guided the "army" of regulars and volunteers back to give the Piutes the bloody licking that ended that trouble.

The Carson Emigrant Road became a real road and coaches and horsemen could use it longer in the fall, earlier in the spring. Snowshoe Thompson was one of those out with oxteams and heavy drags to keep it open as long as possible and reopen it as soon as possible. But in the bitterest months when forty-foot drifts sneered at attempts to break through them, the mail went through on his broad back as it had for eight years now.

The Central Pacific Railroad, creeping for years in short track-laying spurts up the western slopes, reached the crest and was dropping rapidly down to cross the

Great Basin desert. The mail no longer needed to go
over the mountains on the broad back of Snowshoe
Thompson as it had for twelve winters now. But there
were other parts of those mountains and there were
still far lonely foothill and high valley settlements and
cabins that would have to wait the winter through for
mail if it were not for that broad back and those stout
legs beneath and the curve-tipped wings on his feet.

Meanwhile he had been married.

It was lonesome for a lone bachelor in his late thirties
sitting in his cabin reading letters from Wisconsin and
Illinois. Brother Torstein had three children and already
they were growing into long-legged youngsters. Sister
Tina was married and expecting. The little ones with
stepfather Thomas were no longer little ones. Before
long they would be getting married too.

The Alpine Boys were quite a club by this time,
gathering often for skiing sessions near Genoa. Their
families and others came to watch. Some of the girls and
women were skiing too. One day a new young woman
was among them, a bright-eyed laughing young lady
named Agnes Singleton who had recently come from
England with her mother to join her two brothers in
Genoa. She saw Snowshoe Thompson, the unselfconscious
unknowing superb concentrated power of him, swooping
down from the topmost tip of Genoa Mountain, leaping
out from terrace after terrace, emitting the high shrill
Sierra whoop that came automatically to his lips from
the joy of motion. Somehow she had unusual difficulty
staying upright on her own skis and needed considerable
coaching. Somehow Snowshoe, usually clumsy and
tongue-tied around young women, felt easy and compan-
ionable with her in not much time at all. Surprisingly,

he could even talk to her about his mountains and what
they meant to him.

Brothers were a convenient institution. He knew the
Singleton brothers well and could stop by to see them —
and stay to supper and find out what good cooking was
again after his years of doing for himself. But he was
only a poor farmer and rancher and a still-unpaid mailman. Chorpenning had finally gone bankrupt without
ever paying and had retired from the field and new contracts had not been formally straightened out and he had
simply gone on carrying mail to the out-of-the-way other-
wise-unserved places because he was the one man able
and willing to carry it. He thought over his situation and
worried about it. He worked harder than ever and tried
to save money. But he could not be Snowshoe Thompson
and save money. Too much of what he did was again, as
when he was a young man on the farm in Illinois, a free
giving of himself for others. It was the pattern of his life.
He was a poor man and very likely he would always be a
poor man.

What would his mother have said if she were alive and
with him? The same as when she told him to leave and
follow his dreaming. If ever he were to do it, he should
do it now before he was an old man too. That evening he
asked Agnes Singleton would she take him as he was and
would be.

Good heavens, yes! Almost since that first day on the
slopes of Genoa Mountain she had been wondering
when the big gold-headed lout of a slow-thinking Norsky
would get around to doing it.

She was the right wife for him. She made the little
cabin as comfortable a home as a frontier cabin with not
much money ever in it could be and she understood that

he was Snowshoe Thompson and the mails must go through even if there were no pay and when the urge was on him he must be up there in the frozen winter magnificence of his mountains, carrying mail, finding lost travelers — using such things as excuses for just being there. It was the pattern of his life.

And when he came back from one mail trip, hurrying as only he could hurry through those mountains because he knew her time was near, and found that the doctor had been at the cabin before him and he was the father of a lustily yelling boy with a topknot of pale gold hair the color of the lightest corn tassel, his life was complete.

Complete, except for that nagging little ache deep inside him which was more insistent than it used to be and which he refused to let stop him or slow him in the least.

He had really started something fourteen years ago. Skiing was the favorite winter sport nowadays on both sides of the mountains. The papers carried items about it, proudly reporting that it was becoming "scientific." Better and better skis were being made. Ski clubs were coming into existence here and there. Secret formulas for "dope" to be put on the runners to make them slicker and faster were jealously guarded by their inventors.

Northward at La Porte in the Feather River country of Plumas County of California the Alturas Snowshoe Club held annual matches, speed races. A grand prize of $600 was offered.

The Alpine Boys urged Snowshoe to go pick up that prize. He began to think seriously about it. The money certainly could be used by the little cabin in Diamond Valley. With it he could do more for his cheerful uncom-

plaining Agnes and for the small Arthur who was making his own first tries on his own tiny skis. La Porte was
two hundred miles northwestward over the mountains.
He strapped on his old Norwegian snowshoes and
skimmed over the mountains to La Porte.

There were many fine skiers on hand, some of them
originally from far northlands like himself. But they
were all modern, up to date, scientific. They raced down
a prepared track only twelve hundred feet long with a
fifteen-degree slope and a surface glazed almost into ice.
Their skis were doped to a shiny glassiness. They
crouched low on their runners, straddling a stick that
served as another runner under them and steadied and
guided them. Was that snowshoeing, skiing? It was more
like riding a sled downhill. No wonder they were often
called "riders."

They had heard of him and they were happy to have
him with them. They were friendly, too friendly. One of
them, amazed that he used no dope, grabbed his skis and
began rubbing them with his own secret formula. Snowshoe started to stop the man, then shrugged his big shoulders. That was the way they did it here and the man was
trying to do him a good turn.

They ran elimination heats in squads of four. He
stood at the top of the slide with the other three of his
first run and at the starting roll of the drum pushed out
and down. The doped skis rushed over the icy surface
and he fought to control them. He could hear shouts
from the sidelines, shouts of astonishment at his upright
stance with his pole not for riding but for balancing. He
was out in the lead and rushing like the wind. He began
to wobble as one doped ski slid a bit sideways on the
glassy surface. Straddle your stick! people were shouting.

No! That was not skiing! He went down, skidding in
ungainly sprawl into the snow at one side. He was up
and ready to plunge on, but the others were past and
darting toward the finish line.

According to the rules the losers had second chances.
He stood at the top with three others for another run.
Straddle your stick and crouch down, they said, friendly
and meaning well. No! That was not the way he remembered out of his boyhood the men of Norway skied.
They did not make sleds of themselves. They stood
upright like the men they were. He stood upright and
again he was out in the lead — and one of the others accidentally brushed against the end of his pole and he lost
his balance and was down again. He was finished. There
was no third chance.

He trudged back to the top and watched the rest of the
racing. So this was scientific skiing. When some of the
Alturas joshed him about his falls, he burst out with his
own challenge. Let them come over the mountains and
race against the Alpine Boys. Down a real hillside, not a
little hillock. Then down another well forested, zooming
in and out among the trees. Then down another with
natural terraces for leaps outward. Then finish off with a
run from the tip of Silver Peak the long miles to the bottom.

They stared at him. They grinned. Oh, no. They were
interested in their kind of skiing, not in breaking their
necks.

He scraped the dope off his skis and started on the two
hundred miles back to Diamond Valley. He was ashamed
of himself for talking like a hotheaded fool to men who
had welcomed him and would have cheered had he won
in their races. He was just an old-fashioned stubborn

Norsky fool of a snowshoer too stubborn and old-fashioned to take to the newfangled methods. Now that he
thought about it, there had been some mighty fine skiers
among those men. They had really gone whizzing. He
pushed on, taking the miles and whole ranges of hills
and mountains in his stride, in his slow-thinking unselfconscious way not realizing that in the going of the
long way to La Porte and now in the return he was
doing what not a one of the Alturas men would dare
even to try to do. He pushed steadily on, alone with his
mountains, not noticing that he was casually skimming
down steeper slopes than a one of them would think of
taking, was casually climbing great grades whose winter
tops they would never see.

To him, he was merely going home.

For fifteen winters he had been carrying mail and
emergency supplies to the lonely lonesome places no
other carrier would try to reach while the great drifts
barred the way. In all that time all that he had been paid
for the mail-carrying was one payment from one contractor of something like eighty dollars and sixty-six
cents. There had been promises aplenty but nothing had
come of them. The people of the Carson valley country
thought it was time something was done about that. They
prepared a petition to the national government in Washington suggesting a modest award of $6000 for his long
service. Circulating a petition in sparsely settled Nevada
was no easy matter, but in a short time this one had one
thousand signatures. The governor and other state officials in Carson City signed it too. The Nevada legislature
passed a resolution urging the national government to

take action. Nevada's senior senator introduced the petition in Congress.

Snowshoe Thompson was summoned to a hearing in Washington before the committee on post offices and post roads.

He boarded a train at Reno and started eastward. This was the winter of 1872–73, a wild wicked blizzarding winter. On in Wyoming, in the Medicine Bow Mountains, those first he had seen on his journey westward more than twenty years before, the train stalled in the drifts. Snowshoe was out with the train crew, a shovel in his hands. Other passengers joined them. All day they dug while the train crept in little spurts behind them and at last managed to crawl into a section station where more engines could be hooked on. Even with four pulling, the train stalled again. Shoveling was useless. Huge drifts were piling across the tracks faster than they could be shoveled away.

All the next day Snowshoe fidgeted and worried with the other passengers in the cramped quarters of the cars. The government of the United States had summoned him to the national capital — but he would never get there in time at this rate. If only he had thought to bring his skis. He fidgeted and worried through the night. In the morning he picked up his suitcase and started out on foot, battling the drifts, following the rail line. Laramie was somewhere fifty-some miles ahead.

In the dusk of that day he was tramping into Laramie. There was another train there all right — trains, quite a few of them, but not a one running. Dozens of locomotives and about eight hundred freight cars were piled up through the town. A snowplow was going through the futile motions of trying to clear track and making no progress at all. Oh, well, Cheyenne was somewhere fifty-some miles on down the track.

Two days later Snowshoe Thompson and suitcase tramped into Cheyenne, the one person to emerge from the blizzards behind him in more than two weeks. While a Cheyenne newspaperman was concocting a headline, CALIFORNIA MOUNTAINEER OUTRUNS THE IRON HORSE, Snowshoe was boarding a train for the East. He was in Washington in time for the hearing.

Worse than any snowdrifts was official red tape. Delays, delays, delays. The dragging of feet and the dragging of the hearing. He was there nearly two months and not much had happened. Eventually there would be a committee report and eventually, if Congress ever got around to it, there might be some action. Very likely not. Business was business and contracts were contracts. The committee had been sharp with its questioning and had kept talking about contracts. He should have had them, signed and sealed and approved by the proper authorities, before he went ahead carrying mail. But if he had waited for that, the government way of doing business being what it was now showing itself to be, would the people of the far lonely places ever have received their mail through the long winter months? He was just a big not-too-bright Norsky. Something had needed to be done and he had done it and kept on doing it. That was the pattern of his life.

It was time for spring plowing and planting. Next winter's food supply for the cabin in Diamond Valley depended on the summer's crops. The irrigation system for his orchard would have to be repaired soon or there would be no fruit this year. He boarded another train and started back home.

More winters came and with them the deep snows gripping the mountains and when other means failed and there was mail or emergency supplies to be taken to isolated cabins, Snowshoe Thompson took them. When reports came of hunters or travelers lost in the snows, Snowshoe Thompson strapped on his old undoped Norwegian snowshoes and found them and guided them to safety. Unmatched strength still surged in him and the people of the Sierras still thought him as indestructible as his mountains. But his wild Sierra whoop did not sound quite as often and sometimes the great shoulders sagged a bit and the ache deep inside him was more insistent than ever and growing.

It was January of 1876 and word reached the cabin in Diamond Valley that the Carpenter boy who lived with his widowed mother at Silver Mountain had taken a tumble on the skis Snowshoe Thompson had made for him and had broken an arm. A bad break. But he would not let the doctor set it, would not let anyone touch him. He kept calling for Snowshoe Thompson to be with him and tell him it would be all right. It was already afternoon and the way was long and over rugged rocky country and the cold was bitter and would be bitterer in the night and snow was flying before whipping winds and Snowshoe was tired from some far deliveries and the pain inside him was bad, very bad. When had such things ever stopped him? He strapped on his old Norwegian snowshoes and was on his way.

See him now, Jon Torsteinson Rui, John A. Thomp-

son, Snowshoe Thompson of the high Sierras, forty-eight nearly forty-nine years old, alone again in the winter night in the high frozen magnificence of his mountains, responding still to the Viking song in his blood, sensing somehow that this would be his last run, feeling in his slow-thinking stubborn Norsky way that somehow this was the most important run he had ever made and must be made in record time, setting himself the task of seeing what still was in him, what he still could do, pitting what remained of his waning strength against the endless enduring indifference of the eternal rock and the snow!

To get there by one o'clock would be a record run for the Alpine Boys to remember.

He was there by twelve!

Spring came on, fresh and reviving, but not so for him. The broad shoulders had a permanent sag now. A slowness was in him and he had to drive himself to hold erect against the increasing ache deep inside and get through the spring plowing. There was no sense in doctoring; medical knowledge did not yet reach to what was hidden within him gnawing inevitably at the very base of his being.

After the plowing, the planting. He could not finish it on his own feet. But on the back of a patient horse, clutching at the mane with one hand, dropping the seed with the other, he made it along the last row.

He lay on the bed in the cabin in Diamond Valley, unable to rise, a big stubborn fool of a man who had poured out his strength in free giving until there was none left to give. Four days later he died.

John Phillips

1832(?) — NOVEMBER 18, 1883

THIS happened in 1866, the first year following the
Civil War, the year that brought the start of another
war, a war usually passed over quickly or not mentioned
by eastern historians because, after all, it was just another
of the western Indian wars — and happened to be the
only one the Indians ever happened to win.

With the Treaty of 1851 the western tribes had agreed
to respect the Oregon Trail, the Overland Trail, which
ran across the southern portion of Wyoming Territory.
In return the land northward, the Powder River and the
Black Hills country, was to remain inalienably Indian.
No white men's road and no forts there. By 1862, with
the discovery of gold in the Virginia City area of the
Montana mountains, that treaty was becoming, as usual
and inevitably, a scrap of paper. For a while miners
headed for the diggings traveled by roundabout routes.
More and more of the daring began to pass through the
forbidden Indian country. In 1863, in direct repudiation
of the treaty, John Bozeman laid out a shortcut from

Fort Laramie on the Oregon Trail diagonally north-westward to Virginia City. Straight through the sacred Powder River country of the Teton Sioux.

Indian patience was remarkable. There were scattered raids by angry and irresponsible young warriors. But the older warriors and most of the chiefs advocated caution and were content simply to stop and turn back white parties seeking to pass through. Then, in 1864, came two developments which tightened the situation toward real trouble. Down at Sand Creek in Colorado Territory white troops attacked a village of friendly Cheyennes, at the time under the supposed protection of a nearby fort, and slaughtered men and women and children in one of the most infamous massacres on record — and soon many Cheyennes were moving northward, joining the Teton Sioux, talking war with the whites. And over in Minnesota the Santee Sioux were provoked at last into an uprising which resulted in their being driven westward to join their tribal relatives, the Tetons. They were pursued by a punitive military expedition which disregarded the treaty and drove deep into the Powder River country, ready to attack any Indians encountered, under orders to let none escape. This First Powder River Expedition had little success and after various disastrous skirmishes with the aroused Indian allies withdrew, leaving as its legacy little Fort Reno on the south fork of the Powder. A fort in the forbidden territory.

Definitely an explosive situation. But still not open warfare on the part of the Indians. They were still undecided, divided among themselves, the older men calling for caution and patience. Meanwhile white pressure to have the trail opened steadily increased. Obviously there was only one thing to do — scrap the old treaty and make another extracting new concessions from the Indians. In the winter of 1865–66 another treaty was made, conceding safe passage up the trail. But not worth much. Only a few Sioux leaders of any consequence signed it; the others were tired old "agency" chiefs known as the Laramie Loafers. None of the new vital leaders signed. Red Cloud, emerging as the dominant Sioux, was not even present at the conference and most of the younger chiefs and their warriors were following him.

So again, in June 1866, there was to be another treaty. Red Cloud and most of the other influential Sioux leaders were there this time, at the great council at Fort Laramie. Some compromise might have been worked out. But again, as usual and inevitably, the white men's attitude was already apparent. Treaties with Indians were to be dictated, not negotiated. The white decision as to terms had been made in advance; only the price to be paid was negotiable. Already, even before the council met, a Second Powder River Expedition had been mounted. Colonel Henry B. Carrington was on his way at the head of a battalion under orders to establish forts along the Bozeman Trail.

Bad timing. Very bad. He and expedition reached Fort Laramie while the council was meeting, before any agreement of any kind had been made. Immediately Red Cloud denounced this as treachery, the expedition as an unauthorized and outright invasion. He proclaimed open defiance if the invasion should move forward and the forts be built, and departed with his followers. More and more of the assembled Indian leaders and their followers slipped away to join him. Quickly the white commissioners slapped through another makeshift meaningless treaty signed by the Laramie Loafers. Quickly orders came for Carrington to proceed at once with his mission.

A tough job for him. His battalion was never up to strength; his supplies were never adequate; always he was worried about ammunition even for the old single-shot Springfield rifles his men carried. Back at district headquarters in Omaha his superior officers refused to believe that the Indians really would fight and consistently ignored his reports and his repeated appeals for more men, more ammunition, better arms.

A tough job — but he went right ahead. Up the trail to little Fort Reno, where he left some of his men to strengthen the garrison. On up to the junction of Little Piney and Big Piney Creeks, whose waters flowed on to join Clear Creek, a tributary of the Powder. There he decided to establish headquarters and in mid-July began construction of Fort Phil Kearny.

Not much trouble to date. He had kept his column in close order and maintained strict vigilance. But his every move had been watched by Indian scouts. Starting this new fort was in effect a declaration of war. Ten days later, at dawn, came the first attack in which many of the post horses were stampeded and two men were killed, three wounded. Always thereafter the fort was under constant pressure from Indian raiders, who picked off any stragglers, any sentry who exposed himself at night, and attacked any party that ventured out not in sufficient force. What would be called Red Cloud's War had begun.

It was a curious garrison to be occupying a fort deep in hostile territory. Many of the men were raw recruits, some enlisted en route. Most of the experienced men, having served through the Civil War period, had been mustered out. The wives of some of the officers, including

Mrs. Carrington, were there, several with children. The
colonel, fond of martial music, had brought along a military band. For a while, inside the stockade, there were
entertainments and attempts at gay social life. Outside,
everywhere, anywhere beyond immediate range of the
fort's few big guns, was constant lurking deadly danger.

Then, again, two developments that further tightened
the situation toward disaster. One was the dispatch, as
stupidly ordered from Omaha, of part of the garrison on
up the trail, past the Montana Territory line, to establish Fort C. F. Smith — leaving Fort Phil Kearny further
undermanned. The other, in November, was the arrival
of a new officer, Captain William J. Fetterman.

A stubborn headstrong fool of a man. He had a poor
opinion of his commander; he himself had a brilliant action record from the Civil War while Carrington did
not. He spoke rather freely his belief that Carrington
was too cautious, ought to be out trouncing the enemy
into submission. He had an even poorer opinion of mere
Indians. Frequently he boasted that with eighty men at
his back he would ride right through the entire Sioux
nation. Eighty men. By now, by reasonable estimate,
there were at least three thousand determined Indian
warriors within striking distance of the fort and more
constantly gathering.

Arrogant ignorance aside, he was a likable man, soon
a favorite with the younger officers and men. And some
providence may briefly have pitied him. He was given a
chance to learn, to acquire some humility and simple
sense. Early in December he led a detachment of forty
men to the relief of the wood train which was under attack — and let himself and detachment be decoyed on
into ambush. A hopeless predicament. What saved him

was the timely arrival of Colonel Carrington with another detachment. The Indians, uncertain how many
troops, perhaps with artillery, were following the colonel, slipped away.

But Captain Fetterman learned nothing.

The morning of December 21, 1866. A cold wintry
day with snow on the ground and the temperature down
around zero. The fort was almost completed. One more
batch of logs would finish it. A wood train started off to
the wood camp in the nearby hills.

Late morning and guns sounded on Pilot Hill, signal
that the wood train was under attack. Quickly Colonel
Carrington organized a relief detachment. Forty-nine
men from the 18th Infantry, twenty-seven from the 2nd
Cavalry. Cool cautious Captain James Powell in command. Two other officers volunteered — Captain Frederick Brown, who was to leave for Fort Laramie soon and
wanted to "get a scalp" before leaving, and young Lieutenant George Grummond, who wanted to lead the cavalry. Two civilians also volunteered, Jim Wheatley and
Isaac Fisher, whose aid was more than welcome because
they had Spencer repeating rifles.

Then Colonel Carrington made the mistake which
blighted his military career. Captain Fetterman, claiming seniority, insisted he had a right to the relief command. Reluctantly Carrington agreed, letting him replace Captain Powell.

Forty-nine infantrymen, twenty-seven cavalrymen, two
extra officers, two civilians. Ironic arithmetic gives a precise total of eighty. Stubborn headstrong fool of a Fetterman starting out with eighty men at his back.

He left under strict orders, repeated orders, to relieve

the train, to drive back the Indians — and under no circumstances to go beyond Lodge Trail Ridge. He reached the ridge, still visible from the fort, encountering some opposition, and occupied the ridge top in good skirmish style. By now signals from Pilot Hill indicated that the wagon train was no longer under attack, in itself an ominous sign that this had been only a diversion, a means of drawing troops out of the fort. Captain Fetterman and the eighty men were seen from the fort for a few moments longer there on the top of the ridge. Then they disappeared down the other side.

They came back, some of them late that afternoon, the rest the next morning, in wagons, brought back by daring forays from the fort, most of them naked, stripped, mutilated, bloodied bodies of all of them frozen in grotesque attitudes of death.

The evening of December 21. The temperature had been dropping, was close to twenty-five below zero. A fierce blizzard was sweeping out of the hills, piling snow against the stockade so high that men could have walked over the top. Fort Phil Kearny was a hushed stricken place. The full extent of the disaster was now known. So too was the fact that the last few mail parties down the trail had been caught and killed. Well over half of the military garrison had been wiped out. The entire remaining roster within the walls, including civilian employees, was one hundred nineteen. A number of them were sick or wounded from previous affrays. Additional cavalry supposed to have been ordered to the fort long ago had never arrived. There was not even one full box of ammunition per man. Arms and ammunition supposed to have left Fort Leavenworth back in September were still lost somewhere en route. In the blank swirling grayness outside were thousands of Sioux and Cheyenne warriors, aroused and encouraged by their victory beyond Lodge Trail Ridge. Their signal fires ranged the hills. It would be impossible for the fort to hold out long in event of a sustained attack.

What could be done was being done. All prisoners were released from the guard-house. All men, soldiers and civilians, were armed. Double sentries were at every post. Squads worked in fifteen-minute shifts, all they could take at a time in the bitter outside blasts, to shovel away the drifts piling against the stockade. Windows of the various buildings were boarded up with loop-holes left for rifle barrels for inside fighting should the stockade be breached. Wagon beds were stacked three-deep around the powder magazine for a final stand there. Orders were issued that in case of attack the women and children should be put in the magazine and at the last destroyed all together lest they be taken alive.

The weather itself offered hope that an attack would be delayed. But the one hope in the longer run would be reinforcements from Fort Laramie. Aid could come, perhaps in time — if the need for aid were known. But Fort Laramie was two hundred thirty-six miles away across winter wilderness held by the hostile Indians. Even Horseshoe Station, the nearest point to which a telegraph line had been strung, was nearly two hundred miles down the trail.

Colonel Carrington called for volunteers to try to take a message through. There was no response.

Soldiers were there whose job it was to face danger. They kept silent. Officers were there who had applauded

Captain Fetterman and echoed his brave statements. They kept silent. Jim Bridger was there, the storied, the legendary, the most famous of all the western scouts. He too kept silent.

Then one man spoke. A smallish wiry civilian frontiersman. Colonel Carrington did not even know who he was, had to ask his name.

John Phillips.

He was born of a Portuguese family on Portuguese soil, the island of Faial, one of the Azores, probably in 1832. He was a man grown, or nearly so, when he came to America, landing on the west coast. That was during or soon after the first California gold rushes. Through the next years he worked and hunted and prospected in California and on into what are now Nevada and Idaho and Montana. Somewhere along the way he married and had two children, a girl and a boy. When his trail can be picked up with certainty, along in 1864–65, he was in Wyoming Territory, an experienced all-around frontiersman, and his family was with him. When the first movements were being made up the Bozeman Trail, he was among the first to pan for colors along the side creeks of the Powder River country.

A man not above medium height, smaller than most men then in the territory, often called "little" by them — not in derogation but in affectionate respect. All the same, stocky and well-muscled. Soft-spoken, olive-skinned, with high cheekbones, thin nose, steady dark eyes, a dark mustache and a short pointed beard. A quiet dependable man — miner, prospector, hunter, trapper, woodcutter, teamster — liked and trusted by the others

of his kind in that dangerous region in those dangerous days. Portugee they called him, Portugee Phillips,
and he smiled at the name because it was usually spoken
in the warmth of friendship.

During the spring and summer of this 1866 he and
Jim Wheatley and Isaac Fisher had been engaged in some
kind of mining venture up-country from the site of Fort
Phil Kearny. They knew trouble was brewing, was ready
to boil over. They had families. Portugee's wife Hattie
was with him, and the two children. Wheatley had a
young wife and at least one child. The only probable
safety through the fall and winter would be in the vicinity of the new fort being built.

They arrived at the fort along in August. Here were
three able frontiersmen, stout workers, armed as the
troops were not with Spencer repeating rifles. Promptly
the quartermaster offered them civilian jobs. Promptly
they accepted and put up two small cabins just outside
the stockade, the Phillips and Wheatley cabins. Fisher,
a bachelor, lived with one family or the other.

Portugee worked as a teamster. He was a good man
with anything on four legs and hoofs, oxen and mules
and horses. When the wood train left for that last batch
of logs on the morning of December 21st, he was not
with it. He was out with a wagon and mule team hauling
water from the Little Piney into the fort. When the relief party under Captain Fetterman was organized, he
was still doing the day's job, hauling water. But when
wagons went out under guard of almost all the able-bod-
ied men remaining in the fort to bring in the first of
the bodies, he was driving one of the wagons and he saw
what was left of his partners, Wheatley and Fisher, ringed

round with shells from their Spencer repeaters, where
they had made a stand to hold back the attacking hordes
so the infantrymen could try to scramble to a better position and had fought right there to a grim finish.

Men could die fighting. But there were women and
children in the fort. His Hattie and his two. Mrs. Wheatley and hers. Over in the officers' quarters was young
Mrs. Grummond, pregnant with an unborn child whose
father was another of the frozen bodies waiting burial.

He figured, said Portugee Phillips, that maybe he
could get through. At least he could try. If the colonel
would let him take the best horse at the fort, Grey Eagle,
the colonel's favorite thoroughbred.

The colonel really liked that horse. So too had Red
Cloud himself, seeing it briefly back at Fort Laramie. For
a moment then the colonel had thought that Red Cloud
would try to steal it and had acted to forestall the attempt. It is a curious small footnote that now the colonel was upset and irritated by Portugee's request. But
there was stern logic to it. Any courier trying to get
through had to have a horse that could outrun Indian
ponies. Reluctantly the colonel agreed — and once
agreed wished he had thought of this himself.

He gave orders about the horse and retired to his office
to write his dispatch. Portugee went about his own preparations. First to his cabin under the shelter of the fort's
big guns to comfort and reassure his wife and Mrs. Wheatley who was with her and to put on double thickness of
clothing beneath his big buffalo coat. Then a brief stop
at the officers' quarters to speak for the first time ever to
the widow of a man he had liked and admired, young

Mrs. Grummond, to tell her that aid would be coming, that he would get through for her sake.

A fascinating figure, this little bearded Portugee Phillips in his big buffalo coat and buffalo boots and gauntlets and cap. American to the core now, a simple old-hand frontiersman deep in the American West — and still a gallant gentleman from a far sunny land.

At twenty minutes to midnight he and the colonel left the colonel's office and leaned against the wind to walk past the cavalry and the quartermaster's stables to the small water gate near the stockade corner close to the Little Piney. A sergeant and two privates waited there with the horse. The sergeant unfastened the padlock and the two privates pulled out the bars and opened the gate. A sentry, true to his post, blocked the way. The colonel himself gave the countersign and the sentry stepped aside. The colonel and Portugee spoke together briefly. Portugee swung up into the saddle. The colonel reached and took Portugee's gloved right hand again and spoke again and the sentry caught the last words: "May God help you." Portugee wheeled the horse and started away at a steady trot. The colonel stood with bent head, listening. "Good!" he said to no one in particular. "He has taken the softer ground at the side of the trail." When the last faint sound of hoofs had died away in the wind, the colonel turned and went slowly to his quarters. The sergeant and two privates closed and barred the gate. The sentry resumed his beat.

Little Portugee Phillips and a greathearted horse were on their way to make good, in strange ironic fashion, on the boast of a man now dead — to ride right through the Sioux nation.

*

Two hundred thirty-six miles to Fort Laramie — by the trail. Did he stick to the trail?

"Hell, no! More'n once I was more'n ten miles off the trail!"

He knew this country almost as well as the Indians themselves. He knew where ambushes would be most likely. He crossed the Little Piney and swung away into the brush, fighting the drifts. He rode the rest of that night and at dawn hid in a brush-cloaked gulch. He had some hardtack in a saddlebag and a small quantity of grain. He and the horse ate sparingly and waited out the daylight, moving about often in their cramped hiding-place to keep their blood circulating in the bitter cold. At dusk they started on and were jumped by a small party of Indians. While bullets whined about them, the horse, bigger, taller, longer-legged, stronger than the winter-starved Indian ponies, leaped and crashed through drifts and won the race to the gap of a frozen creek bottom ahead and plunged on, widening the lead, and at last well away.

In the small hours of that night of the 22nd he reached Fort Reno, sixty-seven miles — by the trail — from Fort Phil Kearny. Hot coffee there for him, some feed for the horse, well earned, but not too much to slow it down. Not a man could be spared from the small garrison to go on with him. He wanted and needed none. One man could travel faster and stay better hidden alone. In a brief while he was on his way again, into the teeth of the wind and the cold even worse than before. He carried another dispatch now, from Lieutenant Colonel Wessells of Fort Reno.

He was into the long stretch, one hundred and thirty

miles — by the trail — to Horseshoe Station. Portugee
Phillips and Grey Eagle, a man and a horse, alone together in a hostile wilderness, on through the rest of that
second night and the next day and the next night and on
through the next day, the 24th, Christmas Eve. He was
riding by daylight now because he was nearing the Station and the worst of the Indian danger should be past.
Late in the afternoon he was jumped again, this time by
a large band. Again the horse outran Indian ponies, took
him to the top of a small conical hill where he dismounted
to make a stand. There was no charge up after him. Darkness was dropping fast. After a few tests of his skill with
his rifle the Indians settled down for the night, waiting
for morning. He could see their campfires ringing the
small fortress of his hill.

Portugee waited too, alert against any night surprise,
sleepless as he had been most if not all of the time since
leaving Fort Phil Kearny. All the long way the cold had
been as deadly an enemy as any Sioux or Cheyenne. To
fall asleep in that cold was to run the risk of never wak-
ing again. Now he was in double danger. He and the
horse waited through the slow hours, moving about cautiously to fight off the stiffening grip of weariness and
cold. He knew the ways of these Indians. They preferred
to attack at dawn, in the first light of morning. At the
first faint coloring of false dawn he was making a run for
it, in saddle again, that tired now gaunted horse taking
him right through the startled Indian lines and well
away once more.

Sometime during the early morning, on the trail now,
at or near Bridger's Ferry, he met two white men, "Captain" Bailey, leader of a mining group in the area, and

George Dillon, rancher and wagon train boss. He rode the relatively short distance on to Horseshoe Station with them, arriving about ten o'clock in the morning, Christmas morning. The telegraph operator was in his log office when Portugee, ice-coated and half frozen, stumbled in.

The operator managed to get Lieutenant Colonel Wessell's short dispatch on the wires, on its way to Omaha. He tried to send a shortened version of Colonel Carrington's long dispatch to Fort Laramie. He had trouble with it. Perhaps the operator at Fort Laramie was not on duty that holiday morning — or had enjoyed too much celebrating the night before. No one at the Station was interested in doing any dispatch riding in such weather. The operator was sure that eventually he would be able to get the message through on the wires. But Portugee Phillips was taking no chances. He had promised to get that dispatch to Fort Laramie. He tucked it in a pocket again, bundled himself against the cold again, and was in saddle again. He and the colonel's horse had forty more miles to go, through swirling snow and the bitterest cold of the bitterest winter of fifty years.

They made those miles. At eleven o'clock that night, Christmas night, a sentry at Fort Laramie challenged a slow-moving mass of ice and snow that was a man on a horse. The sentry called the officer of the guard and the man and the horse, barely able to stumble along, were led to the door of Old Bedlam, entertainment hall of the fort. All other officers and the wives of those who had wives were assembled there. A fine gay Christmas party was in progress, at the moment to the strains of "Oh Susanna." The man literally fell from the horse, staggered

in, made sure the dispatch was in official hands, and collapsed on the floor.

No more dancing, not at Fort Laramie that night.
Sometime during the day General Palmer, new commander of the fort, had received a garbled version of the
message from Horseshoe Station. He had dutifully sent
it on to Omaha — and dismissed it himself as just another of the rumors of Indian raids and massacres constantly circulating through the territory. Now he knew.
There was no more dancing.

Quick good care was taken of Portugee Phillips. He
would be in a coma for hours, would suffer for weeks
from exhaustion and severe frostbite. And outside Old
Bedlam lay the body of a horse that had dropped dead in
the snow.

Up the trail at Fort Phil Kearny no one knew, could
know, what had happened to Portugee Phillips. Within
the stockade the strain was almost intolerable. A few
days after Portugee left, several of the civilian scouts
slipped away on another attempt to reach Fort Laramie.
They were brave men too. But they did not get through.
Their bodies were found later where they had been
caught and killed.

And the winter held, stern and stormy and forbidding,
fortunate for the fort, keeping most of the Indian warriors in winter camps waiting for better weather. Only
scouting parties stayed in the immediate vicinity, harassing but not directly attacking. On December 27 the first
reinforcements arrived, three officers and twenty-two men.
Not from Fort Laramie. They had been on their way for
some time, holing up through the worst storms, and on

reaching Fort Reno heard the word left there by Portugee. Instead of waiting for the weather to improve, they had pushed straight on. They too were brave men. And they were lucky. Had the weather been better, they might have met the fate of Fetterman's eighty.

By mid-January, before any break in the winter, the main body of reinforcements and supplies from Fort Laramie had arrived. Fort Phil Kearny was reasonably safe, strengthened to withstand almost any attack.

So that was that. The word was through and because of it the fort still stood, untaken, deep in the Powder River country, and the stark events there of that year 1866 were done.

But Red Cloud's War continued. On through the spring and the summer and the following winter. There were few definite battles and none decisive, but the Indian tactics were succeeding. Frequent skirmishes and constant raids kept the Bozeman Trail blocked to all but military movements in force. In the spring of 1868 there was another treaty conference at Fort Laramie. Reluctantly the white commissioners accepted Red Cloud's terms: the trail to be closed, the forts abandoned, the Powder River country to remain inalienably Indian. Red Cloud himself did not sign until the forts, Phil Kearny among them, had been abandoned and burned to the ground.

An Indian victory. But not for long in the relentless white onrush. In the next decade, with the discovery of gold in the Black Hills, white pressure would become irresistible and this treaty too would become a scrap of paper. The Sioux would wipe out another headstrong fool of a man named Custer and with him his men —

but in the end would be forced to accept a new treaty on the white men's terms.

Meanwhile, what of Portugee Phillips?

The record is scant. He might have been launched into fame and publicity, as many a man has been by lesser achievement. He was not — and was well content not to be. He himself left no report of his ride. He was not much of a talker, particularly about himself, and he never said much about it, not even to friends, except in brief matter-of-fact answer to a direct question.

That was a terrible winter anyway, the worst within the memory of the oldest Indians, and very little specific information came out of the Powder River country. The military men involved had their own axes to grind, in the confused aftermath of Fetterman's folly were busy thinking of their own reputations. Colonel Carrington, the one man who might have been expected to have most to say about Portugee, was in disgrace. With Fetterman dead, he was made the scapegoat by his superiors — who themselves had been at fault in regard to the whole expedition. He was immediately removed from command of the fort and spent the next decades trying to vindicate his own record. It was not until many years later, well after Portugee's death, that even the bare outline of his ride and a few facts about the man himself began to be known.

The record is scant. But what there is of it fits the pattern. Just another quiet capable western goodman making a living for himself and his in his part of the American west.

While the war continued, he was a scout along the trail and a mail carrier between the forts. Other carriers

were run down and killed. Portugee always got through.
Men who knew him briefly then were astounded later to
learn that he was still alive. One time he came on a
wagon train besieged by many Indians — and got away
to take word to the nearest fort and lead back the detachment which saved the train. Another time he joined a
train headed up the trail and when it was attacked
helped drive off the raiders. In the morning when the
train was moving on, it was discovered that Portugee was
missing. Right enough. He had ridden back to the overnight campsite. One of the mules had been sick during
the night and the escort soldiers had abandoned it. Indignant at this breach of the unwritten frontier law never to
let a horse or mule be taken by the Sioux if that could
possibly be avoided, he had gone back for this one. He
rode straight into an ambush. He rode out, breaking
through the closing circle, and won another race against
Sioux ponies.

Those were times reported by others. No one will ever
know how many times little Portugee fought off or outran death riding alone through the Powder River country with dispatches in a pocket.

After the new treaty he was in the Elk Mountain region of southern Wyoming Territory hauling ties for
construction of the Union Pacific railroad. A few years
later he had the contract to haul timbers for a new fort
west of Laramie. One of history's small ironic coinci-
dences — Portugee Phillips helping build Fort Fetterman.

Meantime he had started a ranch in the valley of the
Chugwater north of Cheyenne. All through these years
he had trouble with the Indians, with the Sioux. He was
a marked man with them. No treaty ended their war

with him. On through the years they continued to harass him, raiding his ranch often in that relatively peaceful valley. Frequently they shot or stole his stock. Portugee Phillips shrugged his shoulders and accepted this as he had other hardships, as part of the life he had chosen in the big land that had given him his chance to be a free and independent individual.

Along in the mid-70's his ranch on the Chugwater was a regular stage station with a well-stocked bar, a reputation for good food, and enough stalls in the barn to take care of fifty head of stock. He ran cattle on the side and served as postmaster for the area. The superintendent of the stage line reported that always in time of trouble Portugee Phillips could be depended upon to "help in the roundup of road agents or outlaws." On into this century old-timers still remembered the sign:

Chug Water Ranch
John Phillips
Hay Grain and Stabling
52 Miles to Cheyenne   45 to Fort Laramie

By 1879 his health was failing. A hard life often lived to the limit of endurance was catching up with him. By now his stage station had become the Chug-water Hotel. He sold out and retired to Cheyenne. He lived quietly there for a few years and died on November 18, 1883.

The man was dead and buried. The Old Pioneers of Wyoming, at a special meeting, had paid their tribute to him as "a true, honest, upright citizen, friend and neighbor." The Indian wars were over and the West was being settled and time was hurrying toward the new century. But always there were people who felt that John Phillips should have received some reward for his epic ride. He himself had neither expected nor wanted any. He was paid three hundred dollars for his services at Fort Phil Kearny, the regular rate for a civilian employee for the time he worked there. Fair and adequate. But others felt otherwise.

Then, too, there was the matter of his Indian depredation claim. While he was hauling timbers for Fort Fetterman under government contract, a band of Sioux ran off his oxen and mules and horses. Red Cloud himself admitted that particular depredation. The usual claim for compensation was filed. It was approved by the Secretary of the Interior and by the Court of Claims. Then some official snagged it on a technicality. John Phillips was not a fully naturalized citizen. He had taken out his first papers years before but had not completed the process. The claim was canceled.

Always some people felt that John Phillips had not been treated fairly by the government he had served. There had never even been any official recognition of his ride. In 1899, sixteen years after his death, a Wyoming senator and a Wyoming congressman introduced a joint resolution in both houses of Congress for the payment of $5000 to Hattie Phillips in recognition of her husband's "heroic service" and in payment of the old claim. Colonel, now General, Carrington, his own record now vindicated, and the onetime young Mrs. Grummond, now the second Mrs. Carrington, came forward with strong affidavits. The resolution passed. A long overdue account was squared.

Wash-a-kie

His life compassed the whole of the nineteenth century, all of it from start to finish, the century of the sweep of the United States from coast to coast of the continent. He was a man who would have risen to prominence at any time anywhere among any people under any circumstances. Only an accident kept his name from being blazoned in history books. An accident of birth. He was born an Indian.

He was pure Indian, but a mixed-blood among Indians. His father was a Flathead, his mother a Northern Shoshone. He was born sometime during 1798 somewhere in the great rugged spaces where nowadays Wyoming and Utah and Idaho and Montana join on the maps. At the time no white man had yet penetrated the region and far to the east John Adams was still in office as the second President of the infant United States. It is entirely possible that a few years later as a small boy he saw Lewis and Clark on their way up the Missouri and westward to the Pacific.

When he was four or five years old, the family village was attacked by a band of Blackfeet. His father and other men were killed and the rest of the people scattered. His mother, with him and her other children, two more boys and two girls, wandered the wilderness barely surviving until she found and joined a group of friendly Lemhis. For some twenty years the fatherless family lived with these hospitable people. During this period he acquired his name, Wash-a-kie in the most used of its thirty variations and spellings, probably derived from "wus-sik-he" meaning rawhide rattle. One legend has it that he was already a fine singer and often accompanied himself with such a rattle. Another that he made one with the pate skin of the first buffalo he killed and in battle would ride among the enemy rattling it vigorously and frightening their horses. Either or both could account for the name.

When his mother and the rest of the family (except one sister who had married a Lemhi) were persuaded by visiting Flatheads, onetime friends of his father, to go live with them again, he stayed with the Lemhis. He never saw his mother or two brothers or other sister again. He was an independent young man who would go his own way.

That way led him a little later to join a party of Bannocks. Renegades of the whole region, the Bannocks; wanderers, freebooters, outlaws. He roamed with them for several years. Had he been a white man, a chronicler would say he was sowing his wild oats. Then he visited a village of Northern Shoshones living in the Green River area of Wyoming. He was a mixed-blood with Flathead and Lemhi and Bannock experience behind him. But now with the Shoshones he knew he had found his true

people. It was not just that his mother had been one of
them. They were his kind of people, strong in body and
mind and spirit. He married a Shoshone girl and was
one of them, now and forever.

The Northern Shoshones were a small tribe, strongly
individualistic. They were divided into a number of
small bands led by popular chiefs and the compositions
of these bands were constantly shifting with the shiftings
of personal allegiances. All of them were often on the
defensive against many enemies. Already the pressures of
the white men's advance far to the eastward were being
felt as other tribes, numerous and warlike, were being
pushed westward seeking new hunting grounds. The Shoshones needed a man like Wash-a-kie.

He was an orphan in the tribe with no family to back
him or give him prestige. He had no need of that.
Within a few years he was a subchief with increasing willing followers.

He was a superb orator and when he spoke in council
everyone listened and what he said was good to hear and
what he advised was good to do. He was a thorough
craftsman in the making of weapons and the use of them.
He was a mighty hunter and trapper. The white men's
fur companies were penetrating the region now and by
trade with them the Shoshones could obtain the even better weapons of guns and ammunition for defense against
their enemies. Wash-a-kie led in this and encouraged
others to do the same. He came to know many of the
French voyageurs who worked for the fur companies out
of Canada and to speak their language. He came to know

and know well such famed free trappers as Jim Bridger and Kit Carson and to speak their language too. He saw that it was wise to be the friend of these new people with the pale skin and to learn from them and to obtain from them the means to fight tribal enemies.

And he was a mighty warrior, one who delighted in war. Even when enemies were not close at hand for fighting, he went off on lone forays to find them to fight. He brought back many scalps. Once he brought back too a double scar on his left cheek under the eye made by a Blackfoot arrow. But it was in pitched battle leading brave followers that his fighting quality showed best. He was a born strategist, a commander to rank among the great soldiers of any land and any people. In later years warriors like Red Cloud and Crazy Horse, who had fought against him, would say that he was the greatest of them all.

When the Blackfeet struck in force in the Green River country and killed many Shoshones and stole many horses, it was Wash-a-kie who emerged to leadership in the long pursuit and the running battle that wiped out most of the marauding party and recovered most of the horses. Soon afterward, in a big battle with the Crows, it was Wash-a-kie again who led the way to victory.

By the time of the first known mention of him in white men's records, in the journal of trapper Osborne Russell under date of 1840, he was cited as one of the three "pillars of the [Shoshone] nation at whose names the Blackfeet quaked with fear."

By 1843, when the other two pillars had died, he was the lone pillar, the acknowledged leader of his chosen people, and more and more of the scattered Shoshone

bands were gathering about him, strong in loyalty to
him.

That was the year of the beginning of the Oregon migration. The beginning of the white advance directly
through the Indian country of the West. White men in
increasing numbers and sometimes with them their families were moving westward to claim Oregon from the
British just as a little later they were moving westward to
grub gold in California.

That was the year too of Wash-a-kie's great decision,
in the making before and forced now by the onrush of
events. He foresaw the inevitability of the white advance,
the inevitability of the eventual white conquest, and deliberately he chose for himself and his people what he
knew would be the winning side in the long bitter strug-
gles ahead.

The whites were already fighting and would be more
and more with the big tribes that were enemies of his
tribe, that were pushing in under the white pressures
trying to take the hunting grounds of his people. It was
logical that for temporary advantage he would side with
the whites. But he was thinking too of the long-range advantage, of the long future when the white conquest
would be complete and he and his people dependent
upon the conquerors for continued existence itself.
Their lands would dwindle and dwindle and the buffalo
be gone. Like this or not, and he did not like it, if he and
his people were to survive, were not to be crushed in the
conflict of races and ways of life, they must be friends of
the whites and learn to travel the white men's road.

Along the Oregon trail Indian depredations began

and increased and were many. Battles between Indians
and wagon trains were frequent occurrences. Raiding parties struck and struck often. There were no Shoshone war
parties among them. But there were Shoshone war parties that fought side by side with the white men. There
were Shoshone parties under a strongly built mighty warrior with a scar on his left cheek and these fought with a
skill and precision that made them worth many times
their number and they rescued many travelers and they
helped the weary and fed the hungry. "If we can only
make it to Wash-a-kie's camp we are safe," was the saying
along the Oregon trail.

It was a measure of the man that he took that small
individualistic tribe of scattered bands and welded it
into an effective cohesive unit. He was a stern leader who
demanded absolute obedience — and obtained it. By the
mid-1840's he had a thousand warriors, well armed and
well mounted, and good horses too for the women and
children. The Shoshones could go about with heads high
through these years of the mid-century. They were a
small nation surrounded by others bigger and more
powerful and constantly pressing them. But they were a
a fighting nation, well organized, able to move about
swiftly and efficiently as circumstances demanded. Their
warriors were as disciplined as those of any white army.
They had a head chief who was one to be followed anywhere into anything. His plans were good and he was
always in the forefront of battle, showing the way to
those who followed. The Shoshones held their own
against the more numerous Blackfeet, against the proud
warlike Cheyennes, even against the multitudinous
Sioux who were pushing ever westward under the white
pressure from the east.

In 1851 the white men's government called a great council at Fort Laramie to try to make peace among the warring tribes and, more important, to barter for the security of the emigrants traveling the Oregon trail. Word spread all through the Indian country. The Shoshones were not officially invited; they were not to be a party to the treaty. They had not been troubling the whites, quite the contrary, and they were only a small tribe anyway. But Wash-a-kie would not let himself and his people be ignored, perhaps be left out of any agreement allocating territories and hunting grounds. With about two hundred and fifty of his warriors and with their women and children too, he journeyed eastward to Fort Laramie.

They came to the fort as a proud people should come, fearless and with heads high, and the famous Jim Bridger, old friend of Wash-a-kie, announced their coming. Very many times their number of Sioux and of other tribes with whom they had fought so successfully these last years were there before them, were edgy and angry at their coming. On the way some Cheyennes, treacherously in this time of talk of peace, struck in a surprise raid and got away with two Shoshone scalps. But the Shoshones came steadily on. They came to the fort with Wash-a-kie trotting proudly on his favorite war pony well in the lead, with his warriors, well armed and well mounted, in battle formation some distance behind him, with the women and children following on their good horses too. Bitter words spread among the massed Sioux watching them come. The few white soldiers there could do little if trouble should break forth. And a Sioux warrior, whose father had been killed by Wash-a-kie in battle several years before, dashed out intent on revenge.

Not a Shoshone slackened or quickened pace. Wash-a-
kie swung his rifle up to the ready and came steadily on.
His warriors gave one great shout of defiance and then
there was silence and they trotted forward as before, holding their distance behind him, holding their ranks with a
precision the finest white soldiers could envy. And the
women and children followed, straight toward the possible attack of many many times their own number.

What impressed the white observers present was the
simple unshakable steadiness of the Shoshones, all of
them, quietly following that lone figure in the lead. Even
the women and children. There was no scattering toward
safety and no holding back. Quietly they came on, following their men. They had absolute confidence that their
chief would take care of this attacking Sioux and that if
worse trouble started their warriors would take care of
that too.

There was no trouble. An interpreter with the white
troops, a brave and quick-thinking man, galloped out
and seized the Sioux warrior and disarmed him. No irre-
trievable shot had been fired. The Shoshones came steadily on, firm in formation behind their chief, and mur-
murs of respect ran through the massed ranks of the
Sioux and of the other tribes. This was a brave thing
they were seeing done this day. And the Shoshones came
steadily on to be greeted by the white commissioners as a
proud people should be greeted.

"These are the finest Indians on earth," said Jim
Bridger to one of the white soldiers. "Awfully brave fellows . . . honest, too; can take their word for anything;
trust 'em anywhere."

When the council sessions started, Wash-a-kie sat with
the other chiefs and his voice was as strong as any. Before

he would take the peace pipe that was passed around, he
demanded that the Cheyennes return the two Shoshone
scalps taken on the way to the fort. They were returned.
Then the Cheyennes countered with another demand.
They brought forward a twelve-year-old Cheyenne boy
whose father had been killed by a Shoshone some years
before. Would the Shoshone chief do as a Cheyenne
would do with this fatherless boy? Wash-a-kie bowed his
head and according to the Cheyenne custom accepted the
boy to be of his own family, to be a Shoshone and treated
as his own son.

As the sessions continued, Wash-a-kie spoke in his
turn and his words were good and were heard by the
others. When the treaty was signed, pledging presents
and the annual distribution of $50,000 in goods for fifty
years in exchange for free passage of emigrants along the
trail and permission for the building of certain roads,
Wash-a-kie's signature was with the others. He did not
like the territorial allocation that had been made. It gave
to the Crows the Wind River area of west central Wyoming he wanted for his Shoshones. But he had managed
to hold for them, under whatever authority the treaty
would have, the Green River area they were currently
occupying. At least his people and their right to territory
had been recognized at the white men's council.

It was an uneasy peace that followed. The boundaries
for the various tribes were vague and did not mean
much. The major tribes were not accustomed to being
cramped in their movements and they were crowded into
less space than in the past and the game was getting
scarce. The competition for hunting grounds continued.
And from the Indian point of view the treaty was not

satisfactory at all. The white men's Congress in its usual
niggardly wisdom where Indians were concerned cut the
fifty years the annuities were to be distributed to ten and
was never in a hurry to appropriate the necessary money.
The goods usually came late and somehow the expense
of getting them and distributing them put more money
in white men's pockets than goods in Indian hands and
what was distributed was usually cheap and shoddy.
Moreover, too many white men seemed to think that the
treaty gave more than mere permission to travel through
the Indian country. More and more of them came to
stay, to take up lands, and they acted as if they had a
right to do this and the Indians were interlopers. Too
many of them liked to hunt and not just for food. They
were wasteful of the game that was the major food supply of the Indians. There were even some who thought
Indians were to be hunted too.

It was not so much a peace as an often broken and
patched up and broken again truce. Time and again angry young warriors could not be held back by the older
men of the tribes and perhaps even these did not always
have much desire for holding back. There were sporadic
raids along the trail and at places where white men were
settling in disregard of the treaty.

But as before there were no Shoshone raids. As before
there were Shoshones who helped emigrants on their
way, helped them make the dangerous crossing of the
Green River, recovered lost or stolen stock for them,
gave them food and protection, sometimes fought with
them against the raiders. Wash-a-kie never wavered in
the course he had chosen. He liked to say that no true
Shoshone had ever harmed a white man. He held his
people to this, not out of any love for the whites except

for those who became and remained his personal friends, but out of his long wisdom for the future. A big tribe like the Sioux might wring concessions from the whites by fighting them. But the Shoshones could not fight their Indian enemies, made increasingly so by the competition for hunting grounds, and fight the whites too. They were caught between two forces, each much stronger than they were, and it was the duty of the leader of his people to make the right choice for them amd hold them to it.

When the Mormons came into Utah and Brigham Young was named governor and head of Indian affairs for Utah territory, Wash-a-kie and his Shoshones were their friends too. Wash-a-kie went to Salt Lake City to arrange for trade with the Mormons. He and Chief Walkara of the Utes signed a treaty of peace with Governor Young. Within a year Walkara and the Utes were at odds with the Mormons and raiding widely through the territory. But Wash-a-kie and his Shoshones kept this treaty as they were keeping that signed at Fort Laramie. And they continued to learn from the whites. Wash-a-kie listened to Governor Young's advice that soon the game would be scarcer than ever and in time almost gone and the Indians would have to learn to raise crops as the white men did. He watched the Mormons at work with farm tools and irrigation ditches and he encouraged one of his subchiefs, Bazil, the adopted son of the Shoshone woman Sacajawea who had guided Lewis and Clark many years before, to try this new work and Bazil raised the first Shoshone crops with fair success.

Then there was a serious situation to consider. The whites themselves were at odds with each other and soldiers were on the march. The government in Washing-

ton had deposed Brigham Young as governor of Utah
Territory and he had refused to step down and was
gathering forces to oppose the 2500 Federal troops which
were on their way to the territory. General A. S. Johnston (of later Civil War fame) was in command of these
troops and Jim Bridger was guide for them. General
Johnston wanted Wash-a-kie to join in the campaign
with his warriors. Here was a lesson in the strange ways
of the whites. Wash-a-kie had taken a vow not to fight
them; he had signed papers that he would not fight
them. And now one group of whites wanted him to fight
against another group. He would not do it. He kept his
people out of this trouble. When it finally faded away
without serious fighting, he knew he had been right. His
record as a friend of the whites, of all whites, was unbroken.

The year 1863 was an important one. Not because of
the great war that was being fought far to the east by
whites against whites. That had little impact in this part
of the West, except in the withdrawal of some of the
troops from the forts along the Oregon trail. But Indian
troubles along that trail and elsewhere through the
whole area were increasing. The tribes were becoming
ever more restless and angry at the constant white advance which even the great war in the East did not slow
much. And Wash-a-kie's authority over some of his people was dwindling. These were not so sure now that his
way was the right way. Small bands of Shoshones were
drifting away, scattering the tribe as in the old days.
Some of them were mixed up in some of the depredations against the whites, were allied with the renegade
Bannocks in raids. They were with the Bannocks when

white soldiers under a Colonel Connor cornered them in southern Idaho and administered a crushing defeat.

The surviving Shoshone outlaws began to drift back to Wash-a-kie's camp. When the first one of them arrived, Wash-a-kie refused to recognize him. "Who are you?" he said. "I am a Shoshone," said the man. Wash-a-kie shook his head. "You have been whipped," he said. "Shoshones are never whipped. You are no Shoshone." It was his way of exiling the man from the rest of the tribe who had remained loyal to him. But in time he accepted again the survivors. The others who had drifted away came back too. They saw that they had been foolish to leave his leadership. His hold on his people was firmer, stronger than ever.

In that same year there was another treaty. It seemed that the white men wanted more, always they wanted more. They wanted permission to use some of the Shoshone land for more roads, for military posts, for white settlements. That was a hard proposition to take when game was already scarce. But Wash-a-kie took it. He signed this treaty too and his subchiefs followed his lead.

It was the right course for a small tribe of proud people beset by many enemies coveting their hunting grounds. During the next years the Shoshones were relatively prosperous and increased in number and with the steady supply of weapons and ammunitions they obtained by trade with their white friends they fought successfully against their Indian enemies. The Crows, for example, were encroaching on their land and a large party of them was near. Wash-a-kie followed his policy of peace if possible — and if not peace, then hard fighting. He sent one of his men and the man's wife to the Crow camp to talk peace. The Crows killed the man. The squaw escaped and took the word to Wash-a-kie. He gathered reinforcements from among some friendly Bannocks and with Shoshone and Bannock warriors under his command attacked the Crows and after four days of battle defeated them utterly. The Crows were wary of encroachment on Shoshone land after that.

The Sioux were even worse offenders. Once when Wash-a-kie and one hundred of his men were returning from a buffalo hunt, two hundred Sioux suddenly dashed from nearby timber and attacked them. Wash-a-kie, in the forefront of the fight, killed the first of the Sioux to fall and rallied his men and they drove the Sioux back into the timber. There was a lull then in the fighting and during this lull the oldest and favorite son of Wash-a-kie, who had been off somewhere, came riding up. Wash-a-kie was angry that his son had not taken part in the fighting and spoke bitter words, accusing the young man of cowardice. "I will make for myself a name as great as yours!" the young man shouted — and wheeled his horse and galloped straight for the Sioux in the timber. They leaped out to meet him and he killed one, two, of them and then he was down and Wash-a-kie, who had hurried to his own horse to race after him, saw him scalped and cut to pieces. The other Shoshones were close on the heels of their chief. If they had fought well before, they fought doubly well now, and they killed many of the Sioux and drove them away in defeat.

All that night Wash-a-kie sat alone away from the Shoshone camp. It was not much solace to know that the Sioux themselves, a brave people who bowed their heads before bravery when they saw it, would tell the tale for years around their campfires of a brave young Shoshone who had ridden against them alone. It was his doing. He had killed his son as surely as if he himself had struck the blows. In the morning his warriors saw that his hair, which had been as dark as the wing of a raven despite his years, was streaked with gray. And there was a new sternness and at the same time a new gentleness in him.

Friendship and weapons from the whites were good things during these years. They would not be enough in the years to come. Wash-a-kie wanted security for his people. The vague boundaries set by the treaty of 1851 were all but meaningless. He wanted a reservation specifically bounded and guaranteed by the white government and he wanted it to be in the Wind River country. His course of cooperation had been aimed at that for a long time. In 1868 it paid off .

The first transcontinental railroad, the Union Pacific, was being built. It was typical of the whites that they planned this and pushed ahead with it before the way had been prepared by treaties with the Indians through whose lands it would pass. They were busy with such treaties now. There had been another council at Fort Laramie with the Indians of eastern Wyoming. The commission came on west to talk with the Indians of western Wyoming and Utah.

The ablest statesman there, even by the accounts of the white men, the most impressive in appearance and action and word, was a seventy-year-old man named Wash-a-kie. He spoke for his people with the vigor of youth and the wisdom of age and could demand out of a right long earned. The even older Sacajawea was permitted to attend the council and speak and she too could argue a right long ago earned. When had the Shoshones

troubled the whites, been anything but a help to them?
There would be no Shoshone interference with this railroad. But the Shoshones deserved consideration in return. They wanted a reservation all their own and they
wanted it in the Wind River country.

They obtained it, firmly written into the treaty of
1868. A reservation in the Wind River and the Sweetwa-
ter area of west central Wyoming. A reservation almost
equal in size to the state of Connecticut, two and three-
quarters millions of acres of mountains and plains and
well-watered valleys. A small tribe under a great chief
had won a place in the white man's world of the future.

"I am laughing," said Wash-a-kie, "because I am
happy; because my heart is good."

To have written in a treaty was not the same as to
have in fact. Portions of other tribes, big tribes, still
roamed that country. Wash-a-kie would not take his people there until he felt certain they could be reasonably
secure against their enemies. Young warriors among the
Shoshones began to grumble. Their chief had been a
mighty warrior in the past. But he was old now. He had
associated too long with the whites. He had become
womanish; he no longer could perform mighty deeds and
bring back scalps to bear witness for him.

Wash-a-kie overheard some of them talking. Quietly
he took up his weapons and mounted his favorite war
pony and rode away alone. Two months he was gone, no
one knew where. When he returned he carried seven enemy scalps. There was no more grumbling talk. As long
as he lived he would be head chief of the Shoshones.

But the whites too kept pressing him to go to the reservation. They wanted the Shoshones out of the Green

River area so they could take all of it over and exploit it in their manner. In 1871 he led his people to their new home and an agency was built and he started his people on the white man's road of erecting houses and farming and bringing water by irrigation. It was a slow process because there were enemies to fight — but the Shoshones under their Wash-a-kie could still hold their own and perhaps do even better.

One time there was trouble with the Arapahoes and a party of them attacked a Shoshone camp and killed a Shoshone boy. Wash-a-kie and some of his warriors were out to punish the Arapahoes and drive them away. They traveled with supplies and tepees because they expected to be on the march several days. Then scouts brought word that very many Sioux were in the area, all about them, stopping any retreat in any direction. Quickly Wash-a-kie made his plans and they were good plans.

He chose a large meadow dotted with buffalo wallows. He ordered the tepees set up over these wallows and his men to crouch down low in them with their ponies well hobbled nearby. When the Sioux saw the camp, it looked to them like a quiet unsuspecting village. They charged and rode right through, firing as they went. The Shoshones crouched low in the wallows were untouched by the bullets and arrows whipping through the tepees above them and they held their own fire. Wash-a-kie had said to do this and what he said they did.

The Sioux were convinced now that this was a poorly armed village much afraid of them. They regrouped and put on fresh war paint and reloaded their guns and came charging again. Recklessly they fired as they came, believing they would not have much use for their guns and this would be a matter of war clubs and knives. As they swept into the camp with guns empty, the Shoshone guns went into action. From each tepee poured deadly fire. Many Sioux went down and the rest dashed away in disorderly retreat. Then the voice of Wash-a-kie rose in orders and the Shoshones sprang from the tepees and to their hobbled horses and were away in pursuit. For thirty-five miles they chased the disorganized Sioux, killing many more, wiping out small bands that tried to make stands.

With such battles, against Sioux and Crows and Arapahoes and Blackfeet and Cheyennes, the Shoshones, small in number but strong in action, held their own and there was no grumbling among warriors of any age that their chief, despite his many years, was not a man to follow anywhere into anything.

In 1872 the whites as usual wanted more. They wanted to take back the southern portion of the reservation, 600,000 acres of it, where white settlers were continually pushing in and white mining camps were springing up. A council was held for yet another treaty. When Wash-a-kie spoke for his people and the white commissioners desired to know if he spoke for them all, he could say simply, "Whatever I say they all say; it is satisfactory to all of them," and he spoke the simple truth. He signed this treaty, giving the whites what they wanted, but he made them pay for it. Cattle for his people, $5000 worth each year for five years. Now the Shoshones could begin building herds of the white men's cattle to replace the buffalo that were almost gone.

Then he made the one trip of his lifetime all the way to Washington to plead for schools and more farm equipment and all such things for his people. As he traveled eastward and saw the towns and cities and the great num-

bers of the white people, he knew again that the course
he had followed for so long had been the right one. He
met President Grant and the two men, two mighty warriors each in his own way, took well to one another and
they talked together of battles and brave deeds as two old
soldiers should talk. And they talked too of what could
be done to help the Shoshones along the white men's
road.

He was into his late seventies now, but still straight
and strong as a pine tree. It was hard to believe that this
man who still leaped to the back of a horse with no use
of stirrups had been young with the now legendary Kit
Carson who had been laid to rest in a grave southward at
Taos some years ago and with warriors whose grandchildren were now warriors in their turn. He was stern and
dignified enough and more when he was directing his
people in their efforts to walk the white men's road and
when transacting business for them at the agency. But
when he led them on a hunt for the buffalo that still
lingered, the last of their kind, in their Wind River country, he was another man entirely. He was a chief again
out of the old days, joyous and full of enthusiasm, calling
forth good talk around the campfire at night, speaking
himself with smiles on his face and laughter on his lips,
telling of the great hunts of the past and prophesying
good hunting this time. When buffalo were found, he
was a hunter still, using by choice the arrows of his
youth, riding right along with the young men, and when
the killing was finished, he saw to it that the butchering
and preparation of the meat were done properly and with
no waste.

Then it was 1876 and in the Big Horn country to the northeastward the whites were fighting the Sioux and the Arapahoes and the Cheyennes. They had decided that all Indians must be driven onto reservations. Generals Crook and Terry and Custer were in the field with the largest forces yet sent into the Indian country. They would need such forces. They were fighting the largest mobilization of Indian warriors in the whole long roster of the Indian wars.

Word came to the Shoshone reservation. Would old Wash-a-kie, the friend of the whites, send some of his men to serve as scouts with General Crook? He would do more than that. He picked one hundred fifty or more of his warriors and he himself rode with them, taking them to fight the longtime enemies of his people side by side with the whites. It was fortunate for General Crook that Wash-a-kie and his Shoshones were with him in the fighting.

On the march with the white troops he rode sometimes with his warriors and sometimes by the side of General Crook and he and the general were like two old friends who understood each other well and his warriors scouted for the white soldiers like the veterans of this kind of warfare they were. But always, when there was fighting, he was where he should be, in the forefront of battle, leading his men. He could no longer do much active fighting himself, but he was there, where his men could see him fearless of the flying bullets and could hear his shouted orders and follow him anywhere into anything.

Then Crazy Horse with thousands upon thousands of Sioux warriors caught Crook's command in the valley of

the Rosebud and there could have been a disaster worse
than that which overtook General Custer not many days
later on the Little Big Horn. For hours there was bitter
fighting and the troops were stopped, blocked, being
driven back in ever more confusion. The Shoshones and
some Crows, no longer enemies but serving together
with the whites, had been fighting bravely but they were
few against the multitudinous Sioux. An orderly retreat
to a better position alone could save the whole
command. Already one troop under a Captain Vroom
had been cut off, surrounded. A Captain Henry led a
countercharge to break through to the surrounded troop
and to give time for a regrouping of the whole command. He had broken through and was covering the
retreat when a bullet struck him full in the face and he
fell from his horse, seriously wounded, and his men,
seeing him fall, began to scatter in disorder.

The Sioux saw their chance, a leader down, his soldiers uncertain and close to panic. They charged with
increased fury and smashed forward. In a few moments
they would have split the command apart. Already they
were swarming to the very spot where Captain Henry lay
wounded on the ground.

Old Wash-a-kie saw too. His war cry rose as in the old
days. His Shoshones heard, and the Crows, no longer
enemies but allies in war. They followed him straight
into the massed ranks of the Sioux. This was not gun-
fighting, the exchange of shots at a distance. Guns
were emptied in the first moments of attack. This was
hand-to-hand with the knife thrust and the war-club
blow and the grapple of body to body. They drove the
Sioux back and stood over the wounded Captain Henry.

They drove the Sioux back and held them back while the captain was carried to safety and the white soldiers reformed for close-fighting again in orderly retreat.

Victory belonged to the Sioux that day. But the command, though badly battered and mauled, was saved to rest and recuperate and to fight on other days. Wash-a-kie and his Shoshones were with it on the one of those days it drastically defeated the Cheyennes in the Big Horn mountains and the Sioux lost some of their best allies. Then Wash-a-kie and most of his men had to return to their reservation because there was still trouble with Indian enemies in that area too. But he left a few of his best men with General Crook and Shoshone scouts served to the end of the campaign and the surrender of the Sioux.

Far to the east old soldier Ulysses S. Grant read the reports that came to the presidential office and he remembered old warrior Wash-a-kie and sent a present of a fine fancy specially made saddle. At the fort called Fort Washakie in honor of the old chief the military commander made the presentation.

Old Wash-a-kie stood speechless, tears dropping down the scarred face that many whites said reminded them of George Washington. It was not just the saddle. It was that the chief of all the whites had remembered him. He was told that he must say something, some message to be sent to the great white chief.

"Colonel," said Wash-a-kie, "it is hard for an Indian to say thank you like a white man. When you do a kindness for a white man the white man feels it in his head, and his tongue talks. But when you do a kindness for a red man, the red man feels it in his heart. The heart has no tongue." And his words went out on the wires, all the way to the far-off capital on the Potomac, to the great white chief whose hand he had shaken in friendship.

A fine saddle was a fine thing. But it was a present for one man. What about his people, the men and the women and the children who had followed him so faithfully in his course of friendship with the whites? One would think that the whites would be generous to such people, or if not generous at least honest in dealings with them. But too many of the whites and particularly those far away in places of power regarded them as just Indians, lumped together with the other Indians, not really people but some kind of alien creatures to be treated meanly and exploited always to the white men's advantage. It seemed that to have been friendly with the whites, to have helped them, brought no more reward than to have fought them.

Schools had been promised to the Shoshones. There was not a single school on the reservation. Farm implements had been promised. There were only a few and those not worth much. Food had been promised, flour and sugar and beef, and seed grains for planting. The food distributed was scant and of poor quality and the seeds were forgotten and when some did arrive they were not enough for much planting and some did not even grow. The reservation had been promised as their own, to be theirs and theirs only forever, with white men barred from it except for agency employees who were to help them. Part of their reservation had already been taken away. And still white men continually trespassed and shot their game and trapped their furs and stole their cattle.

Now, only a year after they had fought for the white

men against the Sioux and the Arapahoes and the Cheyennes, what did the white men want? They wanted to
settle those same Arapahoes, longtime enemies of the Shoshones, on the Shoshone reservation and on the best portion of it and have the Shoshones share annuities with
them.

When white officials, led by the governor of Wyoming
territory, came to talk about this, old Wash-a-kie, almost
eighty now, received them courteously. He could not do
otherwise. Neither could he help speaking his mind.
With fire and eloquence and the vigor of his long-ago
youth he threw straight into their faces the fact that their
government was greedy and faithless and did not keep its
word. Honor was something which seemed to be unknown to the whites — but it was well known to the Shoshones. He had kept his word all through the years and
he would keep it now, his vow of friendship and cooperation. The whites wanted to put Arapahoes on Shoshone land. Very well. He and his Shoshones would accept them — but only as visitors, to stay only until they
were given a reservation of their own. Quickly the white
officials promised it would be so. They made promises
very easily.

When one of his sons, aroused and angry, talked of
going off to join a band of Bannocks who were raiding
white settlements in the Jackson Hole country, old
Wash-a-kie stopped him with firm words:

My son, with twenty-five other chiefs I signed the Great
Treaty to keep the peace with the Great Father and
his children. I, alone, of the whole number who
signed it, have kept my word, and now, rather than see

you take up arms against the white man, I will strike
you dead at my feet.

These now were the years of peace as the nineteenth
century moved toward its close. The Shoshones were
traveling the white men's road, but slowly, because they
had not much help from the white men. With every
change of administration in Washington there were
changes in Indian policy and in the personnel of the
Indian service. Agents for the Shoshone reservation
changed often and only one or two of them were capable
men who knew much or even cared to know much about
their charges and how to help them along the way. The
others were mere political appointees who were ineffectual fools or whose primary interest, like so many
in the Indian service, was how much they could transfer
to their own pockets of the scant moneys appropriated
for the Indians.

One of these, for example, was a man who had been
nothing more than a tailor by trade, but he had cam-
paigned actively for a new winning president and thus
could claim a profitable appointment. His most frequent
occupation as agent was the consumption of whisky. Another was a major who apparently was appointed because
his superiors did not know what else to do with him.
The Shoshones had to regard him with some compassion
because obviously he was simpleminded. Another was a
professor who promptly got rid of most of the experienced employees of the agency and replaced them with
his relatives. The only thing the least bit admirable
about him and them was their ability to grow big beards.
Still another was a captain, named to the post because his

fellow officers wanted to get rid of him. He was a stiff-
necked martinet of a man and while he was agent, many
Shoshones left their farms and moved back into the
mountains to be away from his immediate influence.

The ways of the white men were beyond reason. Once
when there was a new Indian commissioner in Washington, suddenly there was farm equipment being sent to
the reservation. That was good; it was needed. But
more equipment came, and more, and still more.
Many times more than could possibly be used. What
barns had been built were filled to overflowing with
threshing machines and plows and wagons and rolls of
barbed wire. And still more came, to be piled in heaps to
rust away. The Shoshones thought it strange that so
much equipment should come and yet requests for lumber to build sheds to protect it should be ignored. They
had a good agent at the time and when he objected to
this foolishness, he was dismissed from the post.

But the Shoshones were industrious and hardworking
and they made progress. Slowly, but progress. Under better management they might quickly have become self-
sufficient again, no longer so dependent on the white
government. Sometimes it seemed that the government
wanted to keep them dependent. That made jobs and
money chances for white people. All the same, they were
acquiring houses and barns and considerable land was
under cultivation. They got along.

And these were the years of honorable old age for old
Wash-a-kie. He was the complete, the absolute leader of
his people. Whatever he said, they all said. Well, most of
them most of the time. Which was all even he would expect from a proud and individualistic people in these

times when there were no more enemies on the warpath against them.

He was as stern as ever, when he felt that sternness was needed. One time the then agent was concerned about wife-beating among the Shoshones, about one man in particular who beat his wife too often and too much. Would it not be better, he said, for the chief to do something about this instead of having white men interfere? Yes, it would. Some days later old Wash-a-kie reported that he had disposed of the matter. The man would beat his wife no longer. Wash-a-kie had told him that it must stop. Two days later he had found the man beating her again. He had shot the man and dragged his body out on the rocks. That was that. Wife-beating declined drastically among those Shoshones who had been addicted to it.

The gentleness was there too. It showed best with the children. He loved children. He had had twelve of his own and they had known him as a stern but kind father. Three of the boys, one of them the Dick Wash-a-kie who would be chief after him, were still alive and were middle-aged men with children and grandchildren. All their little ones were as if they were Wash-a-kie's own. And beyond these all Shoshone children were as if they were Wash-a-kie's own. They were not at all afraid of him despite his still stalwart six feet of old, old dignity and there would be a smile on the scarred face which resembled that of George Washington while he watched them at play.

His Shoshone wife, who had kept his tepee during the long hard years of welding the tribe into a unit and holding the Indian enemies at bay and who had given him strong sons, had died many years ago. He had another

wife, a Crow woman who had been captured as a young
girl after a battle with her people and who had been
adopted as a Shoshone and become one of them. She kept
now the house the government had built for him and
was proud of it. But she did not mind, she understood,
that much of the time he preferred to live in a tepee and
use part of the house, which was hard to keep warm in
winter, as a stable for his favorite horse.

If at times it seemed that the Indian Service had forgotten him, the Army had not. There were old soldiers with
stars on their shoulders who remembered. He was on the
Army rolls as a sergeant with no duty, so that in effect he
had a small pension he could spend as he wished helping
his people.

He was listed too as a Christian, an Episcopalian. That
was because, when the white men under President Grant
had parceled out the Indian reservations among the
Christian sect, the Shoshone had been given to the Epis-
copal Church. One of the missionaries, a Reverend John
Roberts, was a fine man and became a firm friend and
old Wash-a-kie listened to him carefully. Once when
Wash-a-kie was ill, he asked his friend to baptize him.
He recovered soon after and immediately many Shoshones wanted to try this "good medicine." Wash-a-kie
had papers drawn and one hundred and sixty acres of
Shoshone land were donated for a church building and a
mission school.

Another time he was ill and in the hospital that had
been built on the reservation and he was on a white
man's mattressed bed. The Reverend Roberts came to
see him. "White Robe," said Wash-a-kie, "I am going to
die if something is not done for me while I am here. My
bed is so soft that I cannot sleep, nor can I rest. I ache all

over." What was it he wanted done? To watch out for the hospital attendants with their silly notions and when they were not looking to take the room door off its hinges and the mattress off the bed and put the hard flat door in its place on the bed. That was done and Wash-a-kie was comfortable and on the way to good health again. He was a firm friend to Wash-a-kie and the Shoshones, the Reverend Roberts.

There was no fighting now, no more battles to be fought, except in memory. But the memories were good. Wash-a-kie made a record of some of them in his own way and with the sly humor that was always in him behind the dignified appearance. Strips of white cloth three feet wide were stretched around the inside walls of his house and on these he sketched pictures with paints made from the colored stones that could be found along the Wind River. He delighted in showing them to visitors. And of course he was the important figure in each picture. There he was, behind a tree, as two Sioux charged toward him on horseback. There, in the next, he had loosed his arrow and it had transfixed both Sioux at once. There, in another, he was crouched behind a log and a whole party of Sioux charged him. There, in the next to that, he had risen and his arrows were flying and all of the Sioux were reeling back and many of them falling to the ground. So they paraded, his pictures, around the walls of his house. If only he could have shown them to the old soldier who had given him a fine saddle.

The whites at the agency and important visitors there and Army officers liked to invite him to dinner with them. They were surprised that he knew how to use their table utensils as they did and that he could speak both English and French. But sometimes he made a mistake in gram-

mar and that amused them. It did not amuse him. So he
took to turning things about so that the amusement
could be his. He would insist upon using an interpreter.
The fact that the interpreter could not speak Shoshone
was what astonished the visitors. Wash-a-kie, with a
chuckle inside him, would converse with the interpreter
in sign language and smile to himself as the signs were
translated into English. The visitors could scarcely believe that so much could be said so quickly and fluently
with mere signs. They would be startled too at the end of
the meal when he would gather what food remained on
the table to take away with him. Did they not know that
to do otherwise would be not to appreciate fully the hospitality? He did not bother to tell them that there were
Shoshone families who needed that food.

When President Chester A. Arthur toured the West
and visited the reservation, the then agent thought that
Wash-a-kie should come to the agency to greet him.
Wash-a-kie arrayed himself in his finest but he would not
leave his own quarters. No. This was Shoshone land and
he was chief of the Shoshones. Here, on this land, the
great white chief should come to him. President Arthur
came.

The years drifted on toward the end of the century
and in 1896 again the whites wanted more. They wanted
a piece of land in the northwestern corner of the reservation, 64,000 acres of it, where were the Big Horn hot
springs that were becoming known for their medicinal
properties. Old Wash-a-kie, ninety-eight now but still
speaking with one voice for his people, signed this treaty
too. But written into it, at his insistence, was a provision

that a portion of the springs should always be maintained for free use by Indians.

The years drifted on and the United States was at war with Spain. Old Wash-a-kie listened eagerly to all the news about it that reached the reservation. When word came of the final surrender, he was happy that the great white chief had "whipped" these enemies too.

He was very old now, past his own century mark, and he had to be helped up into the once-fine saddle that had been given to him as a present long ago. When he rode about and stopped to talk to his people or to white visitors, he stayed in the saddle, erect and dignified, looking down. Some people thought this a show of arrogance. They said he sat there like a king on a throne, deliberately looking down. But the Shoshones knew. They knew that their Wash-a-kie had always had pride but never arrogance. He did not want to make a weak show of himself, to have to be helped to dismount and then to remount again. They did not mind looking up to hear his words.

Then it was 1900 and the new century of the calendar was beginning and old Wash-a-kie knew that his spirit would soon be departing for "the land of the stars." He was worried that perhaps by being baptized and accepting the God of the white men he might have offended the Great Spirit of the Indians. He asked one of his oldest white friends about this. He was told that the God of the white men and the Great Spirit of the Indians were one and the same only called by different names. He was content.

On the 20th of February he summoned his family about him. He told them he wanted them to open their ears and their hearts so they would know what he said. He wanted them to follow in the footsteps he had made for them so that always they would have the respect of their own people and of the whites among whom they must live. Quietly, sometime during that night, his spirit departed on the long journey from which there is no returning.

He was buried in the cemetery at Fort Washakie with a full military funeral and the honors that go to a white man with the rank of captain. The coffin was strapped to a caisson with an American flag draped over it and the procession was a mile and a half long. All the Shoshones were there. And there too were very many Arapahoes, still on Shoshone land after the promise that had been made, paying their tribute to the man who had defeated them as enemies and had accepted them as brothers.

And the white men, only two years later, wanted more and took away more than half of the Shoshone reservation that still remained, leaving not much more than a fifth of the original reservation of 1868. And kept the Arapahoes there too. But a small tribe that could so easily have been scattered and crushed away to nothingness in the conflict of the races still had some land and good land and in the Wind River country.

They are there still, a proud people, on what remains of the land he won for them.

John Simpson Chisum

AUGUST 15, 1824 — DECEMBER 22, 1884

CATTLE kings were not as numerous in the old West as they were and are and will be in western fiction. Most of the really big outfits were partnerships, companies, syndicates. Absentee ownership was common. Individual men holding and personally operating what could be called cattle empires were rare. But there were some here and there across the great spaces. John Chisum was the prototype of them all.

He would have laughed outright if he could have seen a movie or television version of a big-time rancher. He was too busy being one to resemble any romantic notion of one. What he did resemble, most of the time, was one of his own hard-working dust-chewing hard-bitten cowhands. He had the big-boned spare-fleshed angular structure of an old-time Remington cowboy. Dark brown hair topped and a heavy mustache fronted a face which seemed thin because of a long jaw and a prominent nose and was sunbaked the color of old leather. He did have his special clothes for what he called "state occasions" and he could be at ease in them. But his niece Sallie, who was his housekeeper and tried to make him wear them often, soon discovered that his notion of a "state occasion" differed considerably from hers. He usually went about with a soft gray hat set squarely on his head, in a blue flannel shirt with trousers stuffed into boots, all such items much the worse for long wear. Sometimes he worked around the ranch headquarters in a battered straw hat and overalls and heavy brogan shoes. There was the time a natty stranger rode up to the big ranch house at South Springs and saw him at some chore and took him for the tag end of the hired hands. The stranger nodded in a condescendingly democratic manner. "Working for Old Chisum?" he said.

John Chisum grinned. "Yes," he said. "Working for Old Chisum."

He had no need to try to look the part of a cattle king. He *was* the part and his career covered every aspect of it. At his peak he had the widest range and the largest herds of any single individual in the history of the western cattle business. He was in that business from its beginnings and put his mark indelibly on it. He had the flair and the zest for the role. Open-handed, generous, stubborn as the mossiest-backed old longhorn, he was as ready to lose a fortune as to make it. Once he made up his mind to do something, he did it come hell or highwater or Comanche raiders or the loss of his last dollar. He took the good and the bad — there was plenty of both — with the same grin at fate. He liked the ladies and he sparked quite a few of them all through his life but not a one ever put a halter on him. He was a man among men at a time when that took a lot of doing. He needed rough tough hombres for his crews and he found them and he asked no questions about their pasts and was concerned only with their present abilities to work cows and obey orders. They worked for him with a will and he treated them right and he won and held their respect.

And he knew cows, all kinds, from the wild rangy Texan-Mexican longhorns to the squat purebred shorthorns he imported to upgrade his stock. Knew them as few other men have ever known them. The western ranges were once spotted with cowmen who learned the business under Uncle John Chisum. His quick visual verdict on one animal or a herd of ten thousand was as sound and dependable as any official inspector's report after a careful checking. "He could count three grades of cattle at once," said Charles Goodnight, quite a cowman himself, "and count them thoroughly even if they were going in a trot." There was the time he was trailing a herd into New Mexico and another herd belonging to a man named Adams was following and every night the Adams herd stampeded. John Chisum rode back to see what was the trouble. When the Adams herd was bedded for the night, he ambled about, looking it over. He pointed at a big razor-backed one-eyed longhorn. "Cut that steer out," he said. "Drive him down to the river and kill him." There were no more stampedes.

His father was of Scottish ancestry, his mother of German, both from families that had been American for several generations. He was the second of their five children, the oldest boy. He was born in 1824 in Madison County, Tennessee, on his paternal grandfather's big plantation which was being managed at the time by his father, Claiborne Chisum. He spent his early years roaming the place. Land and livestock and the handling of both — he was absorbing knowledge of such things even in childhood. "Cow John," the family called him because of his eager interest in cattle.

When he was thirteen the Claiborne Chisums moved to Lamar County in east Texas just below the Oklahoma–Indian Territory line, among the first settlers on the site of the town of Paris, soon to be the county seat. This was raw frontier then with no schools. There is no record that John Chisum ever attended any school anywhere. But he contrived to pick up a fair education, adequate for his purposes, and in later life was able to write, in letters and other papers, a vigorous prose all his own.

He was a boy stretching into a young man and living in Texas, birthplace of the western cattle business. He was to play a big part in the burgeoning of that business. But not yet. He was a late starter. The cattle business was not yet his style, was still eastern in methods and management, small-scale, barnyard and feedlot. He helped his father on the family farm and held various jobs in the growing town. He did manage to wangle financing and drive a herd of five hundred cattle eastward to Shreveport in Louisiana, the first cattle drive of any consequence ever made out of Texas. Insects and forests and mud and swampland and broad rivers made the driving difficult and killed off many animals. He lost money on the venture. He tried another drive, eastward again, to Little Rock in Arkansas. He made a bit on that one — but knew by now that driving cattle to eastern markets was a poor business. Geography was against it. Not until there were railroads could cattle be moved to eastern markets at a profit. He tried other things, bought and sold real estate, became a building contractor and put up the first courthouse in Lamar County. He ran for county clerk against the popular incumbent and was licked. He ran again in the next election against the same man and won. He made a fair-to-middling county clerk.

He sat in the little office and felt cabined, cribbed, confined. He stood in the doorway and sniffed the winds blowing in from the great spaces sweeping westward. Cattle country! Bigger, vaster, more challenging than anything eastward. If it could support the hundreds of thousands of buffalo that roamed there, it could support cattle the same. Cattle country! Ready for a new kind of cattle business as wide and as free and as rugged as the land itself. Waiting to be taken by the men with the vision and the verve and the downright guts and the hard stubborn persistence required for the taking.

Then he met a man named Stephen K. Fowler.

This Fowler was an easterner with money and thoughts of investing some of it in Texas cattle. He knew nothing about cows but he knew something about men. He gave John Chisum $6000 and a promise of more as required and a ten-year partnership was launched.

John Simpson Chisum, thirty years old, closed the door of the county clerk's office behind him, swung into a saddle, and rode westward into the future.

That was in the spring of 1854. By the end of the year he had put together a herd of twelve hundred head, had enlisted a crew of tough Texan riders to tend it, and had established his range well westward in central Texas in what are now Denton and Tarrant counties. Fowler-Chisum cattle were grazing where the city of Fort Worth now stands. He was the first rancher in the area and all around spread open range. With characteristic foresight he applied for a patent to a large tract in Denton County and established ranch headquarters there. He knew cows and he was learning more all the time and the herd became herds by natural increase and judicious buying and proper care and the partnership prospered and by the Census of 1860 he could put down the value of his share at $50,000.

Then came the Civil War. It was good for business at first. Confederate forces in the trans-Mississippi area needed meat and the Fowler-Chisum partnership had plenty of beef on the hoof that could be driven where needed. John Chisum and his tough Texan cowboys drove it where needed. And again with characteristic foresight plus a suspicion that Confederate money would not hold its value John Chisum regularly put the proceeds into more cattle.

Then the war was not so good for business. Ranch crews dwindled as men drifted away to join the military forces. When troops were withdrawn from the forts in and about the Indian Territory for service in the war campaigns, armed warriors began to slip away from the reservations and raid down into Texas. They wanted horses and they took horses, crippling ranch operations. With the fall of Vicksburg and the Mississippi in the control of Union troops the Confederate markets faded and disappeared. The weather was bad too. Prolonged drought hit the Fowler-Chisum range. John Chisum found himself with only a skeleton crew of loyal men trying to take care of the partnership cattle and those of half a dozen other ranchers too. He looked about for new and better range. Only one direction ever made sense to him for the kind of cattle business he was pioneering. Westward. He started moving cattle deep into west Texas, set up new headquarters on the Concho River near the site of present-day San Angelo. As the war approached its end, most of the cattle for which he was responsible had been established on open range there and the Fowler-Chisum partnership was one of the major cattle-owning outfits of all Texas.

Meantime the ten-year agreement with Fowler was expiring. It had been an amicable and successful relationship. Fowler had supplied the capital. John Chisum had supplied the knowledge and the active management and had made money for them both. But he was through with partnerships. He would run only Chisum cattle, said John Chisum, or get out of the business altogether. He made Fowler a straight offer — buy or sell. Fowler sold. That is, he swapped his share in the cattle for Chisum's patent land in Denton County. John Chisum, forty years old, was on his own, running only Chisum cattle.

This was the period, the postwar period, when cattle drives out of Texas would soon be streaming north up the Chisholm and other trails to the new rail-side cowtowns in Kansas for shipment to eastern markets and Texas cattle would be stocking all the ranges of the West. Most cattlemen looked north, to the shipping towns and the new ranges opening all the way up to the Canadian border and beyond. John Chisum refused to waver in his own directional allegiance. He continued to look westward. On across the Comanche-infested Staked Plains of west Texas, in New Mexico and Arizona, the

government was building forts, was rounding up the
Navajos and the Apaches and penning them on
reservations. That meant government beef contracts.
Charles Goodnight and Oliver Loving, cowmen of his
own caliber, had recently joined forces and headed a
herd in that direction.

His brother Pitzer was with him now, working for
him. He sent Pitzer westward to look over the rangeland
along the Pecos River in New Mexico. Pitzer's report
was enthusiastic. John Chisum decided to see for himself
and ramrodded his own crew on a drive of a thousand
head through drought and Comanche country and to
Fort Sumner in the upper Pecos valley. He arrived too
late to sell his steers that season. He grinned at that minor setback and went to work with the usual Chisum energy. About thirty-five miles downriver from the fort at
Bosque Grande, site so named from the big cottonwoods
that grew there, were a store and several other buildings.
He bought out the owner and set up New Mexican headquarters. During the fall and winter he sold most of the
herd in small batches at a profit as chances offered. He
looked over the rangeland and found it all Pitzer had
reported. When he started back to the Texas ranch on
the Concho in the spring, leaving Pitzer in charge at
Bosque Grande, he had in his pocket a contract, acquired
by underbidding all competitors, to supply ten thousand
steers to Fort Sumner and in his head an agreement,
confirmed by a handshake, to supply trail herds to
Charles Goodnight, who had lost his partner Loving to
Indian arrows not long before. It was a simple arrangement between two independent pioneer cattlemen who
were opening up new cattle territory. John Chisum

would bring herds out of Texas and turn them over to Goodnight, who would drive them up into Colorado to stock new ranches there and to supply meat to the new mining camps.

During the next years John Chisum shunted cattle by the thousands westward out of Texas. His cattle drives made cattle history and entered into the folklore of the cattle kingdom. There were times when he had half a dozen herds on the move at once. The Chisum name was a byword in the business. There was John himself, boss of the whole shebang, all-around cattleman who knew more about cows than any two others put together, a match for any of his men in the skills of the working trade. It was said that if he thought the price was right he would drive a herd straight through hell and deliver to the devil himself. There was brother Pitzer, a younger edition of somewhat the same, to take care of things at the New Mexico headquarters. There was Frank, the dark-skinned Frank "Chisum" who had been a family slave before the war and was a hard-riding cowman now more than ever a member of the family, quite capable of carrying out any assignment given him. There were lean squint-eyed rawhided trail bosses who had learned the game under John Chisum and would take herds anywhere John Chisum said to take them. He himself was free to shuttle back and forth between Texas and New Mexico and roam far and wide on the scent of business and know that the Chisum cattle were in the hands of loyal Chisum men.

Herd after herd he sent westward and his tough trail crews battled outlaws and rustlers and Indian raiders and everything perverse nature could throw at them and took the cattle through. It was a risky dangerous business and the losses often were large. John Chisum grinned — and kept right on.

He liked, when he could, to ride the trail with one of his herds. His men liked that too. They could do the job all right without him, but they could do it even better with him along. He did his share of the work and took all the rigors right with them and his unfailing good nature and ready quick grin kept them all in fine fettle. He was never afraid of anything or anybody, and yet he was slow to anger and easy-spoken even in anger and always ready to talk out an argument to a sensible solution. His chuck wagons were always well stocked and he hired the best cooks he could find. He was a great one for companionship around a campfire at night and he liked to hear and to tell tales, chuckling often and invariably ending an anecdote with a burst of hearty laughter. He tried always to have at least one man along who could provide a bit of music. An old cowhide would be rolled out flat and cowboy boots would stomp merrily on it to the strains from a banjo or mouth-organ or fiddle.

There was little or no law in the land the Chisum crews traveled and they made their own and used rope and lead to make it stick. There was the time a quarrel on the trail exploded into the deliberate murder of a young Chisum cowboy and John Chisum nodded his head and quietly and efficiently his men strung up the murderer to the nearest tree and the herd was on its way again. There was the time outlaws ran off a batch of Chisum horses and John Chisum and a few of his men tracked them across a hundred miles and killed three of them — and recovered the horses. There was the time a big bunch of Apaches, who had made a habit of leaving their poorly garrisoned reservation to dine off stolen Chisum beef, raced into one of his herds and killed some scores of cattle just for the hell of it — and John Chisum gathered his men and rode to the reservation and passed out whisky to the few soldiers and officers there until they were blind drunk then waved his men on and they raced through the reservation leaving quite a few cases of sudden death from lead poisoning behind them. He had little trouble with those particular Apaches after that.

One time brother Pitzer lost a whole herd. Eleven hundred head that had cost twenty dollars apiece in gold. John had driven them to Horsehead Crossing on the lower Pecos and Pitzer had picked them up there to take them on up to Bosque Grande. Indians in large numbers were on the prowl. Pitzer tried to get a military escort and was turned down. He drove ahead anyway and some dozens of redskins managed to stampede the herd and run it into nearby mountains. Pitzer and crew put up a good fight and accounted for a fair share of the Indians and followed right into the mountains but were unable to recover more than a few steers. Disgusted and discouraged, several of them wounded, they rode back to find brother John and report. Word of what had happened had preceded them. John Chisum grinned at his downcast younger brother and battle-scarred crew. He waved a hand at another herd gathered and ready and waiting. "Here's another," he said. "Try her again."

The ranges of the West were once spotted too with men who liked to remark that in their time they had ridden for Uncle John Chisum.

Those were wild and woolly days in west Texas in the aftermath of the war with branded and unbranded cattle running wild and free and rustlers rampant and markets far away and Indians lurking along the trails. Only big outfits like John Chisum's, well manned, ready to take losses, ready to fight, could survive. Many of the smaller ranchers were desperate, eager to sell out. John Chisum was here and there and everywhere, ready to buy, to give notes for cattle, to take them on consignment. Scores of brands began to show up in his trail herds.

The story started that when making up a herd he paid no attention to markings, just gathered everything in sight that looked like a cow and took off. When he lost most of a herd out on the plains and turned back and scooped up another in record time and was on the trail again, the story really took hold. John Chisum merely grinned that now well-known grin. Such talk was part of the game in those wide open days. When Goodnight, a somewhat stiff-necked man, heard the story and noted the multiplicity of brands and became huffy about it and went his way, refusing to accept that herd, John Chisum took no offense. He had plenty of other uses for the cattle and he knew what he had stashed away in a metal cylinder he could lay hands on whenever he really needed it. A little later Tom Catron, ambitious young territorial attorney general, heard the story too and brought suit against him on a charge of bringing stolen cattle into New Mexico. John Chisum grinned — and produced that metal cylinder. It contained a roll of manuscripts, records of every Texas brand he had been handling — hundreds of them — with powers of attorney from the previous owners. The charge was withdrawn.

It may be, as some people who had axes of their own to grind insisted, that John Chisum never cleared all those Texas cattle accounts. It would have been surprising if he did. Amid all the troubles in Texas in the wake of the war it was often difficult if not impossible to trace a small-time operator who had sold out and drifted away. Those who knew John Chisum best always maintained that he never dodged a debt he felt he honestly owed. He would fight to the last legal ditch what he regarded as a false claim. But he would pay and sometimes overpay an honest obligation. There is little doubt that in one way or another and at one time or another he met most of those Texas cattle notes. It is a simple fact that many and many a discouraged onetime Texas rancher who had turned his cattle over to John Chisum made a new start in something else on the stake John Chisum got for him. There was the time, too, a few years later, when he delivered a herd out of New Mexico into Kansas. Instead of the cash he expected, which he needed badly, he was handed a batch of those notes which the man to whom he was delivering had bought up at a fraction of their value. John Chisum grinned — and accepted them at full face value. And there are tales of men, long lost track of, who met him in later years and stepped forward to identify themselves — and saw John Chisum grin in recognition and reach into a pocket for a roll of bills.

He may not have tried overhard to trace all those notes. But he never dodged one when it was presented to him.

Westward out of Texas the Chisum cattle came, by the thousands, by the tens of thousands. Fort Sumner had its beef. Other forts had theirs too. Charles Goodnight had all the herds he wanted to drive up into Colorado until he quit trail-driving and settled there. And still more cattle came, stocking the rangeland along the Pecos. By

1871 when John Chisum closed out operations in Texas and settled permanently in New Mexico, despite all the contracts and commitments met, more than twenty-five thousand Chisum cattle grazed on the new Chisum range.

That was only a beginning.

There was no other important rancher at the time along the whole upper reach of the Pecos. John Chisum's empire of open range, his by right of occupation and use, spread until in general outline it spanned nearly a fifth of the whole of New Mexico Territory. It ran southward down the Pecos from what is now the town of Anton Chico for 150 miles and more to what is now Carlsbad and beyond. It stretched eastward from the river all the way to and across the New Mexico line into the Staken Plains of Texas, westward from the river seventy-five miles and more to the mountains scattered down through the center of the territory. Roughly a great jagged square 150 miles each way, swallowing and surrounding the few settlements within that wide perimeter. His line camps dotted the vast expanse and he had a hundred riders at a time on his payroll. His Rail brand, a straight line from shoulder to hip along a cow's left flank, and his distinctive Jinglebob earmark were known wherever cowboys jingled spurs. When Philip Ashton Rollins, annalist of the open-range cattle industry, wrote a book about a typical cowboy, though he placed him in Wyoming, he tagged him "Jinglebob."

The Chisum cattle multiplied steadily, rapidly. During the first full-time years in New Mexico few deliveries were made anywhere. The cattle stayed on the range. Indian activities, particularly horse-stealing, kept ranch activities to the minimum of necessity. John Chisum and his men were too busy establishing their range and fighting off raids to do much else. The Indians took regular toll and innumerable rustlers preyed on the cattle and many a small-time rancher got his start mavericking or brand-changing Chisum cattle. John Chisum figured that his crews, capable as they were and hardworking as they were, managed to brand about three-fourths of the annual calf crop — that other people got the rest. And still the Jinglebob herds increased. By 1875 it was estimated that seventy to eighty thousand Chisum cattle roamed the Chisum range. He began making major deliveries that year and trailed more than ten thousand head westward to Arizona markets and twenty thousand more northward into Colorado and northeastward into Kansas — and failed to make much of a dent in his holdings.

He himself did not know how many cattle he owned in the peak years. When asked for a figure he shrugged his shoulders and said that if anyone popped up with a quick order for forty thousand steers, he reckoned he could fill it without trying too hard.

The headquarters at Bosque Grande were abandoned and he moved downriver about forty-five miles, much closer to the approximate center of his range, to a site near present-day Roswell. For twenty-four hundred head of cattle he acquired from a James Patterson a forty-acre tract and improvements on South Spring River, an artesian-spring-fed stream that headed there and flowed five miles east to the Pecos. The improvements consisted primarily of what was called the Square House, eight small rooms enclosing a small patio. Not exactly adequate headquarters for the Jinglebob king of the Pecos and the family he was gathering about him. Brother Pitzer, of course, was with him and faithful retainer Frank.

Brother James would soon be coming from Texas, bringing his daughter Sallie and two young sons.

The Square House was razed and replaced by the Long House, once known all through the Southwest. This was a solid adobe structure 148 feet long and 39 wide with a 10-foot hallway dividing it in the middle and broad verandas running the full length front and back. A canal, the "drinking ditch," was dug from the little river and cool clean spring water ran right under that central hallway through the house and on to gardens and orchards. Though the ranch was two hundred miles from any railroad, the house was equipped and furnished in the best contemporary manner. The equal, said visitors, of anything the East could offer.

There was one room which some visitors thought out of keeping with the rest. John Chisum's room. He wanted the place comfortable, even luxurious, for his "family." But for himself, no. His was a combination bedroom and office, neat and plain and almost bare, containing only a bed, a small safe, a walnut writing desk and chair, and a small wire stand supporting a big dictionary. The bed was made up daily — but at night John Chisum pulled the blankets from it and spread them on the floor and lay down on them to sleep the sleep of an essentially simple straightforward uncomplicated man. He had slept too often and too long on the ground by his herds to be comfortable on the softness of a fine mattress.

Here at the Long House the Jinglebob king of the Pecos dispensed hospitality like a king — western style. Here his niece Sallie reigned over the household with its two full-time cooks. She was only sixteen when she arrived but she took hold at once and was immediately a favorite with every male and particularly those of the cowboy persuasion within a long-riding radius. She thought her Uncle John the best of men, the biggest-hearted, the most generous. He talked little and then right to the point (except when telling tales by a fire), but even his silence was genial and there was usually a kindly smile on his sunbaked face. But he *would* insist on that silly sleeping on the floor — and on wearing his state-occasion clothes so rarely that moths got more out of them then he did.

Anyone who came along, friend or mere acquaintance or complete stranger no difference, was welcome to board and bed at the Long House. The big table in the dining room could seat twenty-six people easily, twelve on each side and one at each end. It was set for twenty-six three times a day, breakfast and dinner and supper, and not often through the years was a chair unoccupied. Everyone worth knowing in the Southwest and many more perhaps not worth knowing stopped and were fed under Uncle John's roof and like as not stayed the night or nights. Governors, legislators, distinguished and not-so-distinguished travelers from the East and from Europe, army officers, ordinary soldiers, businessmen of every variety, immigrants on their way to California, cattlemen big and little, cowboys of every description, gamblers, outlaws, gunmen, drifters, tramps — they were all treated alike. That was Uncle John's one invariable rule. Under his roof all men were equals, fellow humans on their stubbornly long or suddenly brief journeys to their own individual destinies.

A man might dash up on a well-lathered horse, grab a quick meal, dash away again. A while later a whole posse might arrive and repeat the performance. Pursued or pursuers, renegade or the righteous, when they rode to his door to partake of his food and friendship, they were all the same to Uncle John.

An immigrant family on the way past might stop with team gaunted and rickety wagon almost empty. When they moved on, they would be rested and fed and their horses would be full of good feed and their wagon would have been repaired and there would be sacks of food stowed in it. Like as not Uncle John would have given them sound advice on routes to follow and where to find good homestead land. He might even have encouraged them to stay in New Mexico and nibble a piece out of his own range.

There was the time a neighbor, a novice at the game, started a ranch just north of the Chisum range and stocked it with a good-sized herd. A storm came whooping out of the north and drove the neighbor's cattle southward until they were far-scattered among the Jinglebob cattle. The neighbor called on John Chisum in a state of worried frustration. He lacked the men and the money to hire men to untangle that mess. Quite a job, agreed Uncle John. He was already calculating what men he could spare to get the job done for this neighbor who was being decent and straightforward about it. But no, said the neighbor. He was fed up with ranching and wanted only to get out of it without losing his shirt. Easy done, said Uncle John; just let the cows stay where they seemed to want to be and name a price. The neighbor thought fast and named a price. A stiff one. Uncle John knew it was a stiff one and he could easily beat it down. He merely grinned — and went to his room for his checkbook.

Two other buildings were built close to the Long

House, closer than the big barn and the horse corrals. One was the commissary, kept well filled, the other set aside for a dance hall. Many were the dances held there in the slack times, in the slowness of the winter seasons, the festivities often lasting for days. Uncle John was aging now and no longer quite up to the cowboy stomp; a more or less sedate waltz would satisfy him. But he enjoyed seeing the young ones kick up their boot-heels — and properly appreciate Sallie.

He worked hard, doing much of the labor himself and personally directing the rest of it, to make the whole place a positive oasis in that semi-arid land. He brought cottonwoods down from Las Vegas and planted them about the house and along a quarter-mile avenue leading to it. He had fruit trees of many kinds brought from Arkansas for the orchards, rosebushes from Texas for a fine flowering hedge. He imported scarlet tanagers and bob-whites from his native Tennessee and let them loose to nest in the neighborhood. He introduced alfalfa to the southwest and sowed and irrigated eight hundred acres of it. He experimented with various grains. Uncle John Chisum, old-timers long remembered, plain liked to see things grow.

He traveled often on business, had to, and was an old hand at getting about by stagecoach and train. One time the coach in which he was a passenger was held up by masked bandits. He was carrying $1000 in currency. He shoved the money down a bootleg and when it was his turn to be searched handed over a small sum. The ruse worked. He chuckled prodigiously whenever he told that tale. But what he liked best, when he had the time for it, was to jog wherever he was going in saddle on a stout horse. One of the popular stories about him was that he

went his way, wherever he pleased, often alone, through
Indian and outlaw country, and never carried, never
even owned, a gun. Nonsense. True enough, he never
wore a gun and cartridge belt as did most range men of
the time. But he carried a gun all right when he went
riding — in a special holster fastened to his saddle. He
had used it some and to good effect in the trail-driving
days out of Texas, but there is no record that after he
settled in New Mexico he ever used it on anything more
than rattlesnakes. His reputation went with him and was
more protection than any gun. He was asked once why
he never seemed to be worried that some gunman (the
territory had many) might use him for a target. He
grinned and remarked that in his experience most gunmen had more sense than to shoot a man of any real consequence.

When he was at home he rode out often, from camp
to camp, to check conditions on the range. He ambled
about, usually on a roan horse he called Old Steady, and
carried binoculars to extend vision of his vast domain.
His cowboys liked to see him come jogging along because
he gave orders not as a boss to hirelings but as a man to
men and was easy-spoken even when correcting them for
work done wrong. They rarely mistook that easy manner
and rarely tried to take advantage of him. They knew he
would fire a man on instant notice who played a mean
trick or shirked on the job but never for an honest mistake.

During these peak years of the 1870's John Simpson
Chisum, the Jinglebob king of the Pecos, Uncle John to
all who knew him, was a living legend, perhaps *the* living legend of the open-range cattle business of the West,

a man who had ridden to power and brief passing glory in worn work clothes on the back of a western cow pony.

Change is the one unchangeable rule of life. And change came fast to the open-range cattle business, particularly in New Mexico.

John Chisum differed from the usual cattle king of fiction in one important respect. He was no ruthless monarch determined to hold what he had. He did not cling to his empire and fight to hold it in the face of changing conditions. With the same foresight which had taken him into the open-range business in the beginning he foresaw that the free use of public land could not last, that it had hit its heyday and was doomed to swift extinction. He held no grudge against the honest nesters and small-time operators and the homesteaders who were soon invading his range. As a matter of fact he encouraged them, particularly those who wanted to settle down and farm where irrigation water was available. He had something of that instinct himself.

He foresaw too that the raising of what were essentially scrub cattle in vast numbers on steadily dwindling range would soon be uneconomic, impractical, that the market trend was toward quality beef, raised in smaller herds in large fenced pastures where breeding and upgrading could be controlled. He became more interested in quality than in quantity of cattle and was among the first ranchers of the West to import good bulls and pay whatever was required to get them.

The big-scale open-range business was becoming ever more difficult anyway, again particularly in New Mexico. As the territory filled in, more and small ranchers ringed his range, the newcomers' cattle mixed with the Jingle-bob. Claims were made that some of them were driven off with his own when he made deliveries. He could counter with the more valid claim that their herds grew remarkably fast and at the obvious expense of his calf crop and that they had a suspicious fondness for brands into which his Rail could easily be converted. Bitterness and bad feeling were on the increase.

Indians were no longer much of a problem, but white rustlers were, more than ever before. Indians had usually stolen cattle solely for meat, in a sense a form of tax on the cattle which had displaced their buffalo. White rustlers stole for money. They ran off cattle in bunches, often hundreds at a time. The ruggedness of the country and the nearness of the Mexican border were major assets to them. Now and again, under particularly strong provocation, John Chisum led his men on armed forays to recover stock. It was like trying to plug the holes in a sieve one at a time with new ones popping open faster than the old were plugged. And John Chisum was older now, mellowing more. He was no longer as ready to fight, foreseeing the ultimate uselessness of it. He tried appealing to the military and was rebuffed. He tried appealing to the law but without much success. What passed for law was a bitter joke in those days in the territory with its racial mixture, Spanish-Mexican and Anglo-American, and the resultant and perhaps inevitable political corruption. Men holding official positions were themselves rustling Chisum cattle — or so jealous of his supposed wealth and prestige that they looked the other way while the rustling went on. Nipping off Chisum cattle was said to be one of the most popular pastimes in New Mexico.

Uncle John Chisum considered all aspects of the whole situation. In typical fashion he decided on a drastic move. He would dispose of most of his present cattle and concentrate on the development and raising of much smaller herds of better quality. At one stroke he sold the bulk of the cattle currently on his range to Hunter & Evans, a big beef commission outfit in St. Louis which controlled ranches relatively free of the rustling problem in Kansas and held heavy government beef contracts. He was to remain in charge of the cattle, holding them on his range, and during the next few years move them to the Kansas ranches or to contract delivery points as directed from St. Louis.

The arrangement with Hunter & Evans included two provisions which would have later repercussions. As surety bond for completion of the agreement, title to all the Chisum holdings in New Mexico was turned over to Hunter & Evans in temporary trust. And brother Pitzer, in recompense for years of loyal service, was to choose several thousand fine heifers from the herds while deliveries were being made. These would be kept apart and when all deliveries were completed, Hunter & Evans would transfer title to them to Pitzer.

John Chisum, in his own blunt stubborn way, was straightening out his affairs and changing his style of ranching.

Meanwhile there was the bloody nuisance of the Lincoln County War.

More nonsense, more mere rumors and farfetched hearsay tales and outright lies and distortions have been perpetrated and put down on paper about the Lincoln County War than about any other such episode in all the

West. Billy the Kid emerged from it for his brief inglorious career and that alone has guaranteed a constant flow of fable and misinformation.

Actually it was a struggle, which eventually erupted into open warfare, for dominance in the county between two factions, the entrenched Murphy-Dolan group backed by what was known as the Santa Fe Ring in the territorial capital and the opposition McSween-Tunstall later-comers. John Chisum's connection with it was chiefly incidental. Part of his range extended into the county. His South Spring headquarters was not far away in neighboring Chavez County. He had no liking for Murphy, who owned a herd of cattle which increased remarkably fast at the obvious expense of the Chisum herds. It was well known that Dolan dealt often in stolen Chisum beef, buying it from the small-time rustlers. On the other hand, McSween was Chisum's lawyer on various occasions and Tunstall, a wealthy and likable young Englishman recently come into the territory, was a good friend of his. John Chisum let the two use his name, putting him down as president, when they started a bank in Lincoln County in competition with the Murphy-Dolan interests. His own interests, of course, went far beyond that one county and he was rarely there. But it was inevitable that his sympathies and his friendship were aligned on the McSween-Tunstall side.

But when young Tunstall was deliberately murdered by a posse under a Murphy-Dolan sheriff and McSween, though a Bible-reading man who never used a gun, launched a vendetta in revenge and the war was on, John Chisum stayed out of it. He tried frequently to keep McSween out of immediate trouble and used his influence to clear McSween of some unfounded court charges. But

he himself took no part in the fighting and sent none of
his men into it. A few of them (he was reducing his
crews during this period) drifted away and joined the
McSween forces on their own. By then they were no
longer Chisum men. He had plenty more on his mind
than a factional war in one corner of his domain. He was
busy gathering and dispatching herds into Arizona and
Kansas under orders from Hunter & Evans. He stayed
out of a war that was not his and was none of his making.

When the war really boiled over in pitched battle in
the town of Lincoln and McSween was killed and the
Murphy-Dolan faction was riding high supported by the
military under orders influenced by the Santa Fe Ring,
John Chisum moved what remained of his cattle (really
Hunter & Evans cattle) northward to Bosque Grande
then eastward out on the plains into the valley of the
Canadian to wait out the storm. When President Hayes
at last took action and ousted the territorial governor
and sent General Lew Wallace to take over the governor-
ship and restore order to Lincoln County, it was John
Chisum who prepared and sent him an impartial plan
for maintaining law and order in the Pecos valley. It was
John Chisum, among others, who recommended the Pat-
rick Floyd Garrett who became the sheriff who did the
final cleanup in Lincoln County.

The story persists, as perennial as publishers' lists, that
Billy the Kid was hired by John Chisum to fight in the
war and later was refused payment and thereupon vowed
to kill Chisum men at five dollars a head until the debt
was squared. There are enough versions of that one, each
wilder than the last, to fill a fat volume. The facts behind
it are few and slim. Billy knew John Chisum (everyone
in the territory did) and had eaten quite a few meals

(just about everyone had) at the Long House in earlier days. He may have "worked" for John Chisum in the sense that he may have taken advantage (many young drifters did) of Chisum's offer of five dollars a head for any mavericks found roaming his range and given his Rail brand. Then, in the aftermath of the war when Billy was broke and hunted as the outlaw he had become, he apparently felt he had some claim on John Chisum because he had fought on the side of Chisum's friends Mc-Sween and Tunstall and he slipped up to John Chisum one day and asked for money. John Chisum grinned, grimly this time. "You know as well as I do," he said, "that I never hired you to do anything for me." Billy backed off and went his way toward frequent rustling of Chisum cattle and Pat Garrett's final bullet and that was that.

Meanwhile again there was the legal nuisance of the packing-house claims.

On a visit back in Denton County in Texas, about the time he was starting his drives to New Mexico, John Chisum had signed a fool paper. A man named Wilber had come to him and said that he and another named Clark planned to start a packing house in Fort Smith, Arkansas, and wanted John Chisum to be associated with them. This Wilber was a persistent talker and at last John Chisum put up a proposition: if they would raise $66,666.66 and invest it in a building and all necessary equipment, he would furnish $33,333.33 in beef. He and Wilber wrote out two copies of the proposal and signed it, each taking one.

John Chisum remained in Denton several months, but heard nothing more from Wilber. He did hear, in an-

swer to inquiries, that the unknown Clark was a dead-
beat and one to leave alone. Then John Chisum was off
to Concho headquarters and busy sending and taking
herds to New Mexico. More than a year later, back in
Texas, he heard the disquieting news that a firm calling
itself Wilber, Clark & Chisum had been operating in
Fort Smith, doing things on a lavish scale, all on credit,
scattering promissory notes right and left — on the
strength of the Chisum name. One of his brothers (probably James) had got wind of it, gone to Fort Smith, exposed the swindle, and the business had been closed
down. But those promissory notes remained, floating
about.

John Chisum went to his old friend, Governor E. M.
Pease of Texas, for an opinion on the agreement he and
Wilber had signed. No, said the governor, that did not
make him a partner in the business that had been ille-
gally started and he should not be responsible for the
notes. To play safe, he should publish the facts. He did.
In Texas and Arkansas newspapers.

All the same he was sued on several of the notes while
he was still in Texas. The courts there held that he was
not a partner of the defunct firm and was not liable for
the notes. That ended the matter. In Texas.

Now, at least ten years later, some of those notes were
appearing in New Mexico. Men who relished the notion
of getting something out of John Chisum's hide had got
hold of them. Lawyers like Tom Catron, who still remembered his defeat on the Texas cattle accounts and
was one of those behind the Murphy-Dolan faction in
Lincoln County, were only too glad to have such cases to
handle — in their own controlled New Mexico courts.
They had a fine time harassing John Chisum with suits

and judgments handed down by the obedient courts. They cited the transfer of title to his New Mexico holdings to Hunter & Evans (done before any of the New Mexico suits were started) as a deliberate device to defraud New Mexican creditors. They cited the provision that title to some of the cattle would be transferred back to Pitzer Chisum as further evidence of fraudulent intent. On one occasion, when he was on his way to Texas to visit relatives, they had him stopped at Las Vegas on the claim he was running away to avoid judgment and he spent some time in jail before his lawyer had that tangle cleared and then they promptly followed it with an indictment on a charge of resisting arrest.

It would be easy to depict Uncle John Chisum, during these last years with the Lincoln County War embroiling one flank of his kingdom and rustlers preying on his herds and legal sharpshooters busy sniping, as an old lion at bay with jackals yapping all around. The picture would be all wrong. Such things were nuisances only, part of the great game of living. His grin stayed the same and with it his zest for life and his capacity for unflagging friendship. He was still the Jinglebob king of the Pecos, known and respected wherever honest cattlemen congregated and a staunch member of their organizations. Through it all Chisum men under the personal orders of the best cowmen they ever worked for were taking Chisum cattle westward into Arizona, northward into Kansas — forty thousand of them before the Hunter & Evans deal was completed.

As for those packing-house notes, John Chisum never regarded them as honest obligations. He was damned if he would pay them. He ignored the judgments. When a bunch of them were piled up and the New Mexico courts were really after him, his lawyer concocted enough injunctive objections to keep the whole business tied up in red tape for years. When such things as that silly indictment for resisting arrest were slapped on him, he simply put up bond and went his way.

Twenty-six places were still being set at the big table in the Long House and as before rarely was one unoccupied. Out in front of the house by the canal the three willows that had been planted close together and trained to twine into the one tree, the Tree of the Three Brothers, John and Pitzer and James, were as strong and flourishing as the relationship between the three men. John, unmarried as he was, had a fine family to head. He was raising quality beef, graded Jinglebob cattle that were winning a wide reputation. With the passing of the big herds, most of his men had drifted away to other ranges but twelve good ones, several of these with him from long ago in Texas, were still on the payroll. He was still watching things grow, experimenting with the newer grains.

John Chisum could look about him and feel that he had met his honest obligations. All of the Texas accounts that had ever turned up had been met. Brother Pitzer, with those chosen heifers for a start, had his own fine herd and brother James was in on that too. The faithful Frank was acquiring cattle too and would be a successful independent small rancher the rest of his life. Niece Sallie was married to a man named Roberts who was a better cowman than either Pitzer or James and would carry on John Chisum's work. And to hell with those packing-house notes.

*

1884. John Chisum was sixty years old. His grin was somewhat lopsided now. He had a tumor on his neck which had been giving him trouble the last few years. In July he attended a cattleman's meeting in Las Vegas, then went on to Kansas City for surgery. He seemed to be doing well. His grin was as hearty as of old when he received word that he had been named to represent the cattle industry of all the western territories at the Southern Industrial Exposition to be held at New Orleans the next year. He started back to New Mexico and at Las Vegas was struck with post-operation complications. The doctors advised him to go to Eureka Springs in Arkansas for the mineral baths there.

The family, all of them, had gathered at Las Vegas to be with him. He seemed to know that he would be leaving New Mexico forever. The old familiar grin showed through tears when he left.

He died at Eureka Springs during the night of December 22d.

He did not know that just a few weeks before, an omnibus suit covering those packing-house notes had been decided against him. The jackals finally got out of his estate what they could not get while he was alive. Even so, he would have grinned in the face of that too. The Jinglebob empire was still strong enough to pay them all — and have plenty left for his "family."

Thomas J. Smith

183? — NOVEMBER 2, 1870

NEVER confuse him with the Tom Smith who was mixed up in the Johnson County cattlemen's war in Wyoming and recruited the imported gunmen for that silly, nasty business — or with any of the other Tom Smiths who were born to or used the name in the wild days of the West. He was Bear River Tom Smith. A man of mystery out of an unknown past — and for a single six-month period as fully known, as fully realized, as clean-cut and distinct as a Remington drawing.

He was born in New York City sometime during the decade of 1830 — 1840. His parents were both of Irish blood and he was raised in the Catholic faith. That is all that is known about his early life. All else is pure conjecture or stray rumor unauthenticated. Even the name he used, Thomas James Smith, may not have been that by which he was baptized.

It is a fair guess that he came of a good family and was well raised. He was intelligent, soft-spoken, well-spoken, gentle in manner, neither drank nor gambled, and was never known to use a profane word. It is a fair guess that the rumor he had served for a time on the New York police force was true. He knew quite a bit about police work and was courteous and deferential to official superiors like a man trained to be. It is a fair guess too that something happened in New York to make him cut himself off from his past and everything connected with it and go west to lose or to find or to redeem himself in new country. He had a strong, a violent temper. He never referred to his early life or mentioned a living relative.

When did he go west? One rumor claimed that he was among the victims of the Mountain Meadow massacre in Utah and was left for dead when the renegade murdering Mormons departed and revived later and crawled away to survive his wounds. That would place him in the west by 1857. There were other rumors of wanderings in Utah and Nevada during the following years, of work in Iowa and Nebraska with wagon trains hauling materials for the construction of the Union Pacific Railroad. What is certain is that in 1868 he was at the temporary railhead of Bear River, Wyoming, working for a construction firm with headquarters there.

A fine figure of a man, this Tom Smith. Five feet eleven inches in height, 170 pounds in weight, erect, broad-shouldered, well-muscled, a natural athlete who kept himself in superb physical condition. Handsome in a rugged way, with a strong chin, fair complexion, auburn hair, light mustache, and gray-blue eyes which were suddenly his most impressive feature when that violent temper took him. He carried two guns in holsters at his sides.

Rough tough places, those railhead camps established

at intervals as the Union Pacific built westward toward its meeting with the Central Pacific to complete the first transcontinental line in May of the next year. Construction crews lived in tents and ramshackle shanties and freight-car flophouses, rode out to work aboard the "track trains," came back at the end of the day ripe for a riotous evening. They were racing westward against time, racing to get down more track than the Central Pacific coming eastward out of California. They worked hard during the day and expected to play hard during the night. Hundreds of saloonkeepers, gamblers, prostitutes, speculators, outlaws, outcasts, unsavory characters of every description were constantly about, eager to grab off the hard-earned dollars. When fifty or sixty miles of track had been laid on ahead, the whole shebang was dismantled, piled on flatcars, and moved up. "Hell on wheels" was the popular name for it.

Bear River was one of the camps, only more so. It was a bit more of a permanent settlement, had some regular residents and permanent log structures. When rail activity was at its height there, the "businessmen" organized what they called a town government, adopted some laws to their own liking, and appointed a marshal. Stirred by articles in the *Frontier Index*, a flimsy newspaper published in a tent that followed the work camps along the rail line, they formed a vigilante committee and began rounding up known desperadoes and locking them in a little log building converted into a jail. That was fair enough. But the vigilantes took to locking up some of the construction workers, among them a good friend of Tom Smith, whose sins were merely the customary ones of drunkenness and disorderly conduct. That was outright interference with the right of the work crews to cut loose of an evening after a hard day of laying rails. They retaliated promptly and vigorously. They invaded the "town," destroyed the newspaper "plant" on the way, ripped open the "jail," released the prisoners and tried to set fire to the building. It was built of green logs and refused to burn. Meanwhile the vigilantes had grabbed their guns, gathered together, and barricaded themselves in a log storeroom about fifty yards away.

That was the situation, construction crewmen milling about without a leader and taking cover as shots came from behind the barricade, when Tom Smith appeared on the scene. When he knew what had happened, his friend jailed and for nothing serious and the vigilantes making a gunfight out of the affair, that temper took him, roused him to fury. He ran straight toward the blazing guns of the vigilantes and at immediate close range emptied both his own into the barricaded storeroom. The battle was on.

Quite a lively little battle too. Fourteen men were killed and at least that many more wounded. Troops arrived from nearby Fort Bridger and imposed order. In a few days the "town" was abandoned and the "hell on wheels" moved on to the next location. One of those wounded had been Tom Smith. Hit again and again by shots from behind the barricade, he had stayed erect until his guns were empty, then had walked to the cabin of another friend some distance away, where he collapsed and for days was close to death. Only the superb strength in that rugged body and the iron will that was part of the essential man pulled him through. The crisis passed, he quickly recovered.

And all the way on across Wyoming and into Utah it was Bear River Tom Smith who was chosen to keep order in each new camp of the "hell on wheels." And he kept order — did it quietly and efficiently. There were no more riots. There was no more spectacular gunplay. There was no need for it. No one who had seen him at Bear River when that fury took him or even had simply heard of it wanted to cross him. He was the man who advanced straight into the muzzles of blazing guns. He was the man who, ripped by bullets, could not be knocked off his feet.

There was another reason. A reason in Tom Smith himself. He was as good with guns as any man who walked the West. He could shatter the center of a target with the best. He was unacquainted with fear in any form. Had he been of the caliber of a Wild Bill Hickok, he could have found plenty of opportunity, of excuses, to use the two guns he still wore under his coat. But something had happened to Tom Smith there at Bear River. As he lay still, recovering from his wounds, he was ashamed of the uncontrolled fury that had taken him, was thankful that, so far as he knew, none of his bullets had killed. Never again would that fury be uncontrolled. Lying there, still and thoughtful, he had found the finer courage of the man who does not need to kill.

1870! Abilene, first of the rail-end cow towns, known from coast to coast, trail's end for Texas cowboys, bonanza for barmen and gamblers and thieves and prostitutes who fleeced them, lit the Kansas prairie all night long, wild and woolly and wicked.

Every hotel had its bar, usually occupying more space than the lobby and desk. There were thirty-two licensed saloons — and many another place where a man could get all the liquor he wanted, day or night. Seven were of the full-blown variety. The Alamo, naturally with a name like that, was the ritziest: wide front embracing three huge glass double-doors never closed, a vast brass-fixtured bar, flashing mirrors behind it, big paintings of well-fleshed nudes on the walls, gaming tables in every available spot, an orchestra that played almost around the clock.

Temporarily more famous was the Bull's Head, made so by a dispute that had rocked the town last season. Its owners had had painted a big red bull across the front of the building. The artist, an uncompromising realist, had included all anatomical details. The Texans thought this an appropriate symbolic sign. Many local citizens thought it too realistic, an insult to virtuous women. Their position was hardly logical since bulls in the flesh on the hoof were a common sight in and about town. Their complaints finally produced a formal order that the owners turn their bull into a steer, add a bush to hide the controversial details, or paint it out altogether. The Texans rallied to the bull's defense. At last, to forestall possible pitched battle, the owners had the picture painted over.

That was the perfect solution. Everyone was satisfied. The order had been obeyed. Virtue had been protected. And the outlines of the bull were still quite visible through the new paint.

Each full-blown saloon was of course also a dance hall. All of them tried to outdo each other in luring the freshly paid trailmen in through their open doors. It made no difference that not much luring was needed; they were intent on outdoing each other anyway. And when the herds were streaming onto the grazing grounds waiting shipment, there were more than enough trailmen, cash in pockets, anticipation in minds, to crowd all bars and dance floors.

Almost everyone more or less permanent in town was after those trail dollars. There were the railroad men and the commission buyers and the respectable merchants operating clothing and outfitting stores. There were hotel and restaurant and boardinghouse people. There were the gamblers, honest and dishonest in all shadings, dealing faro and monte mostly but adept at any game. There were thieves and pickpockets and all manner of assorted con men from the big cities to the north and east who came for easy pickings and found them not always easy. There were gunmen and outlaws of varying reputations constantly drifting through, unworried about the law in such a wide open lawless town. And there were, in the judicious phrase of the time, the "women of ill repute."

The first red-light district, known as Fisher's addition, was right in "Texas Town," the main cattle and saloon area just south of the tracks. That was too close for the comfort of respectable folk. At any time they might be forced to see, brazenly in sight, in the words of one of them, "the soiled dove . . . bedizened in her gaudy dress, cheap jewelry, and highly colored cosmetics." A petition from the women of good repute led to a shifting of the district to the outskirts of town. The result was the Devil's Half Acre. "Hacks were run day and night to this addition. Money and whisky flowed like water down a hill" (this is a local lumber dealer of the time speaking) "and youth and beauty and womanhood and manhood were wrecked and damned in that valley of perdition."

John Wesley Hardin, an expert in such matters, with a good share of his final forty notches already on his gun, dodging sheriffs by taking a herd up through the lonely spaces as trail boss for some relatives, looked Abilene over — and added somewhat to the general explosive excitement before he moved on. "I have seen many fast towns," he remarked later, "but Abilene beat them all."

Now in 1870 the town itself, the sober settling portion, was not happy with this state of affairs. With the money flowing in from the cattle trade, yes. Oh very much yes. But not with the wildness and the woolliness and the wickedness that went with it. The town had been legally incorporated in the preceding year and a council of trustees elected with T. C. Henry the first mayor. These town fathers felt that Abilene lit the prairie too brightly, had too many sudden funerals, smelled gunpowder too often and too pungently. Prospective settlers were being frightened away from the area. Travelers were refusing to pass through, even by train. With the start of the shipping season this year, certain to be the biggest and boomingest yet, the trustees adopted a batch of restrictive ordinances, in particular one banning the carrying of firearms within the town limits, and looked about for a marshal to enforce them.

One of the first applicants, brought down from Colorado by a reputable Abilene citizen who vouched for him, was a big quiet man named Tom Smith. Mayor Henry, who had heard tales of happenings in Wyoming, was surprised at sight of him. The personal appearance and gentle courtesy of the man belied his fearsome reputation. Mayor Henry consulted with the other trustees and they hemmed and hawed for a time. After all the publicity about the inauguration of good government in Abilene, should law enforcement be entrusted to so notorious a man? No. They made excuses. Tom Smith smiled a bit grimly, understanding their reasoning, and quietly left town to return to Colorado.

The trustees decided to use home talent. There were local citizens eager at first for the job. One after another was appointed — and quickly resigned. The Texas trailmen regarded them as fair game and ragged and bullied them with Texan exuberance.

The firearms ordinance was publicly posted. The Texans used it as a target and obliterated it. The trustees started to build a jail. The Texans tore it down. It was rebuilt, under guard, and the first prisoner was a cook from one of the cow camps, jugged for shooting out street lamps. The Texans used the padlock for another target and let him out — then rode about town enforcing their own ordinance, that all businesses not needed for their own immediate merriment should close down for the day. Businessmen who objected had their premises well trampled by mounted cowboys who rode right in through the doors.

Mayor Henry was on a hot spot. He was the head of the supposed town government. That made him the major object of ridicule. He could not walk along the street without being subjected to abuse. Anonymous threatening letters were being sent him. The blinds of his office were in ribbons from frequent shots by Texans galloping past. He knew too that the turbulence in Abilene was not all merely the ebullience of trailhands out for sprees and the meanness of those who sought to prey on them. In the background was the inevitable antagonism between the settlers, the farmers, coming into the area and the free-ranging cowmen. And there was an ugly undercurrent of feeling in town, legacy of the re-

cent Civil War, that could easily get out of hand. Most of
the regular townspeople were northerners. Most of the
trailmen were from the south.

Mayor Henry tried more marshals. They resigned
faster than he could find replacements. He telegraphed
an appeal to the chief of police of St. Louis for two good
men. They arrived one day — and took the return train
out of town that night. The Texans had enjoyed working on them.

By now Mayor Henry and the other trustees, as he recalled later, had reverted to "primal instincts." They
were no longer interested in "turning the other cheek."
They "craved a couple of eyes for one eye; several teeth
for one tooth."

Mayor Henry remembered a big quiet man and a jaw
that looked like it was made of rock and the glint in a
pair of gray-blue eyes. He went over to the telegraph
office.

A Saturday morning late in May, 1870. A big quiet
man on a big gray horse rode into Abilene and stopped
at the mayor's office and went inside.

Mayor Henry could not help it, was surprised again.
Such a gentle, self-contained, noncommittal, respectful
man. Mayor Henry began to tell his troubles and as he
talked he began to be worried. This was Bear River
Tom Smith who was said never to back away from anything. To send him out against the Texans could be to
send him to his death. He was so serene and leisurely in
the few things he did say that he seemed unaware of
what he would be up against. It was only fair to try to
make him understand. Mayor Henry suggested that be-

fore he decided whether to take the job he ought to look the town over and see for himself.

Bear River Tom Smith smiled a bit, said he did not think that was necessary, but if Mr. Henry thought he should do it, he would. He left the office, swung up on the big gray he called Silverheels, and rode away.

He returned just before sundown and stood outside by the office door. Mayor Henry came to the open doorway, bareheaded. Tom Smith respectfully removed his own hat. What did he think of the proposition now? The same as before; he had not seen anything in town much different from what he had expected. Mayor Henry was still worried. He was even more worried when questioning revealed that the man had occupied most of his time during the afternoon looking over the stockyards and the new bridge over Mud Creek. How about Texas Town? Just about what he had expected.

If he took the job, what would he do? Well, it was basically a simple matter. The combination of liquor and guns caused most of the trouble. Liquor could not be eliminated without discouraging, sending elsewhere, the very cattle business that made Abilene prosperous. The sensible thing was to eliminate the guns. Enforce the firearms ordinance.

But how? Bear River Tom Smith simply shrugged his broad shoulders and said he thought it could be done.

Mayor Henry, only twenty-nine years old at the time with responsibility heavy on him, was baffled. He wished he knew more about this man, so cool and calm and respectful, so apparently unaware of what the job might mean — wished he could get the man to tell something of the past behind the Bear River business. But that was a closed book the man would not open.

Mayor Henry made his decision. He reached back into the office for the Bible kept there and a silver badge with it. Tom Smith laid his hat on the ground, put his left hand on the book, raised his right hand, and repeated the oath of office. He picked up his hat and put it on. He pinned the badge to his shirt. He said he would see the printer at the newspaper office about getting some copies of the firearms ordinance and post them the next day. He said it would probably take a few days before they knew just how things would be. Meanwhile he would look over a few of the tough spots. He turned and walked away, leading the horse, toward Texas Street about a third of a mile away, the mainline of Texas Town.

Mayor Henry watched him go. Mayor Henry thought it would be a miracle if forty-eight hours later the man should still be alive.

There was no need to wait forty-eight hours to find out what would happen. In less than twenty-four hours Bear River Tom Smith had taken over Abilene.

The first act occurred almost immediately. He had been seen going into the mayor's office in the morning, strolling about town in the afternoon, calling on the mayor again in late afternoon. The badge on his shirt was sufficient declaration of the new development. He had not gone far along Texas Street before he was confronted by a burly brute, name recorded as Big Hank, a onetime cowboy now taking life easier as a town toughie, who had made himself a reputation bullying previous marshals. No one, Big Hank had often boasted, would take his gun away from him.

A Saturday evening. Big Hank was in fine liquored

fettle. As usual he had a gallery of admirers. Here was a brand-new marshal ripe for ragging. Big Hank marched out into Texas Street and blocked the way.

Was this the man who proposed to run the town? Why, yes, it was; he had accepted employment as marshal and he intended to maintain order and enforce the laws. What did this ambitious new marshal propose to do about the firearms ordinance? He intended to enforce that one too.

He tried to do that decently by asking Big Hank, quietly but firmly, to turn over his gun. The response was a burst of Big Hank's best profanity. He asked again, as quietly but even more firmly. The result was an even better burst of profanity and personal abuse.

Like the striking of a match, that fury took Tom Smith. Not lethal and uncontrolled but concentrated and directed by the clear clean intelligence behind it. He leaped in close and laid Big Hank flat in the dust with one terrific punch. He bent down and ripped Big Hank's gun from its holster and told Big Hank to get out of town for good. Big Hank staggered to his feet and looked into a pair of gray-blue eyes that shook him as no blow could. Big Hank got. For good.

The gallery gaped. The suddenness, the completeness, the effectiveness of the action shook them all. They drifted away, scattering, to spread the word. Tom Smith continued on his way toward the newspaper office to see about the printing of copies of the firearms ordinance.

The second act occurred the next morning. All Abilene knew what had happened. Every cowboy at the camps for miles around knew too. They had spent most of the night discussing it. At one of the camps another burly brute, this one known as Wyoming Frank, had taken to bragging, wound up with a bet he would take care of the new marshal. He was in town bright and early, gun conspicuous at his side. It was Sunday morning and the new marshal was nowhere in sight. Sunday meant little in Abilene and the saloons were open. Wyoming Frank indulged in drinks and more bragging. About the time he was boasting that the new marshal must be dodging him or had run away, Tom Smith came into view, walking quietly down the middle of Texas Town's Texas Street.

Wyoming Frank stepped out and started his play, aiming to force a quarrel, to turn it into gunplay. Tom Smith stepped in close, almost chest to chest, too close for Wyoming Frank to go for his gun without instant interference. Wyoming Frank backed away and Tom Smith pressed close after him. Wyoming Frank backed along the street and into a saloon, already feeling a sense of retreat, of being pushed into a corner. Tom Smith asked for the gun. He asked twice. That was his way. To ask twice, quietly, decently. The result, as the evening before, was a display of profanity. Plus further quick backing to get space for gunplay.

Again that fury took Tom Smith. As Wyoming Frank sought to bring his gun up, Tom Smith leaped and with two terrific punches laid him limp on the floor. In the same flash of movement he bent down and ripped the gun from Wyoming Frank's hand and beat him bitterly about the body with the barrel. He stood over the thoroughly cowed man and told him to get out of town and stay out. This time he set a time limit. Within five minutes.

Wyoming Frank faded. Well within the five minutes.

A startled, baffled silence held the men in the saloon.

Respect and admiration for a man staking everything on his own lone gamble and for a pair of gray-blue eyes glinting the unmistakable message that he would stand up to them all struggled against ingrained antagonism for authority in general and town officers in particular.

The proprietor of the saloon stepped forward, his gun in his hand — held by the barrel with the handle extended toward Tom Smith. He figured he would not be needing it any more, not as long as this new marshal was around. Suddenly the others realized they figured the same. They crowded forward, proffering pistols, buzzing with admiring remarks.

Then the touch of genius. Just check your guns with the bartender, said Tom Smith, and pick them up when you are ready to leave town.

That simple rule did more to tame Abilene than any ordinance devised by the town trustees.

No distasteful submission to authority in the form of having to hand over a gun to a man wearing a badge. No nuisance of a side jaunt to some official place for this. Simply a cooperative process in the simplest manner. When coming into town check your hardware at the first stop, hotel or store or bar, and when leaving pick it up again.

You mean if we give 'em up, we get 'em back again?
Certainly. They're yours; they belong to you.

During the next days Tom Smith visited most of the establishments in town, explaining his simple rule to the proprietors. It would be good business. The trailmen would patronize the places where they checked their guns — and come back a second time to pick them up. Right. Before long barmen, storekeepers, hotel clerks

were becoming expert at persuading gun-toting strangers
to part temporarily with their weapons. Once in a while
they failed — and like as not, after a while, after hearing
talk about town, the man would be back.

Guess I'll leave this here after all.

*Thought so. You're lucky you didn't bump into our
new marshal.*

Already he was receiving cheery salutes from passing
cowboys who patted gunbeltless waists and grinned at
him. Somehow most of them felt no shame at being made
to behave by a man like that, a whole man, a bear cat in
action and so damned decent too. They were even somewhat proud of it, proud it took a man like that to ride
herd on them. They would put pressure themselves on
the more belligerent of their kind to shed metal weight
while in town.

This marshal played fair, right down the line. Remember the ruckus the evening he went over to the Devil's
Half Acre and made the women shuck all their hardware
too? Collected a wheelbarrow nearly full of small pistols
and derringers.

And he was no persnickety pious man passing judgment on human frailties, interfering with any other
man's right to go to hell in his own way. Abilene was as
woolly and wicked as ever — it had to be to hold the
cattle trade. It was merely not so wild. It lit the prairie
with a steadier more welcoming glow. It smelled gunpowder rarely and the funeral business fell away. Inevitably
there were quarrels and brawls and crimes of one kind
and another. But the instant decisions and efficient actions of this new marshal took care of such things
promptly and with a minimum of fuss and feathers.

This season Abilene was a place where a trailhand could ride in and find the sky the limit and spend his hard-earned dollars with a whoop and a holler and in as wicked ways as his heart desired — as long as he did not try to mix whisky and weapons. That meant a certain collision with Bear River Tom Smith.

Mayor Henry and the other trustees were delighted with their good luck. The first week in June they held a meeting to give formal approval to the appointment and fix his salary at $150 a month, excellent pay for the period, plus a $2 fee for each arrest. Early in August, on their own, out of sheer gratitude, they insisted on making it $225 a month, a record for the time. A group of townspeople got together and presented him with a pair of pearl-handled revolvers. A somewhat ironic gift. His guns were the least conspicuous feature of Tom Smith. Not once while marshal of Abilene, except in target practice which had its own salutary effect on would-be troublemakers, did he fire a gun. In later years oldtimers had difficulty remembering whether he ever carried one.

I guess you're right. Yes, he wore two. But we hardly ever noticed them.

What they did remember, distinctly, was a jaw and a pair of gray-blue eyes and a cool courtesy — and two fists that could move with the speed of snakes striking and the power of hard-swung sledgehammers.

Through the summer and into the fall Tom Smith patrolled Abilene. Townspeople looked out and saw him pass and felt better about their town. He checked in regularly at the mayor's office, hat removed, respectful, and made report and went out and swung into saddle. He

had an assistant named Robbins to handle routine matters and paperwork. His place was in saddle, on patrol.
He ambled easily along, down the middle of the streets,
vantage line for close watch on both sides and into the
alleyways. No loitering in saloons, bending an elbow. No
sessions at the gambling tables. No hobnobbing with particular cronies. Cool and courteous to everyone alike,
making no distinctions. A lone man, hammered into
what he was by a mysterious past and his own stern will,
doing steadily and efficiently a job he had applied for and
had accepted.

Nothing was ever static in Abilene. New trailherds
kept coming, new trailhands kept riding into town. Some
would not accept the new regime willingly. Every now
and then townspeople would look out a window or doorway and see Tom Smith walking past, leading his horse,
with a limp cowboy or would-be outlaw gunman over
one shoulder, bound for the rebuilt jail. A cooling-off or
sobering-up period and the man could go forth for gun-
less fun.

*Name the place where you want your gun checked;
you can pick it up when you leave town.*

He could knock out a man almost as easily from horseback as from a standing position on the ground. Sometimes, not often, on a man judged to be really tough, he
used a gun barrel. Usually just those fists. He would
come up alongside a gun-toting galoot and ask for the
weapon. Twice. Then a lightning sweep down and the
man would be sprawling in the dust. Once a man,
smacked full in the forehead, turned a complete back
somersault. Another had his tongue cut half in two when
his teeth snapped together from an uppercut. That one
was a walking testimonial for days as he went about with

his face bandaged. Another had two ribs broken by a single side swipe.

Word spread down the trail from cow camp to cow camp. Not much sense spending your trail's-end spree recovering from such sudden ailments.

Nothing static in Abilene. Not just trailmen coming in. Hardcases of every kind drifting through. Shots were fired at Tom Smith, usually from ambush, not once but many times — and to no effect. The fact was, of course, that he was not hit. But this, coupled with his evident lack of any fear of being hit, created a legend of invincibility. Some men swore that he had a steel plate under his shirt. Others preferred to believe that he simply could not be hit — or, if hit, could not be stopped.

There was the night of his raid on the Old Fruit saloon, one of the worst joints in town. A Texan for whom he had a warrant had slipped in there and was taking on a cargo of liquor in company with other men applauding his defiance of the law. Suddenly they were aware that Tom Smith, alone, a gun in hand, had entered by the front door and was moving to cut off any retreat through the only other exit, a side door. The man he wanted backed away to the rear of the long narrow room. Tom Smith advanced toward him. The others, wavering, uncertain, partly awed by his very approach, parted to each side as he advanced. They began to close in behind him.

One of them snatched one of the three lamps in the place from its bracket and threw it at him. It fell to the floor and flickered there, dripping oil. In a moment the flimsy room could be in flames — as had happened, tragically, at several other places in Abilene. Tom Smith strode right on, had his man, disarmed him, heaved him up on a shoulder with a hand tight on his windpipe.

Then the general melee cut loose. The other two lamps were blown out. Guns were grabbed from behind the bar and shots fired. Men milled about in the dimness. Through it all strode Tom Smith, battering his way to the front door and out and away with his man to the rebuilt jail.

The Old Fruit emptied fast. Nothing fazed that marshal. He might be back to find out about those shots.

Several of the men who had fired them insisted they had hit him. The legend was clinched. The hardcases began to avoid Abilene.

The first and worst of the wide open cowtowns in its biggest season. One man tamed it without once firing a gun at another man.

It was well into the fall now. The shipping season was over. The town was quiet without the Texans and their exuberance. No more herds would be coming up the trails until next spring.

Tom Smith was no longer marshal of Abilene. He had accepted a bigger job with a wider territory. He wore the badge of a deputy United States marshal. But Abilene slept better at night knowing that he was still there, was living there.

Some distance out of town some cattle belonging to a man named John Shea damaged a cornfield on a home-

stead claim worked jointly by an Andrew McConnell
and a Moses Miles. In the following argument Shea tried
to shoot McConnell but his gun failed to fire. McConnell's gun did not fail. McConnell turned himself in and
after an investigation was released — a clear case of self-
defense. But friends of the late Shea insisted on a trial
and wangled a murder warrant. The county sheriff went
out to serve the warrant and returned, saying that Mc-
Connell had fortified his dugout, a sod-roofed room dug
into a hillside with a narrow trench leading in to the
doorway, and had refused arrest. The sheriff was not
interested in another trip — unless Tom Smith would go
with him.

This was not Tom Smith's responsibility. It was a local, a county matter. But Bear River Tom Smith never
backed away from anything, least of all a request for help
on any official duty. He took the warrant and swung up on
Silverheels and rode out and the sheriff went with him.
That was a mistake, letting that man side him. Even
across the decades since, the stench of that sheriff's
cowardice is strong.

When the two of them approached the homestead and
dismounted, McConnell and Miles were standing outside
the dugout. McConnell retreated into the dim interior.
Miles stayed outside.

Tom Smith strode straight in. If there were any trouble outside, the sheriff should take care of that.

There was trouble outside. Another man had seen the
two officers pass his place and had trailed along. Hidden
in bushes nearby, he saw it happen. He too was not
much of a man.

Miles had an old carbine. He turned it on the sheriff

and pulled the trigger. The hammer snapped futilely. Again and again in mounting anger and exasperation Miles tried to make the old gun fire. The sheriff, forgetting his own gun, forgetting everything but his fear, backed away. Then two shots sounded inside the dugout — and the sheriff turned and fled. He did not even try to mount his horse, simply ran across the fields in headlong flight.

Inside the dim dugout Tom Smith was doing the job. He told McConnell he had a warrant for his arrest. McConnell had already snatched up a rifle and he fired and the bullet ripped into Tom Smith's body. The legend held — no bullet could stop that man. He replied once, the one shot he fired at another man in the Abilene area. It hit what he intended it to hit — the gun in McConnell's hands and one of the hands holding it — forestalling another shot. Then Tom Smith plunged forward and grappled with McConnell and dragged him to the doorway. As he backed out, holding his man, into the narrow trench that led to the doorway, Miles swung the old carbine like a club and brought it smashing down on his head. He fell, unconscious. Miles and McConnell quickly dragged him further into the open and one of them picked up an ax.

When the body was found a few hours later, the head was severed except for the skin at the back of the neck.

All Abilene, hushed and quiet, marched in the long procession to the cemetery, led by a big gray horse saddled and riderless with two pearl-handled revolvers in their holsters hanging from the saddlehorn. All businesses were closed for the day, even the saloons. All Abilene knew that something fine and decent had been among them and was gone.

"Any officer can bring in a dead man," Tom Smith had said. He died living up to that hard-won creed.

Valentine T. O. McGillycuddy

FEBRUARY 14, 1849 — JUNE 6, 1939

His parents gave him a mouthful of name and a long lean body full of energy.

They were Irish both, the father a McGillycuddy of a family which had turned Protestant generations back to save its property at a time when Catholic lands in Ireland were declared forfeit, the mother a Trant, of a family which had held to the Catholic faith. They met on the boat bringing them as immigrants to America and were married when they reached port. Catholic Trant carried a letter of introduction from a family friend named O'Connell to the Archbishop of New York which she never presented because she had just married a Protestant McGillycuddy. But she kept it as a prized possession.

They traveled inland and settled in Detroit and there, on February 14th, 1849, St. Valentine's Day, their son was born. All the names were gathered into his name: Valentine Trant O'Connell McGillycuddy.

A mouthful of name. A name that for a seven-year pe-

riod would be remarkably well known and remarkably
vilified and remarkably defended in the terse form in
which, during that period, he invariably signed it to letters and documents and proclamations: *McGillycuddy
— Agent.*

Indian agent. Autocrat of the **Pine Ridge Sioux** reservation. A rare and remarkable phenomenon in nineteenth century United States — an able and honest man
in the government Indian service.

He started out to be a doctor. At seventeen he was in
his first year as a medical student at the school connected
with the Marine Hospital in Detroit. The staff physician
at the hospital was a confirmed drunkard. Dr. T. A. Mc-
Graw, head of the school, recommended young McGillycuddy as a substitute for him, to make his regular rounds
for him. Young McGillycuddy accepted the assignment.
In some respects it was better training than the formal
studies. Sailors of the Great Lakes in all stages of disease
and corruption were his patients. At any hour of the
night he might be called out to handle emergencies at
the brothels along the waterfront. He learned much and
fast about the darker aspects of existence and man's capacity for inhumanity to man. He carried that load for six
months before other arrangements were made at the hospital and he could again give full time to his studies.

While still in his twentieth year, already the slim spare
figure he would be for the next seventy years, one
hundred thirty-five pounds of him spread over six feet of
bony frame, he graduated from the school and promptly
joined the faculty. Lectures on splints and bandages were
his specialty. Administering anesthetics for operations
was a regular chore. Work with the Detroit police-ambu-

lance corps was a busy sideline. There were still a few
spare hours out of the daily twenty-four. He added service as physician at the county insane asylum.

Young McGillycuddy was not aware of it, but that
energy burning in him, coupled with an ingrained urge
to take hold and do anything and everything that needed
to be done, was driving him toward serious trouble. Already he was nipping often at a whisky bottle. Dr. Mc-
Graw, who kept a watchful eye on his favorite pupil, became worried. He ordered a thorough examination. Just
in time. Young McGillycuddy was straining, weakening,
his heart. A year of life in the open was prescribed for
him. His place at the hospital would always be waiting
for him.

Young McGillycuddy had studied a bit of engineering
along the way. He went to the office of the geodetic survey
of the Northern and Northwestern Lakes. In a few days
he was on his way to join the expedition surveying Lake
Michigan as assistant engineer and recorder.

Week after week in an open boat on the open water in
all kinds of weather in charge of a sounding crew and
young McGillycuddy became sun-and-wind-tanned and
his body hardened and his heart beat strong and steady
and he knew he was meant for life in the open spaces. To
Dr. McGraw's surprise and regret, when the year was
over, he stayed with the geodetic survey, as surgeon as
well as assistant engineer. When Chicago was devastated
by the great fire of 1871, it was young McGillycuddy
who was picked to take a crew there and resurvey the
entire Chicago district. A competent man, this energetic
beanpole of a young Irishman. He could boss a crew of
men twice his age — and make them like it.

Word spread among men in the field, spread all the

way to the headquarters of the United States Engineering Corps in Washington. In 1873, in his twenty-fourth year, Valentine Trant O'Connell McGillycuddy was offered and quickly accepted the position of topographer and surgeon with the International Survey of the boundary line between the United States and British America. He packed a few things, extracted a promise to write to him from the blond blue-eyed Fanny Hoyt he had been escorting to the theater whenever he was home in Detroit, and rode the new transcontinental rails westward into the heartland of the North American continent.

This was the life for a man meant for the open spaces, tracing the Forty-ninth Parallel across the trackless northern plains toward the far Pacific. A two-mile strip twenty miles long was a good day's survey, followed by sound dreamless sleep on the ground inside or better yet outside a little tent under the vast clean sweep of sky. Buffalo meat broiled over an open fire fueled the energy in that lean hard-toned body. For weeks at a time he and crew, an orderly and a sergeant and ten Army privates, would be separated from the main body of the survey, running their lines with the care and precision that marked topographer McGillycuddy's work. At times they might have to wait a day, two days, while buffalo into the tens of thousands passed by and the earth trembled with their passing and instruments jangled and were inaccurate. At times a dust cloud might approach and become Indians on horseback following the buffalo, as happened early one morning, and young McGillycuddy made the acquaintance of Sitting Bull himself and shook the hand of the famous medicine man of the Hunkpapa Sioux and gave him a present of tobacco.

Westward went the survey across the Great Plains, establishing the upper line of what is now North Dakota and eastern Montana, then on into the wild rugged country where the smaller ranges climbed toward the main bulk of the Rocky Mountains. On it went, westward ever westward, across rushing streams and through steep canyons, until at last the monument was found that marked the eastern end of the boundary set by the Northwestern Expedition of 1858. Field work finished, the survey party backtracked to Fort Benton on the upper Missouri, traveled by boat downriver to Bismarck in Dakota for proper celebrating, then entrained for the east coast and Washington, D.C. and the long tedious job of translating field notes into boundary maps.

On the same train eastward rode another man returning from another expedition, General George Armstrong Custer on his way to report on his foray into the Black Hills. History was in the making.

With the treaty that ended Red Cloud's War of 1868, the Black Hills were part of the territory set aside to be inalienably Indian forever. That is to say, to remain Indian until white men should want it in sufficient numbers to make the breaking of another treaty a profitable undertaking. Now the United States was deep in a depression brought on by the so-called Panic of 1873. New sources of gold would be a boost to the economy. There had long been rumors of gold in the Black Hills. General Custer and his 7th Cavalry, in deliberate violation of the treaty, had been sent into the hills to look at the possi-

bilities. The most important finding he was taking to
Washington was that, yes, there was gold in those hills.

But how much gold? Would it be worthwhile stirring
again the Indians, the Teton and the Oglala and the
Hunkpapa Sioux and their Cheyenne allies, who had
fought so well and won an at least partial victory in Red
Cloud's War? Another expedition was planned under
the pretext that it would be solely scientific and geographical in purpose and thus not exactly a violation of
the treaty. Curiously enough, however, it was to be
headed by two experts from the Columbia School of
Mines — and along with it would go experienced prospectors with sharp noses for pay dirt.

Young McGillycuddy, now twenty-six years old, hard
at work on his maps in Washington, was discovering that
a surveying career had its handicaps. Field work was
fine. Endless poring over figures and papers in a stuffy
office in an eastern city was not. He was losing his hard-
won tan and his beanpole body was softening. Then one
day he was summoned to the main office of the boundary
survey and invited to shake hands with a Major J. W.
Powell — *the* Major Powell who had earned fame by exploring the depths of the Grand Canyon of the Colorado.
Major Powell had been named geologist for the new
Black Hills expedition. He had been inquiring if the
young man named McGillycuddy about whom he had
heard would care to come along as topographer.

Would he? His heart was thumping as it never had
under the stimulus of a mere stiff drink. But there was
the little matter of maps he was supposed to finish.
He could forget that. Major Powell had already
taken the liberty of arranging for a substitute for that
particular chore. Could he be at Fort Laramie,

Wyoming Territory, in three weeks ready to go? He most certainly could!

This was the life again, moving westward through the open spaces toward the Black Hills. What if the cavalrymen of the military escort thought at first he was only a city-bred greenhorn and gave him the worst horse available at the post, a big black brute that took the bit in its teeth and bolted for the horizon? They knew better when they heard him curse the brute like a trooper and an Irish one at that and saw him ride it and keep on riding it all the long way, day after day. He was out in the open spaces again, camping and hunting and working with men like Major Powell and Colonel R. I. Dodge of frontier fame and California Joe, scout and guide who was a legend in himself. He was becoming a good friend of a sixteen-year-old girl called Calamity Jane who had tried to join the expedition officially and failed but came along anyway in a soldier's uniform and was ordered to head back to the fort every night and obediently disappeared — and was marching again with the column every morning.

They reached the hills and established camp headquarters on French Creek. While the scientists explored and measured and drove their stakes and made their innumerable notes, the prospectors discovered that, yes, there was gold in these hills — and probably in considerable quantity. Strange that such news was rushed out by courier as if it were much more important than any scientific data. Young McGillycuddy did his work, surveying routes into and about the Hills, and met a few more Indians though most of these seemed to be avoiding the expedition and on one side jaunt he became the first

white man to stand atop Harney's Peak, the highest
point in the whole region.

Meanwhile war clouds were gathering in the distance,
result of the previous Custer expedition and this one.
Some of the chiefs, Red Cloud among them, were summoned to Washington for a council — and returned
after rejecting the terms offered for cession of the Hills.
Another big council was called at Chadron Creek in Nebraska — and was hastily abandoned when open fighting
was narrowly averted. The expedition heard of these developments when mail reached it, but encountered no
Indian troubles of its own. The older chiefs were still
counseling patience, peace, watchful waiting. Perhaps
nothing further would come of these expeditions. Did
not the treaty still stand, protecting their lands?

Young McGillycuddy thought little about such things,
about the ethics and the probable consequences of what
he and the others were doing, about the inevitable fact
that his surveying was part of the preparations for a
white onrush into the sacred Hills of the Sioux. He was
too busy enjoying the outdoor life — and planning an
important personal project.

Then the expedition was back at Fort Laramie and
young McGillycuddy with his voluminous notes to be
translated into maps was en route to Washington again.
On the way he stopped off in Detroit for that personal
project — to acquire a very important piece of personal
property, a wife in the person of blond blue-eyed Fanny
Hoyt.

Once again Valentine Trant O'Connell McGillycuddy, twenty-six years old now, sporting a mustache

and a trim pointed beard, was acquiring calluses on his rump from perching on a high stool before a drawing board in a stuffy office in an eastern city. It was not so bad this time because Fanny was in Washington with him and she so obviously enjoyed the social life of the city. But much was happening far westward in the open spaces he knew so well. As usual the reports of gold in the Hills had been exaggerated by the newspapers and by hearsay out of all proportion to fact. White men were pouring into the area, eager for gold. The Indians were striking back. As usual this provided the excuse for punitive military expeditions designed to whip the Indians into submission and force them to accept a new treaty ceding the white demands. General George Crook was in the field with a large force in the vicinity of the Little Big Horn Mountains, stronghold of the Sioux. General Alfred Terry was on the march too. And General Custer with his 7th Cavalry.

McGillycuddy maps were being used in the field. McGillycuddy himself was sitting on a stool nearly two thousand miles away merely making more maps.

And one day a telegram arrived at the survey headquarters in Washington and was brought to his office and handed to him. From General Crook. *Can McGillycuddy's service be secured for the field? If so send him at once.*

He left by the evening train. Not as a civilian engineer now, but as a soldier-surgeon under contract to the War Department. He had made no mistake when he married his Fanny. Told of the telegram, she simply asked when — and started packing his bags. She would return to Detroit and wait there while he was gone. And hope that no harm would come to "the Doctor." Whatever else he would be called in the years ahead, to her he was always "the Doctor."

The telegram said "at once." He dropped off the train at Cheyenne and made the acquaintance of two Bills — Wild Bill Hickok and Buffalo Bill Cody. They advised him against pushing right on through dangerous country, to wait until General Merritt's command, then forming, would set out for the battle areas with Cody as scout. No. The telegram said "at once." He found a mail carrier leaving on the two-hundred-mile jump to Fort Fetterman and covered that stretch with him. At Fort Fetterman he found a wagon train ready to carry supplies to Crook's command and he rode with it the nearly two hundred miles more to the valley of the Rosebud where Crook was encamped. He was heartily welcomed and assigned as surgeon with the 2nd Cavalry.

The valley of the Rosebud!

He was in the midst of it now, in the midst of history in the making, of the hard fighting and the overall Indian problem brought on by the relentless white advance in which all unthinking he himself had been taking part. There in the valley of the Rosebud he learned what it was to tend the wounded and the dying while fierce battle swirled around him. He was there, in the midst of it, when the Sioux under Crazy Horse struck the command and outmaneuvered it and outfought it and administered definite defeat.

This was the outdoor life with a difference — not just of deadly danger added, but of the whole tangled problem of the clash of two races, of two ways of life, brought sharply into the foreground of thought for a thinking man. He was seeing Indians, both friendly and hostile, in a new light, not just as interesting objects moving about as part of the general background of the outdoor life he loved, but as human beings meeting the slings and arrows of outrageous fortune in their own ways. He came to know well some of the Crows and the Shoshones serving as scouts with Crook, among them old Chief Wash-a-kie himself. He saw Sioux and Cheyennes fight with skill and courage that wrung unwilling admiration even from 'the white troops opposing them. He heard firsthand from Colonel Reno (a friend since the International Boundary days) the bloody details of the fate of Custer and his men on the Little Big Horn only a few days after the disaster occurred. He was in charge of the wounded train on Crook's long "starvation march" to Deadwood in Dakota and was under fire often again on the way. It was during one of these skirmishes that two squaws daringly brought to him from the enemy lines a wounded Sioux, gutshot with his intestines spilling out. As McGillycuddy bent down to do what he could, to give a hypodermic to ease the pain, soldiers cursed him for doing anything for a goddamned Indian. McGilly-cuddy rose to his beanpole height and cursed them even more vehemently. Here was a *man* suffering and dying. Did the color of his skin make a difference? This was no longer quite the same McGillycuddy who had jumped so eagerly at chances to enjoy the outdoor life — and to survey in advance for the white onrush into Indian lands.

Given the time and the place and the character of the new civilization spreading westward, that white onrush was inevitable. The Indians were obstacles, in the way,

when aroused a danger. But were warfare and direct sub-
jugation leading to eventual extermination the only answer? Was the only good Indian a dead one?

When the fighting was over and the Indians, as always
in time and despite their temporary victories, were
driven and harried and starved into submission, Crook's
command and McGillycuddy with it were stationed at
Fort Robinson in western Nebraska while the various
units were being distributed among the western posts.
Here too were gathered most of the Sioux who had surrendered, roughly grouped into two big bands under
Red Cloud and Spotted Tail. McGillycuddy took a brief
leave of absence to go east and get his Fanny. On his return with her he was assigned as assistant surgeon at the
fort. His experience at the Marine Hospital in Detroit
was a help now as he answered calls to handle all manner
of emergencies among the soldiers and the Indians clus-
tered about the fort. Particularly among the Indians. The
fort surgeon was only too willing to leave that kind of
work to the assistant.

When Crazy Horse himself reluctantly came in because his wife was ill with tuberculosis, it was McGillycuddy who took care of her and became the one white
friend of the strange and mystic young war chief of the
Oglalas and heard from his lips too the story of the Little
Big Horn. When white officials, worried over Crazy
Horse's influence among the Sioux, sent orders and he
was tricked into arrest and a mortal wound, it was Mc-
Gillycuddy who jumped into the affair and saved him
the dishonor of being dumped despite his wound into
the guardhouse and stayed with him all the last hours,
easing him into death. And out across the plains and
through the hills wherever the Sioux crouched by camp-

fires went the word: this man, this McGillycuddy, had been a true friend to the finest warrior of them all.

Sitting Bull's band had not surrendered, had fled northward into Canada. Constantly runners slipped southward to urge the Sioux in the neighborhood of Fort Robinson to renew hostilities or to come north. The official decision was made to remove the Red Cloud and Spotted Tail bands further away from such contamination, to establish them on reservations well to the eastward along the Missouri in Dakota. When the great march started, it was McGillycuddy who rode with it as surgeon with the military escort — and with him rode Fanny, the one white woman on the march. When the new reservations were reached, it was McGillycuddy who stayed at what was temporarily known as the Red Cloud Post as its surgeon.

He was in the midst of something else now, not warfare and hard campaigning, but the post-victory handling of the Indian problem. Was the way to treat the conquered to do so with indifference and contempt and to keep them under constant military surveillance? Did these Indians exist simply to be exploited — to provide excuses for keeping up military establishments, to give military men chances for glory and promotions, to enable agents and supply contractors to grow rich by all kinds of clever swindling devices as government appropriations passed through their hands? McGillycuddy said little but he thought much.

Now came the turning point, the sequence of events which changed his career. He was an Army man, under emergency contract to the War Department, and he could easily have remained an Army man. The Army Medical Board had invited him to take the examination for a regular commission in the Medical Corps. He wrote requesting release from his current emergency contract. This was granted and he was told to report to the Medical Director in Omaha for the examination. He and Fanny were preparing to leave when orders came for the troops at the Red Cloud Post to return to Fort Robinson. No other surgeon was available to replace him. He volunteered to postpone the trip to Omaha and serve on this march too.

Winter was setting in, the bitter winter of the northern plains. It would be a rough tough march. He refused to permit Fanny to make this one with him. She left to return to Detroit and wait for him once again. He departed westward with the troops. And thus McGillycuddy was at Fort Robinson for the bloody days of late December of 1878.

Southward in Oklahoma, the Indian Territory, where they had been sent despite the promise of a northern reservation of their own, the Northern Cheyennes were dying from disease and weakness brought on by meager rations and an unaccustomed climate. Within little more than six months more than a third of them had died. Their petitions that the promise be redeemed were ignored. Under Chiefs Dull Knife and Little Wolf they started northward toward their homeland on their own. Relatively few in number, women and children with them, poorly armed and with few horses, they fought off all military forces rushed into the field to stop them, eluded pursuit again and again by incredible exertions, and struggled on northward. Some of them, under Little Wolf, refused to believe any more white promises and managed to get to Canada and join Sitting Bull. The

others, under Dull Knife, made the mistake of believing
a new promise that they would be given a northern reservation and let themselves be taken and disarmed and
brought to Fort Robinson. But when orders came from
Washington, these were that they should be sent back to
Oklahoma.

They refused to go. They would die there in their
northern homeland, they said, rather than return to
slower death in that pestilential place from which they
had fled. They were shut in a big empty barracks, un-
heated in below-zero weather, and left without food to
be starved into submission. They had five old guns
which had been taken apart before the search by the soldiers and the pieces hidden in the squaws' ragged clothing
along with a very little ammunition. On the fifth starvation night they broke out of the barracks and ran for the
bitter winter hills. A suicide squad of young warriors delayed pursuit for a few minutes, then with those slain the
soldiers had a fine bloody time running down the others
in the snow and killing them, men and women and children alike. A few managed to get away and for days were
hunted through the cold and the snow by the troops.
They were hidden in a washout hole in a dry creek bed
when the troops found them, starved and half frozen.
They would not surrender. Again and again troopers
jumped to the edge of the hole and fired down into it,
jumping back to reload. At the last, three Cheyennes,
nearly naked and only one with a weapon, a knife,
leaped out and charged straight into the soldiers and
were shot down. There was no more shooting. There was
no one left to be shot. There were only dead and badly
wounded women and children in the hole.

Valentine Trant O'Connell McGillycuddy was at the

fort the night of the break from the barracks. He had
been there long enough to learn the details of the Cheyenne trek northward and of their treatment at the fort.
He was a free man, the march from Red Cloud Post completed. He was ready to leave for Omaha to take the examination to become a regular Army surgeon. He left —
but not for Omaha. He left — and a deep anger and disgust went with him. He rode the rails to Washington
and he called immediately on the Commissioner of Indian Affairs and he spoke plain facts about what had
been happening at Fort Robinson — and about the
whole treatment of the Indian wards of the nation.

A fool, this McGillycuddy, a stubborn Irish-tempered
fool, forgetting his own career and going to Washington
to talk like that to a dignified government commissioner!
But all his experience to date had been aiming toward
such action. And all unaware he had come at just the
right time. Reform was briefly in the air in Washington
under the administration of that pleasant and well-mean-
ing but ineffectual man, Republican President Ruther-
ford B. Hayes. There were a few good men in the cabinet. McGillycuddy was asked to call again the next day
and was taken to give more of the same talk to the commissioner's superior, the Secretary of the Interior, Carl
Schurz.

McGillycuddy talked. The way he felt he would have
talked plain facts to the devil himself. He answered innumerable questions about the situation at Fort Robinson
and about conditions among the Indians of the West. Answered them plainly and bluntly. Then Carl Schurz
talked.

The most difficult situation for the entire Indian service was that at Red Cloud Post with its vast surrounding

Pine Ridge reservation. The present agent had done well enough when he had been in charge of the peaceful Shoshones. But he was not doing well with the thousands of semi-hostile Sioux at Pine Ridge. Those Sioux were aroused and restless, stirred up by the Cheyenne happenings at Fort Robinson. A new agent was needed, one who just might be able to handle them. Men in the surveying and engineering division of the Interior Department had spoken well of a man named McGillycuddy. So too had certain Army officers. It just so happened that this McGillycuddy's record showed that he had acquired considerable experience among the Sioux, fighting them and working among them as surgeon, and had even been for a time at Pine Ridge. It just so happened, too, that while this McGillycuddy was not active in politics, it was known he was of the right party, the Republican. And now, right now, this McGillycuddy was in the Secretary's office talking like a man who knew what he was saying, like a man who just might be the man for the job. Would he take it?

Would a duck swim? Would a bird fly?

The Pine Ridge reservation! Largest in the country at the time, four thousand square miles of it, in what is now South Dakota, just north of the Nebraska line, ranging almost all the way from the Missouri River on the east to the White River on the west. It was mostly high rolling plateau open to the fierce sandstorms of the summer and the even fiercer snowstorms of the winter of the great plains, but took its name from the long lonely rocky ridge studded with stunted pines that ran along the southern boundary. The agency buildings were one hundred fifty miles from any railroad, fourteen from the nearest Army post, Fort Sheridan.

It was an inland empire four times the size of Rhode Island, geographically part of Dakota Territory, officially independent. The territorial government had no jurisdiction over it. Indian title to it had not been relinquished in any treaty yet made or forced. It was Indian land and the agent, if he had the gumption and enough prestige among his charges, could rule it with almost autocratic power. He was appointed by the President with appointment approved by the Senate and was responsible, through the Indian Bureau, solely to the President.

Some eight thousand Indians had been herded onto the reservation after the fighting over the Black Hills that had come to be called Sitting Bull's War. Most of them were Oglala Sioux with a few bands of Cheyennes scattered among them. They were nearly destitute, stripped of weapons and most of their horses. Only a few crude houses or huts and a few rickety wagons could be found throughout the entire reservation. There was not a single school. Most of the Indians were huddled in ragged skin lodges within a five-mile radius of the agency, dependent upon it for food rations. All were sullen and discontented and semi-hostile still, uncertain of their course in the period ahead. New outbreaks could occur at any time. Only a strong man, fearless and sure of himself, could make much headway with them.

Strong man McGillycuddy, absolutely fearless and utterly sure of himself, came to his empire as agent in March of 1878 after some weeks spent in Washington learning the ways of the Indian Bureau. He and Fanny and a mulatto servant girl named Louise came the last

long stretch from Fort Robinson wrapped in many thick-
nesses of buffalo robe in an Army ambulance through a
wicked late winter blizzard and in the dark of night stumbled up the steps into the unfinished house that would
be their home for the next seven years.

   And out around on the frozen plains the Oglala Sioux,
in the mysterious messaging all their own, knew that he
was coming, knew at once that he had arrived, and they
waited, wondering. The friend of Crazy Horse, a young
man with an old head on his shoulders, a strong-tempered man with a tongue that always spoke what was true
in his heart, had come to be their new Father.

   His first important move was to call a big council of
all the chiefs. Oh, he was sure of himself, this McGillycuddy, knew precisely what he wanted to do. Right or
wrong in the long perspective (the argument still accom-
panies government Indian policy), he was honest in his
conviction and belief and intention. The only salvation
for the Indians, he felt, was to become as white men, to
follow the white men's road, to break away from tribal
organization and tribal customs and seek to become industrious citizens on the best white model.

   One thing was immediately apparent at the council.
There was a schism among the Indians themselves, dividing them roughly into two main factions. One, led by old
Red Cloud, was staunch for the old ways, believed that
the white men owed them a living for the lands taken
from them and the buffalo herds slaughtered, would oppose any efforts to turn them into imitation white men.
The other, led by the family of Young Man Afraid
(Young Man of Whose Horse They Are Afraid), would

accept, reluctantly but wholeheartedly, the new ways forced upon them. Fortunately for McGillycuddy, the second faction was by far the larger.

He wanted them, said McGillycuddy, to spread out away from the agency, to occupy more of their remaining lands, to live in the relatively fertile valleys of the few streams where they could farm and learn to live independently. He would get them the farm equipment needed. He would have houses built for those who deserved them. Red Cloud snorted at such nonsense. Other chiefs were doubtful. Would not that make it more difficult for them to come to the agency for their rations? Certainly it would, said McGillycuddy. But he would increase rations for each group in proportion to the distance from the agency. That simple stroke had considerable success. Before long the spreading-out process was under way.

Then he delivered his master stroke. Other agents at other reservations felt safe only when troops were stationed with them or near them, handy in event of trouble. Soldiers, that is, were used in practically all cases of law enforcement. But McGillycuddy knew that the very presence of troops kept Indians uneasy, restless, worried. He wanted, he said, to recruit fifty young warriors from the various bands to be organized and trained to serve as a police force. That done, he would ask the Great Father in Washington to remove all soldiers from the vicinity and let the Pine Ridge Indians, under their agent, handle their own affairs and enforce the law for themselves.

All the chiefs grunted astonished approval. Even Red Cloud thought this a fine idea. The removal of troops at least. But he saw no need for a special police force. He himself would turn over to the agent plenty of young warriors any time there was a law enforcement problem.

No, said McGillycuddy. Suppose these young men were called upon to enforce the law against Red Cloud. Would they do it? Of course not. What he wanted was men sworn to serve only the Great Father through his agent.

Red Cloud departed in a huff. He knew this scheme would cut across the old tribal organization. But enough chiefs agreed to make the project practicable. Young Man Afraid recommended and McGillycuddy appointed as captain a tall powerful young Indian, Man Who Carries the Sword, who had already earned quite a reputation both as a taker of horses and as a fighter in the pre-reservation days. He had his troubles, this Sword, with Red Cloud opposing him. He obtained a beef from Mc-Gillycuddy and staged a barbecue for selected possible recruits. Red Cloud warriors came whooping and broke up the affair and devoured the beef. Sword staged another barbecue at a more secluded spot. Eventually he had his fifty, stalwart young bucks all. McGillycuddy wangled Spencer rifles for them (he had to go to Carl Schurz and then to General Sheridan for that) and uniforms that pleased their vanity. They drilled like soldiers and they behaved like men. Their first real test was conclusive enough.

Spotted Wolf, an irreconcilable Cheyenne, and twenty-five of his followers were reported to be slipping away from the reservation, heading north in warpaint, probably aiming to join Sitting Bull. They could cause considerable trouble on the long way. Troops might have to be called out and there could be hell to pay. Many Indians might be killed and some white men and more excuses provided for even harsher treatment of all

Indians. McGillycuddy sent Sword and twenty-five of the new police on their fastest ponies to bring the Cheyennes back — above all, to bring back Spotted Wolf, dead or alive. Ten days passed with no word. McGillycuddy was worried, though he let no one know it. Had this police experiment, the keystone of what he hoped to accomplish, failed? Had Sword and the twenty-five themselves defected, gone on with the Cheyennes?

On the eleventh day Sword appeared at the agency, tall on his horse at the head of his twenty-five. With them was a pony pulling a travois with a wrapped bundle on it. Behind them came many more Indians, Sioux and Cheyenne, chanting a death song. Sword gave orders and two of the police carried the bundle into McGillycuddy's office and unrolled it on the floor. Spotted Wolf had been overtaken all right. He had refused to come back and had reached for his gun. He would reach no more for anything.

Oh, McGillycuddy's Sword was a fine and faithful weapon for a strong-tempered man to have always ready at hand all through those seven years!

But he had killed a chief, had Sword. He had done it in line of duty, but there was Indian law too. His own people fined him fifteen ponies. He did not have fifteen ponies. McGillycuddy heard. This was his affair, he said; Sword had simply obeyed orders. Let those demanding the ponies come to him. No more was heard about fifteen ponies. The Pine Ridge Indians already knew the temper of their Father. He could not be pushed around like the agent at the Spotted Tail agency to the north who was afraid of his charges and retreated behind white soldiers in any emergency and rarely seemed really to make up his mind about anything. Their agent was a hard man, quick-tempered and stern, who knew his own mind always and made fast decisions and stuck to them, and what he decided was always, in his own mind at least, for their own good.

They were proud of their own police too, even though in organization and operation it cut across tribal customs. Indians, not white soldiers, enforcing the law and agency rules for Indians. Arresting not only Indians when that was necessary or their Father thought it necessary, but white men too, the horse thieves and the illegal liquor peddlers who hung around the edges of the reservation. Their agent stood straight with a stiff backbone and because of him they could stand straight too.

He knew how to handle them. They were men in their own ways, but in the white men's ways they were as children. He treated them as a stern father who understands them would treat his children. Sternly — but with understanding. There was the case, for example, of Little Chief, another Cheyenne, and his conniving with Red Cloud to flout authority.

Little Chief and some of his followers moved their camp from Wolf Creek to Red Cloud's village on White Clay Creek. This was not only contrary to orders but brought too many of the malcontents together in one place. McGillycuddy sent for both chiefs. He pointed out that there was not enough good land near Red Cloud's village for so many people. Little Chief answered haughtily that it was all Indian land and he could live where he pleased on the reservation and he pleased to live with his friend Red Cloud. This could have been a police matter. McGillycuddy had the power to make it so, as most other agents would have made it a soldier matter. But McGillycuddy merely grinned that rare small lopsided grin of his. Very well, he said. But under the last treaty the agent had authority to withhold rations from those causing trouble, inciting to rebellion, as Little Chief was in the habit of doing. Little Chief could live where he pleased; but as long as he was not where he should be his rations would be cut, sugar the first week, flour the next, beef the next. The two chiefs departed, angry and determined. Surely no agent would dare to hold out against two of their standing.

Ration day of the first week and there was sugar for those of Little Chief's band who had stayed on Wolf Creek, but none for Little Chief and his immediate followers. Ration day of the second week and it was the same with flour. Red Cloud was having second thoughts. He was having to share the sugar and flour for himself and his followers with these visiting Cheyennes.

Ration day of the third week and it was beef, most important item of all. Rumors were racing about that the Cheyennes would take their beef regardless and kill McGillycuddy too if necessary. Little Chief's warriors were at the corrals, armed to the limit of their resources. McGillycuddy came riding up — and with him his Sword and the fifty police in full uniform with Spencer repeating rifles in their hands. There would be no killing of beef at the corrals today, he announced; none of the usual shooting and wild racing about pretending that the steers were buffalo as was the custom. Each band must drive its cattle away to be slaughtered elsewhere.

One by one the various bands, reluctant but wary, left with their cattle. Little Chief's remained. McGillycuddy ordered the corral gates closed. The rationing was over. Little Chief and his followers looked at the impassive

Sword and the equally impassive fifty with their rifles at the ready. They rode away.

The next day they were back at the camp on Wolf Creek. Little Chief came to the agency and asked for his rations. McGillycuddy wrote out an order for him. But he expected more, said Little Chief; rations for the past weeks too. No, said McGillycuddy, a man cannot eat backwards. And that was that.

Or again, there was the case of flying the flag.

He wanted a flag flying over his agency, did this McGillycuddy. He had a fondness for seeing Old Glory wave in the wind. When Fort Sheridan was abandoned (no need for it with the Indian police), he persuaded old friend General Crook to give him the proud flagstaff. This too could be a bad business. Back in 1875 an attempt to raise the flag at the agency, then still known as Red Cloud Post, had been blocked, despite the presence of a regiment of cavalry, by the Indians themselves. To them the Stars and Stripes meant soldiers, ever more soldiers, military action, war. This time, when the flag was to be raised, there were no soldiers. There were only Sword and his fifty in full regalia. There were many other Indians too, most of them apprehensive and resentful, among them Red Cloud shouting against the action.

McGillycuddy lifted his hand for silence. Old reactionaries like Red Cloud, he said, had wrong ideas about the flag. Sometimes it stood for war. More often it stood for peace. It meant that those under it were under the protection of the Great Father in Washington — over whose own house it flew. This flag that he held in his hands had been sent all the way from Washington by the Great Father himself. To belong to the Pine Ridge Indians.

It was Sword who unfolded the flag and fastened it to the ropes and raised it high. An Indian giving it to the Pine Ridge winds. The others departed, many still grumbling, to think all this over. Not long afterwards Red Cloud was at the agency to see about getting a flag for his village. To the crazy white men such a thing was a matter of prestige. Very well, he would have one too.

Or yet again there was the case of the last great Sun Dance of the Sioux.

The white men in Washington in their wisdom had decreed that such a barbaric and pagan custom with its self-inflicted tortures of swinging to the pole must cease. An order like that, enforced as, say, the Army would have enforced it, directly and arbitrarily, could have been a cause for fighting. All the Sioux were affected, not just those at Pine Ridge. But it was McGillycuddy, at Pine Ridge, who found the way for them all. All right, he said, the Sun Dance must cease and perhaps that would be a good thing. But before it ceased there should be a last and greatest Sun Dance for the Sioux to remember as they went forward on the white men's road. He argued and wrangled and fought and he wrung from Washington permission for it. Who now could think of fighting in preparation for such an event?

It was a mighty gathering, lasting for days, held in Nebraska just below the Dakota line, not far from Pine Ridge, a gathering of most of the Sioux from all of the reservations. McGillycuddy and the Pine Ridge Indians were the hosts, were those who would be held responsible for whatever might happen. White people were there too, many of them, Army officers and interested officials from Washington and ranchers from all around and scientists aplenty, historians and ethnologists and archaeologists and anthropologists.

At one point there could have been fighting, erupting into terrible trouble. It was the morning of the first day of the dancing and most of the Indians and visitors were already assembled at the dance ground. McGillycuddy and some white guests were at the agency, preparing to leave. And a big bunch of Brulés Sioux from the Spotted Tail agency, hundreds of them, used to their own weak and vacillating agent, gathered by the Pine Ridge agency, interested in the big "Give-Away House," the warehouse from which supplies were distributed. They demanded a generous handout. If it was refused, they would take for themselves.

McGillycuddy received their old chief in his office. He said that he knew rations for the whole round trip had been issued to them at their own agency. There would be no more. The chief blustered and threatened. McGillycuddy grabbed him, hustled him to the outer doorway, and kicked him into the dust. Instantly, from somewhere, Sword and some of the police appeared. The chief stalked away to his band.

The angry Brulés consulted together for a while, then mounted their ponies and raced back and forth at some distance from the agency, working themselves toward battle pitch. McGillycuddy and the few white employees on hand and the visitors took rifles and positions at the windows. And where now were Sword and his men? They had disappeared, simply faded away.

It was a tight situation, ready to explode at any moment. Time passed and the Brulés worked closer, preparing for an attack. And suddenly another batch of Indians came racing from behind the agency on war ponies! Sword and all of his fifty! Stripped of their fine uniforms, naked to breechclouts, painted for war, with Spencer rifles in their hands! Prepared to die fighting in the old way — but for the new order! They leaped from their ponies and lined up behind the picket fence in front of the agency and crouched down with their rifles ready.

McGillycuddy grinned his rare small lopsided grin and stepped out. It was the proudest moment of his life. No shooting unless he gave the order, he said. The Brulés came charging and saw the reception waiting them and stopped. They milled about, uncertain, indecisive. The old chief seemed to be trying to urge them on.

McGillycuddy called to an interpreter who could speak their language. Tell that old buck, he said, to chase himself back to his camp. "Tell him, if ever he bats his eyes at me again, I'll just choke him to death for luck!"

The message was given. The old chief raged more than ever. But his followers seemed to be losing interest. Their agent could be pushed around. Not this one. After all, the Sun Dance was to start soon. They began drifting away.

It was a good dance, complete and carried through to the last detail as in the old days, and young men swung to the pole with the courage and hardihood of their ancestors and the young girls urged them on and one, to the grunted approval of the whole assemblage, ran out to throw her arms about her sweetheart and add her weight to his and help him rip loose to freedom and honor with the blood streaming down his proud chest. McGillycuddy and his Sword and Young Man Afraid and his followers were watchful and saw to it there were no real disturbances. And the Sioux were satisfied, not fully but enough. There would be no more Sun Dances, at least none that the white men would know about, but there had been a last and the greatest to be carried in memory along the hard path of the white men's road.

He was an autocrat, a tyrant, this McGillycuddy, said some of the newspapers of the time; a cantankerous man, arbitrary and self-willed, who sometimes stepped right over the law. Of course he was and did. More so perhaps than the writers of such articles knew.

He had authority enough over the Indians. White men presented another problem, particularly those who hung around the fringes of the reservation looking for chances to nip off Indian stock or to sell Indians forbidden liquor. Two expedients helped him here, neither one in exact alignment with the law. The boundaries of the reservation were hazy anyway, not well marked, and he developed a convenient myopia about their precise locations. And he persuaded a judge of the United States Territorial Court in Dakota to appoint him a court commissioner. The judge remarked that he did not know whether the appointment was valid, but the title did have a fine legal sound and presumably carried with it authority to issue warrants, to hold preliminary trials, and to bind offenders over for regular trial before the Territorial Court. Armed with these two expedients, McGillycuddy went into action.

One time, for example, following his orders, his police chased a bunch of thieves who had made away with Indian horses not only well off the reservation but sixty miles into Nebraska and caught the leader of the gang and brought him to the agency. The guardhouse there

made an excellent jail. Nebraska citizens and newspapers
were aroused at this affront to their sovereign local rights
(the fact that Indian police had done it was particularly
aggravating) and made the wires hot with complaints to
Washington. Secretary Schurz felt obliged to inform Mc-
Gillycuddy that he had exceeded his authority and
should release the prisoner at once. But McGillycuddy
had already convened his commissioner's court, bound
the prisoner over to the regular court, and dispatched
him under guard on the way to Deadwood. He replied to
the Secretary in all seriousness that he regretted the im-
possibility of obeying the instructions because a United
States Court Commissioner had already disposed of the
matter. He felt no necessity to add that he was the commissioner.

Another time he stirred an interdepartmental row in
Washington. A trader who had a contract to carry supplies and mail to the reservation also had an employee
who had a habit of smuggling whisky along with the
mail. McGillycuddy ordered the man barred from the
reservation. The trader, indignant, insisted the man, as a
sworn mail carrier, was immune to such orders and to
arrest. Not to a McGillycuddy arrest. When the man arrived, boasting of his immunity, McGillycuddy popped
him into the guardhouse and sent the mail on with a new
carrier sworn in by the agency postmaster. The wires became really hot this time. A post office inspector came
posthaste from Omaha. McGillycuddy refused to release
the man. More heat along the wires. In Washington the
Postmaster General himself went to see Secretary Schurz.
Again McGillycuddy was advised that he was exceeding
his authority. Back went a McGillycuddy — Agent telegram demanding to know whether Indian agencies were

controlled by the Post Office or by the Interior Department and whether bootleggers could go scot free simply
because they carried mail. There had been no interference with the mails, it pointed out; deliveries had been
made on schedule and by an accredited carrier.

Whatever else happened in Washington, that was the
end of it at Pine Ridge and the man was bound over to
the territorial court and served a sentence.

It was sheer luck that saved him another time. A man
named McDonald had a ranch in Nebraska, below the
line, where he sold liquor to soldiers and Indians. It was
a trouble spot for Army officers and Indian agents alike.
No one seemed to know what to do about it. McGillycuddy developed another case of convenient myopia
about boundary lines (and he a onetime surveyor) and
with Sword and ten of his police rode to the ranch. He
left the others out of sight and walked in and announced
he had come to close up the place. McDonald and
customers hooted in derision and hustled him back outside. He kept one foot wedged in the doorway to prevent
the door from being closed and bolted and waved to his
Sword. There was a brief bit of flashing action and the
customers were fleeing and McDonald, held by two
husky young bucks, was watching his liquor supply be
confiscated. He bellowed in helpless rage. He would have
the law on McGillycuddy for this.

But that same day a Wells Fargo stage out of Deadwood carrying bullion was held up and one of the bandits resembled McDonald. It was McDonald who was
soon in the grip of the law. It was McGillycuddy who
could testify that McDonald was far from the scene of
the holdup at the crucial time and established an alibi
for him. McDonald figured that squared the account.

He was a high-handed man all right, this McGillycuddy, a tyrant who laid down hard rules and had hard
young bucks in uniform to enforce them. He posted a
McGillycuddy — Agent proclamation banning unauthorized guns anywhere in or about the agency buildings.
And had the effrontery to apply that to white men as
well as Indians. A good look at the big sergeant named
Pumpkin Seed who carried an authorized gun and had a
face as inscrutable as a brick wall and was regularly in or
just outside the agent's office was usually enough to con-
vince the sensible of the wisdom of obeying that order.
Even the not-so-sensible. Like a man named Quantrell,
nephew of the Civil War guerrilla leader, who boasted
that no goddamn Indian agent could make him give up
his gun and invaded the office with a forty-five stuck in his
belt. Pumpkin came in too and stood at one side with his
carbine in the crook of one arm.

Before they could do any business, remarked McGillycuddy cheerfully, his visitor must hand over his gun.
And what, inquired Quantrell, did the agent think he
would be doing if the agent tried to take it away from
him. He would be dead, remarked McGillycuddy. If the
gun were not handed over within one minute, the sergeant there would take it. McGillycuddy took out his
watch. Quantrell looked at the big sergeant standing still
as a statue, impassive. Fifteen seconds, said McGillycuddy. Thirty. Forty-five. Quantrell carefully drew his
gun and handed it to Pumpkin. There is a difference,
remarked McGillycuddy, between bravery and plain foolishness. There certainly is, agreed Quantrell, and shook
McGillycuddy's hand before getting down to the business that had brought him.

High-handed. Particularly with those of his Indians

who opposed him. Above all with old Red Cloud, who would not give in, would not change from the old ways. It was a personal feud between the two, the old war chief and the young agent barely half his age, a matching of wills, each determined to break the other's power. A strange feud in some respects. Red Cloud would come to the agency and sit about and talk in a friendly manner and there was the respect and real friendship of one strong-minded man for another and once in a while Red Cloud would say something about his throat being dry and McGillycuddy would wink at his own rules and agency law and bring out a bottle kept for medicinal purposes and the two would share a drink together. But always, with each new move, each advance into the new ways, Red Cloud opposed it, used his influence against it. Repeatedly he sent messages to Washington demanding a different agent. His talk was strong at councils and in his own village and others. So strong that once eight of his young men plotted to kill McGillycuddy and only advance warning from friendly Indians and adroit maneuvering by McGillycuddy prevented real trouble. Again one young man, very young, stirred by the talk, tried sniping through the office window — and luckily missed his target.

At last Red Cloud, urged on by white men who had their own reasons for wanting to get rid of this agent, sent a message that McGillycuddy and his wife must go. If they were not gone within three days, they would be killed. McGillycuddy seized the chance for a showdown. He called a council of all the chiefs. Red Cloud did not come. Most of the others did. He told them of the message. He told them that word of trouble brewing had reached Fort Robinson and the officers there wanted to

send troops, but he had replied no, that he and his police
and the friendly chiefs would handle this affair. Had he
done right? He had, said the chiefs. Very well. They
would meet again the next day, the third of Red Cloud's
ultimatum.

They met and the whole of the reservation seethed
with talk of the big trouble. They met and McGillycuddy read a telegram from the Commissioner of Indian
Affairs giving him authority to arrest Red Cloud. What
should he do? Young Man Afraid said that he should ask
Red Cloud again to come in and make talk. Twice
couriers went to Red Cloud's village. Twice Red Cloud
refused to come. Meanwhile young warriors by the
hundreds were gathering near the agency, mounted and
armed. They were the warriors of the friendly chiefs,
waiting to be told what to do. A third courier went to
Red Cloud's village, not from the agent, direct from the
assembled chiefs: come — or we will turn our young warriors over to the agent to go with his police to make you
come.

At his village Red Cloud's flag hung at half-mast. He
had heard that was a symbol of trouble. As he stood by
the pole, pondering defiance, the frayed rope broke in
the wind and the flag fell. A bad omen for him; the
Great Spirit had deserted him. He went to the council.

McGillycuddy read aloud the telegram giving him authority to arrest the old chief. He would not do that, he
said. Red Cloud was no longer even worth arrest. He
would simply depose him. Never again would he recognize Red Cloud as a head chief of the Oglalas, only as a
minor subchief and not even as that if he kept on making trouble. Red Cloud leaped up in rage and made for
him — but the friendly chiefs stopped him. McGilly-

cuddy spoke abruptly. It was enough. The council was
finished.

Red Cloud's power was broken. His spirit too. He was
only a nuisance of a bad-talking old man now.

Oh, he was a high-handed, arrogant, hard man, this
McGillycuddy, unfit as some newspapers trumpeted to
serve as an Indian agent. Why then was the Pine
Ridge agency the neatest and best organized of all the
agencies and the best able to handle any kind of trouble
and without the aid of troops? Why did friendly chiefs
and those not so friendly like to visit a neat office and talk
long talks with a strong-tempered Father and stop by to
pay their respects at a neat agent's house with good
gardens around it planted and tended by a Mother who
always had willing Indian helpers and was followed by a
deer and a sandhill crane and other pets given her by
Indians? Why was there more land under cultivation by
far-scattered villages along the streams and more stout
houses up and being built for Indians and more and better farm equipment than on any other reservation? Why
were there six day-schools dotted across the expanse and
a big boarding school with clean beds and running-water
showers and six teachers at the agency while most other
reservations yet had none at all? Why were the Oglala
Sioux and their Cheyenne neighbors better fed and more
prosperous than their cousins the Brulés to the north?
Why did those same Brulés sometimes send petitions to
Washington that they be moved down to Pine Ridge?

When a thousand or more of the troublesome Sitting
Bull Hunkpapas at last came back down out of Canada,
where were they sent? To Pine Ridge, already the most
populous of the Sioux reservations. When individual In-

dians here and there gave trouble and the Indian Bureau
did not know what to do with them, where were they
sent to learn how to behave? To Pine Ridge — where
there was not a single white soldier to keep them in order, where there was only a McGillycuddy and his Sword
and the Man Afraid family, Old Man and Young Man,
and other friendly chiefs.

The most exasperating thing about him for many people was that he was honest. With strong convictions.

Not only was he convinced that Indians should be converted as rapidly as possible into imitation white men,
which meant that the more romantic, the more sentimen-
tal, who believed that Indians should be permitted to remain Indians with as much as could be salvaged of their
culture and customs unchanged, were bitterly opposed to
him. He was also convinced that every dollar appropriated for Indian purposes should be spent for Indian purposes, which meant that those who for years had been
advancing their own careers and pocketing private fortunes at the expense of Indians were even more bitterly
opposed to him. He had the positive effrontery to regard
it as his simple duty to see that his Indians got every last
pound of provisions and every last yard of goods and
every last dollar of annuities which treaties and the law
and government appropriations promised them.

For a long time the Indian service in the field had
been shot through with cheating and swindling and the
kickback system of purchases and other kinds of crooked-
ness. Indians usually received only a fraction of what was
supposed to go to them and what they did receive was
usually cheap and shoddy although fancy prices for it
had been pocketed by white contractors. It was an ac-

cepted practice for political debts to be paid (even Abraham Lincoln unblushingly did it) in the form of agency appointments on the unspoken assumption that the agents would retire fairly soon with many times as much money as their salaries for the periods served. The so-called Indian Ring, whose members managed to divert by devious means more of the Indian moneys into their own pockets than the Indians ever received and were adept at getting hold of much of that too, was politically powerful with influence extending into Washington and into the halls of Congress. Some of its members had even convinced themselves that there was nothing wrong with the whole business, that the sole excuse for not exterminating the Indians was to exploit them — and they were only half human anyway. Here was the biggest agency of them all in the hands of a stubborn strong-tempered man who thought otherwise and was scrupulously honest. An exasperating and frustrating situation.

He was incorrigible, this McGillycuddy. Not only did he think his Indians should get everything due them; he thought they should do as much as possible for themselves. When houses were to be built for them, he not only insisted on good lumber — he had Indians do the building. When his Indians had wagons and some experience as teamsters, he had them haul their provisions and annuity goods from the railheads. He was keeping wages out of the pockets of white workers and freight business out of the hands of white contractors. The sheer impudence of the man!

From his first week to his last as agent he was the object of almost constant attacks, denunciations, investigations. If one believed the tales invented by pamphleteers and newspapers controlled by the Indian Ring and spread across the country, he was the most complete villain in America. With his palace guard of Indian hoodlums he ruled his domain like a ruthless despot. A minor disturbance on the reservation, quickly and easily handled without bloodshed, would become in print a serious bloody outbreak. If he let a band of Indians under such a trusted chief as Young Man Afraid go on a hunt for the last of the buffalo, he was said to be sending warriors on the warpath after scalps and stories of mythical slayings and atrocities were circulated. When he sent an Indian youngster to the Indian school at Carlisle in Pennsylvania and the youngster, required to have a white name, took the name in gratitude and respect of Tom "McGillycuddy," that was instant proof of the man's lascivious immorality. At one time and another he was accused of just about every crime on the criminal calendar.

One time the Indian Bureau sent him a copy of a letter received in Washington, signed by most of the Pine Ridge chiefs with their dashes and X marks. It contained a horrendous list of charges and a demand for a new agent and a threat that unless the present agent was removed he would be killed in a bloody uprising. McGillycuddy called a council and read the letter aloud. The chiefs, even old Red Cloud, were astonished. They had signed a paper all right. But they had been told by the white men who slipped about talking to them that it was a request for more trade goods and farm implements. McGillycuddy grinned his lopsided grin and made a brief report to Washington. He felt neglected, he once remarked, when no one was calling him a thief or a tyrant.

The first investigation was a friendly one. Secretary Schurz came to see for himself what all the shouting was about. He dined in comfort at the agent's neat house

(something difficult to do at most reservations) and slept
in comfort in the same house (without knowing that
each night, after he had gone to bed, McGillycuddy and
Fanny went outside and up a ladder to sleep on a mattress in the garret). He held a council with the chiefs
and heard Red Cloud demand a new agent and many
other chiefs say the opposite and he went about the
reservation seeing for himself while some of his staff
checked the agency account books and Old Man Afraid
gave him his own war shirt that had been worn in many
a battle against the whites and now was given in friendship and when he left, well satisfied, McGillycuddy had a
promise from him of $20,000 for the building of the
boarding school.

The next investigation degenerated into a farce. An
inspector in the Indian service named Pollack, whose ani-
mosity to McGillycuddy was known but whose connection with the Indian Ring was not until later, took advantage of the absence of the Interior Secretary from
Washington one time to wangle an order to go to Pine
Ridge and nose about. He hunted for irregularities and
found none. At last he did discover that McGillycuddy
had let his wife take a pair of scissors from a box of these
to be distributed to the Indians. Aha, the agent had stolen Indian goods! On the basis of that, without mention-
ing the item itself, he built up a scathing report and
wired the Indian Bureau that he was suspending McGillycuddy from office and appointing the chief clerk as temporary agent. Despite a return wire warning him not to
be foolish, he went right ahead. For several days McGillycuddy sat about grinning, refusing to make a single
suggestion, while the clerk, a true and trusted friend,
grappled with the daily problems and took the ribbing

of the other employees and muttered he didn't want the damn job. Pollack had departed in triumph. But a telegram overtook him, from the Secretary now back in Washington, dismissing him from his job and demanding return of the expense money for his trip to Pine Ridge. Another inspector was sent to the agency — and his report was that if all agencies were run as McGillycuddy ran Pine Ridge, the Indian Bureau would be lucky indeed.

A man named Bland, editor of a publication called *Council Fire* supposedly dedicated to the welfare of the Indians but actually more so to the welfare of Bland and associates, was one of those which continually attacked McGillycuddy and continually stirred Red Cloud to oppose him. This Bland obtained a letter from Washington giving him permission to visit Pine Ridge. McGillycuddy received him, read the letter, noted that it contained a condition that the visit was not to interfere with the affairs of the agency — and politely but firmly ordered Bland off the reservation on the ground that he definitely did interfere with agency affairs. Sergeant Thunder Bull of the police saw to it that Bland left.

Red Cloud, indignant that his "friend" had been expelled, went to Washington with new complaints. As a result a General McNeil, title a hangover from the Civil War, known to be the most merciless inspector in the service, came to Pine Ridge. After three weeks of the kind of checking that justified his reputation, he reported that Red Cloud's plaints were nonsense and that more McGillycuddys at more agencies would be a good thing.

Then Grover Cleveland defeated James Blaine for the

presidency. A Democratic administration was in office with a new cabinet and a new head of the Indian Bureau. Could Republican McGillycuddy keep his post?

Bland and others thought not. They invented more rumors of McGillycuddy sins and encouraged Red Cloud to go to Washington again with more charges. They went with him. McGillycuddy was summoned to Washington to answer the charges. Young Man Afraid went with him.

The informal trial was held in the office of the Commissioner of Indian Affairs with various officials assembled to sit in judgment. It was McGillycuddy who was on trial, but the two key figures were the two Oglala Sioux, Red Cloud and Young Man Afraid. And because of that McGillycuddy was unworried. There would be straight talk, honest talk, in that room that day. And it was so.

Despite the bitterness in his heart and the pressures on him from those trying to use him for their own purposes, old Red Cloud would not, could not lie, say that was true which was not true. It turned out that all other charges were foolish, merely objections to things which McGillycuddy had done which he had clear authority to do, and the one important charge was that he had conspired with Young Man Afraid to depose Red Cloud as a head chief and put Young Man Afraid in his place.

Yes, that had been done. But what was the true story behind it? Red Cloud was not a real chief, had never been one. He was perhaps the ablest war leader the Sioux had ever had. A great man certainly. But he was only a warrior who had been made war chief for the fighting with the whites over the Bozeman Trail back in 1866 and afterwards he had refused to step down and had kept

on as a leader. He was not a true chief for times of peace.
And how about Young Man Afraid? Let him speak for
himself.

Young Man Afraid rose to his feet with the eagle
feather of a chief in his hair. He and his father and his
father's father and his ancestors as far back as the
memory of the Sioux could reach had been chiefs. No
man could make him a chief. He *was* a chief. Was that
not so, Red Cloud?

Honest Old Red Cloud bowed his head and could not,
would not, deny it.

And McGillycuddy went back to Pine Ridge and
heard no more of such charges.

But it was only a matter of time. There were other
investigations. A Judge Holman came, prejudiced against
McGillycuddy in advance, and his prejudice faded as he
too saw for himself and was gone entirely when warriors
of the Red Cloud faction, hoping to impress and frighten
him at conditions under McGillycuddy, tried to stir serious trouble and he saw it handled without bloodshed and
saw other warriors, many of them, unsummoned and un-
bidden, gather and keep watch around the agency office
that their Father should not be harmed and insist upon
accompanying him wherever he went and watch again all
night around the agent's house that their Mother should
sleep in peace. Nothing came of investigations. Always
they were blunted against the simple fact of what was
being done at Pine Ridge.

The world is what it is and people are what they are.
It was only a matter of time. Of the right trick being
found. In 1886 the right one was found.

The Democratic administration in Washington was

more than willing to get rid of him so that a deserving Democrat could have the post. But there had to be a reason, an excuse. Too many people were impressed with what he had accomplished and some of the big independent newspapers had not only defended him but had made fun of the many abortive investigations. Well, he was a bonded official of the government through whose hands passed hundreds of thousands of dollars of government money. It was the custom to permit such officers to choose their own chief clerks who acted for them in their absences for any reasons, men personally known to them and trusted. McGillycuddy had his. What if a new chief clerk, appointed from Washington, were forced upon him? Could not his Irish temper be counted on to make him refuse to dismiss his own clerk and accept the new one and thus be subject to dismissal himself?

It could. When informed he must accept a new chief clerk, he wired his refusal. When an inspector arrived to see about this insubordination, he still said no, that he would not deliberately dismiss a good man who had served him and the government well. In that case he was no longer agent. So be it; he could not do otherwise. He and Fanny began packing. They moved to Capital City in Dakota.

Now he was more in the news than ever. A roar of protest came from the Indian country and was echoed in newspapers of the whole area. Some answer had to be made. It was ready at hand. Did not his refusal to accept a new clerk mean that he and his pet clerk had something to hide? An official announcement was actually made that he had defrauded the government of twenty-eight thousand dollars.

Now his Irish temper was really aroused. He thun-

dered through the papers his demand for an honest investigation. The most-investigated man in the country was
himself demanding to be investigated. Public pressure
forced action — made this time by the Treasury Department. The verdict was that one, only one, irregularity
could be found. This McGillycuddy owed the government $128 for expenses incurred on a trip to Washington.
When the Interior Secretary had summoned him that
time, the secretary himself had exceeded his authority.
The trip, even though on official business, must be regarded as a private one.

Valentine Trant O'Connell McGillycuddy wrote out a
check for $128, payable to the United States government,
and put it in the mail.

What does a thirty-seven-year-old man with a lean
body full of energy do when the work for which he is
peculiarly fitted is taken from him? He keeps busy.

He became a businessman, western style. He built a
house in Rapid City and became president of an invest-
ment company and vice-president of a bank. These positions kept him indoors too much. He organized a hydro-
electric power company and superintended its work in the
field. He had a finger in many another enterprise and
was mildly prosperous. The one personal worry was the
recurrent illness of his wife Fanny.

The Ghost Dance craze swept through the Indian
country with its prophecy of the coming of an Indian
messiah and the return of the buffalo and the old free
life for the redmen. The Pine Ridge reservation was a
focus of agitation. The current agent there, frightened,
sent for troops and their presence increased the possibilities of serious trouble. The governor of the new state of

South Dakota, admitted to the Union the year before, sent McGillycuddy to Pine Ridge to do what he could to prevent trouble.

News of his arrival spread fast and the chiefs themselves called a council to talk with their former Father. It was hard for McGillycuddy to have to obtain the permission of an Army officer to talk to his former children. But he saw old Red Cloud, very old now, rise to his feet and he heard old Red Cloud say things he would never forget. When this man, this McGillycuddy, had come to them as agent, he had seemed to Red Cloud to be just a boy and his ideas had seemed to be all wrong. But Red Cloud knew now that this man had been a man with an old head on his young shoulders. He had been right. When he was with them, they were better off than they had been ever since. When he had been with them, they had settled things, much worse things than this present trouble, among themselves and with no white troops coming only to make more trouble. Could he not help them now?

It was hard, very hard, for McGillycuddy to have to say that he could do nothing, he could only talk to the white officers and urge them to act wisely.

It was true he could do nothing. He told the officers that the blunt order that the Ghost dancing must cease and at once was a mistake. If the Indians were permitted to dance, that would occupy them on through the winter and in the spring; when the prophecy failed, they would see that they had been misled by foolish talk and the trouble which was only a final flickering of Indian hopes which the whites were making into a trouble would fade away. But he was pushed aside and his words ignored. He was even refused permission to go to another council

when Red Cloud sent word that he and the other chiefs
wanted their former Father to advise them as in the old
days.

He could do nothing. The trouble drifted on, deepening, and at the Standing Rock reservation old Sitting Bull
was worrying the white officers with his influence and like
Crazy Horse before him was tricked into arrest and a
mortal wound and in the aftermath of that bloody business came the even bloodier fighting in Wounded Knee
valley. It was McGillycuddy who hurried there to do
what he could tending the wounded whose skins happened to be red.

Time passed and McGillycuddy kept busy. The Panic
of '93 carried down with it most of his enterprises. He
became president of the School of Mines in Capital City.
That was not too confining. He could travel about, in-
specting mines.

Time passed, swiftly, and in 1897 his Fanny had another stroke and died and he could no longer bear to live
in the region where she had so uncomplainingly and
helpfully gone through so much with him. He became
medical inspector for the Mutual Life Insurance Company of New York for its western division, with headquarters in San Francisco.

He was still only in his middle years and energy still
burned in him and he married again, Julia Blanchard,
whom he had known as the blond blue-eyed young
daughter of one of the licensed traders at Pine Ridge. It
was a new life he was leading but the past was sometimes
there. When Buffalo Bill's Wild West Show toured the
west coast, some Pine Ridge Sioux were with it, and they
came in full regalia to visit him and tell him there was

poverty and little food on the reservation or they would not be doing anything so silly as this showing off before white people for money and they wished he would come and be their Father again. On the rare occasions he could find business excuses for swings out through the mountains and plains, he met again with hearty handshakes old friends, red and white, and among them a fat too-fast-grown-old woman still known as Calamity Jane.

As his work kept him more and more in an office in a city and he could contrast this comfortable, routine, unexciting existence with that of his own past when he ate game he himself killed and slept under the open sky and marched with troops through blistering heat of summer and bitter cold of winter and was responsible for thousands of semi-hostile Indians and made life or death decisions with the threat of rebellion around him, he began to understand how old Red Cloud had felt as white civilization constricted and crushed the wild free life of his people. He wished he had not been so harsh on the old man, had not been so convinced he must break the spirit of the old warrior. He could see now the essential kinship between them. Had he been in Red Cloud's place, he would have felt as Red Cloud felt.

Time passed, ever more swiftly, and the United States was in the First World War. He was too old for any sort of service, said the military authorities. Too old? What did these soft modern men know of hardship endured to the last gasping breath, to the last flick of energy in the straining muscle? He showed them when the influenza epidemic was sweeping the country, taking more American lives than the war itself. It was "the Doctor," old McGillycuddy, who ranged through much of the West, to the mining towns in the mountains, to the most remote settlements where there were no doctors, surmounting all difficulties, setting up clinics, finding new ways of fighting the disease. When the epidemic reached Alaska, he was there too, carrying the fight to the farthest outpost the disease struck.

Time passed, rushing now with the speed of the machine age, and old McGillycuddy applied for registration as a regular physician in California. He did not intend to practice medicine. He had done that often enough, but always under emergency conditions. He wanted, before he died, to be a fully accredited registered doctor. The first requisite before an examination was a certificate from the state in which he had last practiced. But old McGillycuddy was out of another age. When he had been a "doctor" in Michigan and in Dakota, such things as certificates had not been issued. As a matter of fact, he had been a "doctor" in California before that state had thought of such things. The California Medical Association brushed aside the problem of a previous certificate, staged an examination in the form of listening to one Valentine Trant O'Connell McGillycuddy give a talk on the treatment of influenza, and presented him with a fine new California certificate of registration. Doctor McGillycuddy. He was almost as proud of that as he had once been of the terse signature: *McGillycuddy — Agent.*

Daily, in whatever weather, summer and winter, old Dr. McGillycuddy went for a long walk, his lean old body swinging along with the sure flatfooted gait he had learned long ago on the Great Plains. On June 6, 1939, he died quietly at his home in San Francisco.

The next day at Pine Ridge the flag hung at half-mast on the flagpole that had once stood on the parade ground of Fort Sheridan. Many aging men whose skin happened to be red and who had been children when that pole had been raised in front of the Pine Ridge agency mourned in their own way the death of the white man who had been for seven years their true Father.

Charles Fox Gardiner

OCTOBER 12, 1857 — JULY 31, 1947

HE CAME of an old well-entrenched American family. His ancestors did not come over on the *Mayflower,* but the first Gardiner in this country did come soon afterwards, crossed the Atlantic in 1632 as a lieutenant in the service of His Majesty Charles I of England. While stationed at a fort in what was not yet organized as the colony of Connecticut, this Lieutenant Lyon Gardiner acquired title to the small island almost directly across Long Island Sound from New London which has been known as Gardiners Island ever since, and there he built himself a "manor house." The family was still living there nearly two centuries later in the early 1800's.

Charles Fox Gardiner, named for his grandfather, a banker and shipowner, was born in New York City in 1857. His father had removed to the growing metropolis and was a wholesale tobacco importer and marine insurance underwriter. Young Charles was an only child and a thin delicate one at that, often afflicted with severe migraine headaches. Even when he attained full growth, he was only five feet seven inches tall and never weighed more than 110 pounds fully dressed.

Because of the headaches he attended no regular schools and was tutored at home. Like so many frail youngsters pampered and spoiled and protected against the rough world during childhood, he went to the other extreme in his reading and read all the books he could find about big strong heroes and exploits in far places.

When he was nearly sixteen, he decided to do something about his physical insignificance. He could not increase his size, but he could the quality of what there was of him. He started a strict regimen of stern exercise at a gymnasium, two hours every day. Doggedly he trotted around the track and did work on the parallel bars under Austin Flint, a famous athlete of the time. For years he took boxing lessons under the once famed prizefighter Billy Edwards. He went on long walking trips in the Catskill and White Mountains and slept out with a single blanket and learned to build fires in the rain and to use an ax and a rifle. He canoed up and down the Hudson River and out into the Sound. He became a Rear Commodore of the Lake George Canoe Club and won races in a canoe he made himself. Year after year, as steadily as possible, he plugged away at his program. There was not much of him, but what there was acquired the toughness of a piece of weathered hickory. One year he was Featherweight Amateur Boxing Champion of New York State.

Meantime he was started in his profession. He had accompanied his father on several extended trips abroad and had begun the study of medicine in Berlin and Vienna and London. He had attended what is now

Columbia University's School of Physicians and Surgeons and had interned at Charity Hospital.

In late 1881, turning twenty-four, he was a busy young man. He was surgeon for the prison on Blackwell's Island and in charge of the outdoor medical service of New York Hospital. He was engaged to Miss Daisy Monteith, daughter of the celebrated author of *Monteith's Geography,* one of the most popular school texts of the period. He was a frequent visitor at the Monteith farm in what was still country just above 125th Street. Then something happened which changed the course of his life. He went west.

A serious quarrel with his father tipped the decision, but he had been thinking of it for a long time. To do some adventuring on his own, strictly on his own, and finish the job of building up his health. Surely with all the shootings and knifings and scalpings continually taking place in the wilds of the great open spaces a young doctor could find use for his talents out there for a while. He would go for a year or two, make a fortune or two, then return to settle down.

He started west. He had never paid much attention to money because there had always been plenty of it in the family. What he had now of his own seemed to go remarkably fast. He got as far as Colorado. In the mountains there his money gave out.

It was early in the January of 1882. The mining camp of Crested Butte, north of the county seat of Gunnison in the valley of the Gunnison River at an altitude of ten thousand feet, was all but snowbound for the winter. The snow was six feet deep on the levels and the drifts topped the telegraph poles. People who got about did so on skis and snowshoes. The raised board sidewalks of the little town had been shoveled relatively clear and the snow from them was piled so high in what passed for the main street that it was possible from one side to see only the roofs of the buildings on the other side.

Along the raised sidewalk on one side walked young Dr. Gardiner, looking for the one hotel. Everything about him said easterner and presumably a well-to-do one: his pale citified complexion, the fine leather bag he carried, the derby on his head, his sleek dark overcoat, his polished shoes. He panted for breath in the high thin air and sat down on his bag to rest. A door opened and someone came out and briefly through the doorway he could see a bar doing good business and tables with men around them playing poker. Gambling and in broad day-light! A rumble started in the distance and grew into a roar and the frame buildings along the street shook and he could feel the board sidewalk under him quiver. Good lord! What was that? An earthquake? Just a snow-slide in the hills, said a miner passing by and staring at him.

Dr. Gardiner went on and found the hotel. A group of men were seated on plain kitchen chairs around a big stove in the front room, their feet up on the rail around it. The proprietor was behind a small counter that served as a desk. The proprietor inspected him thor-oughly and his signature on the register the same and began talking. Obviously he regarded the new guest as a well-heeled eastern gent on a vacation for his health.

In simple fact all Dr. Gardiner had left in his pocket was fifteen dollars with no prospect of reinforcements ex-cept by the one expedient he was determined not to use, that of sending an appeal back east to New York. But all unknowing he had something better than money for the time and the place, a matching determination to have things plain and straight. He took out his fifteen dollars and explained in a low voice (a personal matter to his eastern mind) that fifteen dollars was all he had and expected to have and he wanted to stay at the hotel as long as it lasted while he tried to earn some more.

The effect was downright astonishing to him, a lesson in the kind of people, one kind anyway, who inhabited these western mountains. The proprietor pushed the money aside and to Dr. Gardiner's embarrassment shouted to the men by the stove to come on over and listen to a good one. They came. Here, he said, was a young man who could easily have pulled a bluff with his fine fancy appearance and luggage and instead had told the simple truth about himself and his lack of finances. That being about the straightest story he, the proprietor, had ever had told him, he wanted everyone in general and this young doctor in particular to know that he, the young doctor, could stay all winter and to hell with his fifteen dollars!

Young Dr. Gardiner was learning fast. He was joshed with rough good humor and hustled into the bar for a drink. At supper soon after, he was introduced to the proper eating etiquette. Each man wet his hair and slicked it down and then all of them sat at the long table in absolute silence and with earnest concentration devoured vast quantities of food. Tongues were released for talking again only when they had gathered about the stove once more.

When he went upstairs to unpack his trunk which had been brought to the hotel, some of the men followed him

and crowded right into the room with him and derived
uproarious enjoyment from each new item of eastern ap-
parel disclosed. The hit of the evening was the complete
suit of oilskins he had used when fishing in Long Island
Sound, hat and trousers and coat all a bright yellow with
"Fish Brand" in black letters on them. Each man in turn
put it on and paraded about.

After a night punctuated by snowslides in the distances and outbursts of raucous noise from a nearby saloon, he was awakened by shots outside in front of the
hotel. Good lord! Gun battle and murder and sudden
death already? Need for a doctor so soon and so early in
the morning? He dressed quickly, grabbed his little first-
aid kit, and dashed down and out.

One of the men had slipped into his room during the
night and made off with the suit of oilskins, had fastened
it together and stuffed it with straw, and had hung it
high over the street from a telegraph wire. A placard
hooked to it read: *High water doc.* Men were scrambling
for positions on the piled snow and peppering the stuffed
suit with bullets. Most of the town seemed to be gathered about, cheering each new hit.

That was the real turning point of young Dr. Gardiner's life.

Some people from the East took a long time to do it
and some never achieved it. Young Dr. Gardiner, who
had filled his mind with tales of big strong heroes and
exploits in far places as a boy and by sheer will and persistence had made a delicate sickly body into a piece of
weathered hickory, became a westerner finally and forever in a matter of minutes. He gulped down astonishment and indignation and anger. He cheered as lustily as
he could in the thin air with the rest of them. And then

he blew the fifteen dollars treating everyone to drinks. "You're all right, Doc. Here's to you!"

Making a living in a sky-high Colorado mining camp as a doctor was not as easy as it had seemed in imagination. The miners were unconscionably healthy; only bullets and knives and accidents with dynamite seemed to have much effect on them. And in such cases, when a doctor was needed, there were already two of them established in town. They might not be as up to date on medical knowledge and techniques as a bright young man fresh from the East, but they had been there longer and were known and got most of the business. It was disconcerting, too, when an occasional patient did come along, to discover there were ailments not yet known to the eastern medical schools. Cow fever was one. Snow blindness another. Dr. Gardiner had to have obliging old-timers of the area tell him what these were and even suggest remedies. That at least had the advantage of tempering any extra pride in his own learning and skills he had brought west with him.

With business slow and at times extinct he had plenty of time to learn to ski. Not just to come swooping down cleared slope or prepared slides, but to go anywhere and everywhere on them. In that country they were the winter equivalent of horses. A man had to know how to keep them in shape and to repair them as well as how to use them. If a ski broke while he was traveling over snow from six or seven to forty feet deep, which was usual thereabouts, he could be as doomed as a man attempting to cross a desert on horseback if the horse broke a leg. Unless he could make his own repairs, he would be unable to get out to safety. He would break through the

crust or sink into a soft spot and be hopelessly buried in
the snow. A brief struggle to break trail on foot and exhaustion would claim him and sometime later his frozen
body would be found. There were many such cases in
the high reaches of the mountains. But a man who had
made his own canoe could learn to repair skis in an emergency. And Dr. Gardiner's long, stern regimen had given
him trained muscles and good coordination and he was
soon skimming over the deadly depths with all but the
best of them — and occasionally stopping to sit down to
rest on the top of a telegraph pole.

Business was slow but his credit was good, established
by a suit of oilskins. On the main street he built a small
shanty generously called his office though the one room
was kitchen and dining room and bedroom too. Out in
front it sported a resplendent sign, swinging at a right
angle, gold letters on a blue background, painted for
him by a Frenchman stranded in town who could not
otherwise pay for having been safely steered through an
attack of delirium tremens. Such a sign would have been
frowned upon by fellow doctors back in New York. Here
it was right in style. The two other doctors had set the
style with their signs.

Next door was a saloon known as the Slaughter Pen
because of the frequent attempts (some successful) at
mutual slaughter which took place there. One evening
after one such attempt in which many shots were fired
(but only one man hit and he only in the arm), Dr. Gardiner returned to his "office" to find holes in the wall by
his bunk and splinters on the blanket. He promptly put
up breastworks along that wall by the bunk consisting of
double planks with sand packed between them. Naturally he had to take considerable ribbing about his

"fort" — but he could sleep in safety while slaughtering activities went on in the pen.

One of his early patients was a cow, the only one in town not driven with the others down to the lower levels for the winter. She was kept in a small stable which was completely buried by the deep snow and was entered through a tunnel dug down to it. When the time came for her calf to be born, she was in poor condition from lack of exercise and could not give birth. Dr. Gardiner tried everything he had learned in the obstetrics ward in New York. At last he determined on heroic measures and tied the cow to a post on one side of the stable and rigged a block-and-tackle to a post on the other side. Heave-ho! Out came the calf. Mother and child were soon doing well. No one else thereafter could approach that cow or her calf without being hooked or kicked. He could walk straight to her and examine her thoroughly and even pick up the calf and receive nothing more drastic than a mild mooing welcome.

Business was slow and along came a mining engineer who owned a slice of the mines in the Bald Mountain district and who also owned a badly decayed tooth. He was a busy man and did not want to take time to go to Denver to a dentist. He would pay one hundred dollars for relief from the pain and a solution to his problem. Dr. Gardiner recalled a trick the prison dentist on Blackwell's Island had sometimes used and popped some pure carbolic acid into the hole in the tooth. Wonderful. The pain stopped. Then he sent to Denver for some soft dental filling and the next time the engineer came by filled the cavity. That would do for a temporary job. The engineer gladly paid the hundred dollars. And more patients with tooth troubles began to appear.

Being a doctor in a highline Colorado mining camp was a fascinating business. Four-footed as well as two-footed patients. Dental work as well as medical and surgical. Patient after patient unable to pay, then one who would casually hand out one hundred dollars. Unpredictable. But fascinating. Who with life flowing strong and steady in a once delicate sickly body would not enjoy living at the top of the world among men who might well be rough and ignorant and act like overgrown boys and even outsize juvenile delinquents at times but who, with some sorry exceptions, were stout men at their dangerous work and men all through in any emergency and instinctively loyal in friendship? They had something that was fading fast in the older East, lost there in the competition of ever more crowded living and of ever more tenacious pursuit of dollars. They faced the hard facts of existence in their own open-handed elemental way — "simple and true and unafraid."

A doctor, to be one of them, had to be the same.

One night a man named Tom Wilson staggered into the little office. He was so worn and exhausted that he could barely stand. Food and coffee perked him enough to be able to tell his story.

A familiar story in the mining country. He and a brother and two others had a mine up and over the crest of Black Mountain at nearly fourteen thousand feet. They were working it even in winter. The brother had drilled a hole at the inner end of the tunnel, inserted dynamite, fitted a fuse, tamped it well, and lit it. He had waited outside and nothing had happened. A defective fuse. He had gone back in and started to pick out the tamping to try another fuse. His drill had struck a spark from the hard rock and the spark had reached the dynamite. The backlash of the explosion had struck him full in the face. John Wilson had come over the crest of the mountain and the long way down and to town for a doctor. He had already been to the other two in town. One was too old for such a return trip with him and the other had a baby case on the brink of birth and could not leave. Two from three left one — Dr. Gardiner.

They started in early morning on two saddle horses. It was fair going for about ten miles, then they were into the deep gulch haunted by snowslides that was the only way up to the crest of Black Mountain. It was late winter edging toward spring and the snow was soggy with great masses everywhere ready to move. They rode now a hundred yards or more apart so that if a slide came both would not be hit. And a slide came, roaring out of the heights, and the edge of it caught Dr. Gardiner and his horse.

He lay in snow and ice and icy mud, battered and bruised and with a badly cracked rib, and his stomach heaved, vomiting in sickness. The horse lay dead in deeper snow farther down. He sat up and dug snow out of his eyes and ears with hands that were scraped raw and bleeding and felt his own pulse. Not too weak to be worrisome. He was sick again and lay back, dazed and almost dozing. Then John Wilson's hand had him by the coat and was shaking him. "Are you hurt much, Doc?"

Was he? Well, some. But how would one of the husky mountain miners take a tumble like that? He sat up again. Hell, he'd be all right if he could have a shot of whisky. John Wilson got his doctor's bag from the rigging on the dead horse and fortunately the little flask inside was not broken. He had his shot of whisky,

straight, and John Wilson helped him into the saddle of
the other horse and they went on.

About a mile more and the way was too steep and the
snow too deep for the horse. They turned it loose and
started it back down the gulch. They went ahead, both
on foot. They were above timberline now and Black
Mountain rose above them in sharp pitch. The snow was
not more than two feet deep up here but was covered
with a sharp crust. Skis would have been of no help because the crust was rough and jagged. It was break
through with one foot, then the other, heaving always
upward. The temperature was steadily dropping as the
day wore on. This was up where it still fell below zero
the moment the sun was gone. Dr. Gardiner's whole
body ached from the brutal tumbling of the slide and
breathing was painful from the cracked rib in the high
thin air and John Wilson had to reach back and help
him up the steeper places and they could make only a
short distance at a spurt before being forced to stop and
rest, gasping for breath.

They topped out on the crest and lay flat, looking
down the thousand-foot cliff that dropped away on the
other side. About a hundred feet below on a ledge were
the cabin and the opening of the mine tunnel. The way
down was another ledge cut into the rock, thin and small
and angled. Ice coated it from drippings out of the cliff.
They filled their pockets with sand scooped from hollows
in the mountaintop and tossed this onto the ice ahead
as they crept down on hands and knees. Once Dr.
Gardiner, startled by a falling stone that almost struck
him, slipped sideways and almost went over the edge and
hung trembling. In positive panic he scrambled on —
and literally fell into the arms of the two miners waiting

below. Then, not until then, he fainted as he was being carried into the cabin.

He was in need of a doctor himself. If not that, nurses. He had them. The miners stripped him, wrapped him in blankets, put a hot stove lid near his feet, filled him with whisky, and rubbed him thoroughly until his blood was flowing freely again. He dozed off under the treatment — and when he woke soon after went to his patient.

He did what he could, easing the pain with morphia, picking the rock fragments out of the shattered face, dressing the wounds. But these were already infected and pneumonia might soon add its complications. The patient would have to be taken down into town as soon as possible.

As he lay in a bunk trying to sleep in the bitter mountain night, Dr. Gardiner could hear the two miners playing freeze-out poker at the one table. The cabin, which jutted out into empty air from the narrow ledge and was anchored to the cliff wall by heavy ropes fastened to iron staples, shivered and shook in the terrific winds that whipped past, and the two men, dirty and mud-splattered from head to foot and with long hair and shaggy beards, unconcernedly played their game. One of their partners lay nearby so severely hurt he might not survive and the other lay near him in exhausted sleep, and they played their game and argued and joked together. Hard-hearted, callous men? Perhaps.

But they were the ones who had doctored the doctor. In the morning they were the ones who chipped away most of the ice from the treacherous thin trail to the crest and carried the injured man up it in a sling between them, then eased him down the long rough jagged way on a sled made of four skis fastened together, hold-

ing it back with unflagging strength from the certain
death below if the ropes should slip from their hands.
When the tired and bedraggled party reached the lower
gulch, John Wilson hurried on ahead and by time they
were further down many willing hands were ready to
help on the last leg of the way into town.

At his office Dr. Gardiner dressed his patient's wounds
again and did the best possible to make him ready for a
trip to Denver with his brother in the hope an oculist
might save his sight. When they had left, Dr. Gardiner
was himself a patient. Blood poisoning had set in, probably picked up through his raw hands from the injured
man, and a high fever and delirium. Some of those seeming hardhearted callous men of the mountains got instructions from the other doctors and in his lucid moments he could prescribe for himself and they sat up
with him day and night and they pulled him through.

Now he was really a part of the high country. He was
offered and accepted the post of surgeon for the Colorado Coal and Iron Company, which owned many
mines in the area, and he had more than enough doctoring to keep him busy. Jaunts like that up Black Mountain were almost routine items in the week's work of a
weathered-hickory little doctor at timberline.

"You're all right, Doc. Here's to you."

Two years he was at Crested Butte, and mining activity thereabouts was slowing on one of the periodic down-
swings. It was about time to go back east. Miss Daisy
Monteith was waiting for him. Various people back
there were telling him by letter it was time to be
sensible, to settle down in a respectable practice in a re-
spectably civilized section of the country.

He went back east. He stayed long enough to marry Daisy and to find out he had been his kind of sensible in wooing her and she would go wherever he wanted to go. That was west again and into the high country. To the northwest of Colorado, to the small settlement of Meeker in Rio Blanco county, in the high cattle country of the western slopes of the Rockies. He built a small cabin there that again was home and office and once more he was a high-line frontier doctor, this time the only one for a hundred miles and more in every direction.

In this part of Colorado too he needed more skills than those merely medical and surgical. Just to get to a patient could be more of a job than treating him after arrival. Frequently he had to make overnight trips into areas where there were few trails and those hard to follow and even fewer ranches or other stopping places. Since calls came only in serious cases, fast travel was important. Horses were indispensable and only tough western broncos had the endurance for such work. Usually he had three or four in his little corral. Many a time, coming home from one long jaunt, he would find someone sitting on the doorstep with news of another emergency at another distant ranch. Nothing for it but to slap a saddle on a fresh horse and start out again.

Cattlemen, born to and raised in the saddle, could take that kind of riding and like it. But mounting a fresh bronc after hours on another and having it come unwound getting the kinks out of its backbone was an ordeal for an eastern-bred westerner. Jolting along the trails, he indulged in daydreams of the perfect horse for a frontier doctor, one like those in tales from the Arab countries, good-looking and powerful, easy-gaited and

tireless, obedient to the slightest command yet still full
of fire, a friend and companion by day and a guardian at
night. And one day he saw it — kicking and bucking in
outlaw frenzy between the taut ropes of two cowboys.

His dream horse, in physical form anyway, just as he
had pictured it in his mind. But too wild to be of any
use. The boss had told the two cowboys to drag it to
town and sell it for anything they could get. Dr. Gardiner bought it for five dollars. The two cowboys maneu-
vered it into his corral and fortunately that corral had
been built stout enough to keep out the wild cattle that
tried to break through to the hay stored in it in winter.
It was just barely stout enough to hold that horse.

Dr. Gardiner stared through the rails at his dream
horse and wondered what to do next. He was joshed unmercifully by the townspeople about his "pet," told to go
right on in and take its temperature, feel its pulse, give it
pills. Old-timer Dutch Charlie did no joshing. He paid
for having been cured of chronic malaria by giving good
advice. Just keep the critter from food and water until it
collapses, he said, then bring it around again slow and
easy and gentle.

The starving took a whole week, then the horse was
down, strength gone, unable to move. Dr. Gardiner was
appalled at what he had done. The once sleek powerful
animal was thin and gaunted and lay on its side unable
even to lift its head, unable even to swallow. Carefully
he worked over it, massaging its throat to ease down
small doses of whisky and water. By the next day it could
eat a little warm mash. For these first days he had to stay
with it around the clock. If he left, it would whinny and
call to him until he came back. In a few days it could
stand again and move about. In a few weeks it was the

same sleek powerful animal it had been before. And it had adopted him as the one man out of all mankind to be trusted.

Cautiously, taking weeks for it, Dr. Gardiner got the horse used to a rope, to a bridle, to a saddle, to weight in the saddle. At last he swung up. The horse looked around at him, seemed positively pleased at the arrangement, and trotted off as if it had been ridden for years. It was downright eager to please him. In a short time he could guide it simply by pressure of his knees. It would follow him about, come whenever he called, jump or break through fences to get to him.

He had his dream horse, named Chum, one that would take care of him anytime under any conditions, that could carry him at a smooth restful fast fox trot all day and day after day and stick with him whatever happened. It was still a man-killer to everyone else, would let no one else come near. But that was an asset. There was not much chance of anyone's making off with it while he was in some lonely ranch or farmhouse visiting a patient.

Not even Chum could be used much in wintertime when snow lay deep and dangerous over the land. Skis were needed then and his experience at Crested Butte had given him that skill. But long trips on skis over rugged up-and-down terrain could wear out a weary doctor. The dog Czar solved that problem.

Czar, half husky and half wolf, was a native of Siberia and had been sent to a man in Alaska. The man had a brother who was a mine superintendent in Colorado, in the Meeker area. The superintendent had a wife who was pulled through a serious illness by Dr. Gardiner. A result of that chain of circumstances was that the superintendent, wanting to make a proper present to the doc he insisted had saved his wife's life, wrote to his brother in Alaska to send the dog down to Meeker.

Czar arrived in a big crate and most of the town gathered to see it opened. Meeker already had a fair supply of dogs and when the stranger stepped out of the crate, big and powerful and dignified, they rushed to the attack. And stopped. And started to slink away. Czar had not even bothered to growl or show his teeth. He had stood motionless. But the thick ruff around his neck and along his shoulders had silently risen and suddenly he seemed larger and wolf-like and such a symbol of menace that even the men gathered about were shaken.

Dr. Gardiner kept him chained to the outside wall of the cabin and again wondered what to do next. This was no Chum; kindness and gentleness had no effect on him. He remained silent and withdrawn and somehow sinister. Then one day Dr. Gardiner returned from a ride and stepped in close to see if the dog had water and Czar leaped at him and seized his arm, ripping the thick coat sleeve. Dr. Gardiner jumped back. He had a quirt in his hand with a leaded handle and in quick anger as Czar leaped again and again to the chain length at him, he beat the dog over the head until it fell unconscious.

The next morning, head swollen and misshapen, Czar sprang at him again and he struck again with the quirt handle — once only, a strong blow, and the fight was won. In his own wild way Czar had found his master. Dr. Gardiner unfastened the chain from the wall and led the dog around and around the cabin and it followed quietly and obediently. A few days later he took Czar hunting with him. When he had wounded a deer, he slipped the chain and the dog raced forward and pulled the deer down. When he butchered the carcass on the spot and gave Czar some of the liver, the partnership pact was sealed. He had a one-man dog to match his one-man horse.

When winter came and snow began to pile into the hills, Czar was ecstatic. This was weather as it should be. He was as strong as a small grizzly and Dr. Gardiner could take hold of his tail or of a rope fastened to his collar and be pulled at wonderful speed on skis over the crusted snow and up the long hard slopes. On soft stretches where the crust would not hold the dog, Dr. Gardiner would glide ahead on his skis and Czar would follow, spreading legs to straddle the pressed-down ski tracks. Crust again and away they would go, Czar pulling in the lead, tireless, proud of his prowess. High-speed winter transportation, this, to patients at the far lonely ranches and farmhouses! And when caught out at night in the bitter dropping cold, Dr. Gardiner could snuggle down with his dog, the two of them wrapped in the blanket he always carried with him in his pack, and the strong warm thick-furred body would keep him comfortable till the morning light and the onward march.

Fit partners through the seasons for an indomitable little doctor in the high country of the West, those two, Chum and Czar. It was Chum, surefooted and a powerful swimmer, who took him safely across rivers swollen with spring floods. It was Chum who, when they slipped on ice and he was thrown from the saddle with a foot still caught in a stirrup, instantly stopped and stood like a rock while he disentangled the foot. It was Czar who rushed to the rescue when a wounded buck had run him down and was rearing to strike with sharp hoofs and who took him through winter storms he could not have faced alone.

He wanted a "hospital" where he could keep surgical patients close at hand. What their doc wanted, Meeker and surrounding territory would provide. One man donated a lot on the main, the only street. The owner of a sawmill supplied the lumber. Many hands helped build and there it was — a small building fifteen feet square made of unpainted pine, equipped with two bunks, a cookstove and a pile of firewood constantly replenished, a whisky barrel full of water on the porch with bucket and dipper handy. Dr. Gardiner was superintendent, business manager, surgeon, attendant physician, general nurse — the entire staff in one 110-pound man.

A few days after the building was completed, he came stepping proudly along the street to view it in the pride of possession. During the night it had acquired a name. Painted across the front in big black letters was the legend: *The shortest road to Hell.* He heard snickers and from hiding places around emerged some twenty cowboys, delighted with themselves and their joke. For Dr. Gardiner the proper response was reflex action now. He led the way into the nearest saloon for liquid refreshment.

Naturally, when he had to be away, a nursing problem would arise. That was solved by the simple rule that of any two patients occupying the bunks at any time, the one able to get up and navigate by any means possible should be nurse and cook for his bedfast fellow. If neither could get about — well, usually one or the other had friends who would volunteer.

The first two inmates made a strange pair. One was a young cowboy named Joe, wrangler for a nearby ranch, who was as good a rider as ever sat a bronc but had broken his right leg when a mean one crashed him into a corral fence. The other was a middle-aged Mormon from Utah, dirty and mean and whiskery, who had been traveling through in a wagon and had managed accidentally to gutshoot himself with his own gun. Joe could hop about on his good leg and cheerfully did the cooking for the two of them and laughed at his unwilling companion's profanity and bad temper.

Fourth of July was coming up and both hospital patients were doing well, even the Mormon able to get about some. Dr. Gardiner departed on an elk hunt. To be off with Chum and Czar, camping out, taking his time with no emergency case at the end of the journey, was his favorite relaxation. But right after the Fourth his leisurely jaunt was interrupted by a summons to return in a hurry. He did and found both patients in bad shape again. Neither one would say anything, but he extracted the story from people about town.

The Fourth had been a fine day in Meeker. Cowboys came whooping in for fun and frolic from fifty miles and more around. The saloons did wonderful business. An Englishman who had an interest in a big ranch in the area came careening into town in a buckboard with an unusual cargo, six cases of champagne, and invited everyone to imbibe. Free drinks from an Englishman on the American Fourth was enough in itself to promote merriment. Champagne on top of quantities of cheap whisky

completed the process. The crowd surged up and down
the main street, shooting off guns, beating on oil cans.
Then one merrymaker had a brilliant idea — make the
Doc's two cripples run a race.

Joe and the Mormon were plucked from the hospital
porch where they had been seated watching the fun. Joe,
always game for anything, hopped to the starting line,
but the Mormon had to be prodded by bullets at his
heels. At the signal shot Joe hobbled cheerfully along,
doing his best, though the leg bone cracked and the
splint twisted out of shape. The Mormon, after running
a short distance, staggered and fell screaming to the
ground. An ample woman known as Mother White, who
ran a boardinghouse, dashed out and told the suddenly
abashed merrymakers what she thought of them and
their foolishness and in a shamed quiet under her orders
the two patients were carried back to the hospital.

So Joe and the Mormon were still in the bunks with
more time there before them. Joe's leg healed and he was
back at work in the saddle daring more mean ones to try
to break more bones, but the Mormon remained, recovering slowly. Every now and then, all the time he was
there, some cowboy would ride up, hand Dr. Gardiner a
five- or ten-dollar bill, mutter something about having
been locoed by that fancy new drink, and gallop hastily
away. When the Mormon finally left in the wagon, as
mean and ungrateful as ever, one of the boys quietly followed him on horseback to see that he did not bog down
anywhere and forded the rivers all right and got where
he was going.

The entire episode was just about par for the time and
the place and the people.

*

Daisy was pregnant and her time was near and it was late in the year. She had come from comparative luxury in the East smack into the middle of his raw rough West and had taken the change in stride and never complained overmuch about being so far from civilization. But now she might need better care than he could give her or get for her in Meeker. He had been so busy, too, covering his huge territory that they had not had much chance to be off alone together. Here was a fine excuse for a trip. He put her into a buckboard, swung up on the seat beside her, and they started eastward over the mountains, sleeping under the wagon at night. A mere matter of three hundred miles up and over the continental divide and down the western slopes to Colorado Springs. Two weeks later the baby was born there, a boy.

Six more weeks and the three of them were on their way back to Meeker by stagecoach. Not exactly a dull journey. They bumped into a blizzard in one of the high passes and the problem of keeping the baby warm was enough to banish boredom. Then the small alcohol stove carried along to heat the baby's milk upset while lit into the straw on the floor to keep their feet warm and there was a lively scramble to prevent too much sudden warmth in the form of a burning coach.

There was a bad moment after they were back at Meeker when the baby was old enough to begin to toddle about. Czar, big and formidable, lay in front of the cabin gnawing on a bone. Around the corner stumbled the baby and fell right over the bone, between the outstretched paws, under the great jaws. Dr. Gardiner saw and shuddered and grabbed his gun, but was afraid to shoot for fear of hitting the child. Then he saw, too, the expression of idiotic devotion on Czar's face and heard

the soft caressing whining that came from Czar's throat
as the baby kicked and gurgled and reached out to pull
at the thick fur. He called and Czar rose and started toward him and the baby yipped in displeasure, and deliberately Czar turned about and went back and lay
down and rolled over and let the baby climb all over
him and tug at his fur and pull at his ears. He had a new
master; Dr. Gardiner was now only second on the list.

From that moment Czar regarded the baby as his private property, only the parents, if they behaved themselves, permitted to come near. At night he raised such a
fuss that they had to let him sleep inside the cabin, close
by the crib. If as much as a coyote howled in the
distance, Czar would be up and alert and poking his nose
into the crib to make certain everything was all right. In
the daytime the baby could be picketed outside with a
rope from his waist to a stake and left for hours playing
happily in the sun with no fear of any danger approaching. Czar drew an imaginary line around his charge and
let nothing alien cross it. Wild cattle that sometimes wandered near would be sent flying with tails up stiff in terror. A cowboy galloping in with a summons for the doctor would have to make a detour around to the back.
Stray Indians passing by, always fascinated by a white
baby, would have to sit their ponies and look discreetly
from a distance. Until the day a few years later Czar ate
some meat poisoned with strychnine by a wolfer and
died in Dr. Gardiner's arms and was buried by a sunny
corner of the cabin, the Gardiners had a permanent capable never-tiring baby sitter.

Taken all in all, being a frontier doctor in western Colorado was better than reading books about big strong

men and exploits in far places. It was living the material for books.

A call came that the Doc was needed at Old Man Hyde's place on Snake River. Not so much of a jaunt. Merely fifty miles. But when he reached the place, he walked into the middle of a feud transplanted from Tennessee. Shots kicked up dust by his feet as he ducked hurriedly into the incredibly dirty cabin. It was not particularly reassuring to be told by Old Man Hyde that the Becks hidden outside, being Tennessee mountain men, had missed him only because they meant to miss him and obviously were only trying to scare him some. It was not particularly pleasant to take care of the small Hyde boy who had virulent smallpox while the Hyde-Beck feud went merrily on and occasional bullets ripped through the cabin and Old Man Hyde replied to them from a window. The night was reasonably quiet — by the rules also transplanted from Tennessee feuding ceased from sunset to sunrise — but the bugs in the bed given him were too numerous for evasive action and he had to try to sleep on the floor. When he slipped away down a gulch in early morning after leaving medicine and instructions for taking care of the boy, hostilities were beginning again.

Word came that Bill Dern at a ranch on the other side of Coyote Basin had been thrown by a horse and dragged among stumps and was in desperate need of the Doc. To get there as soon as possible meant crossing the Basin — a hundred-mile stretch of sunken desert badlands devoid of almost all forms of life except rattlesnakes, with only one waterhole and the only stopping place the flimsy shack by that waterhole inhabited by a crazy hermit called Rattlesnake Joe and the dozens of big snakes

he kept as pets in a pit under the flimsy pole floor. It was
a devil of a trip at any time. This was a bad time, in the
heat of summer, and Dr. Gardiner had just suffered one
of those periodic migraine headaches which always left
him weak and vomiting. But a man was badly hurt and
needed him. He made it that first day to the waterhole
and the night he spent with Rattlesnake Joe and the pets
was an experience to top all others and the next day he
made it the rest of the way across and found Bill Dern in
very bad shape indeed, all battered and bruised and
scraped and with left hip dislocated. Mrs. Dern held the
chloroform rag to her husband's face to render him unconscious on the floor and relax the strained muscles and
Dr. Gardiner wrestled with the leg until at last the bone
snapped back into its socket — and then Mrs. Dern
fainted and the children began to yell and the Dern dog,
convinced the medical intruder was trying to kill them
all, rushed in and bit him on his saddle-sore rump. Just a
routine scene in frontier practice. He stayed three days
starting tough Bill Dern on the road to recovery, then
took the long way around the Basin to avoid Rattlesnake
Joe and the pets on the return trip. As usual he found
doctoring to do along the way — pulled a few teeth, extracted a piece of steel from an eye, rigged a truss for a
man with a rupture.

A rancher from over by Sand Creek brought his wife
into Meeker for an operation. She had a wen on her head
that had grown to prodigious size, so large that it pulled
her scalp to one side and hung down on her shoulder.
Dr. Gardiner had a separate office now, a small adobe
building with a dirt roof that had been built as a fort
during an Indian scare, and he prepared for the operation there. Word had spread and most of Meeker gath-

ered around, determined not to miss such an interesting event. Dr. Gardiner was just as determined not to have his operating room jammed with people. A reasonable compromise was achieved. The foreman of a local ranch stood inside by a window and in colorful range language reported the proceedings as they proceeded to the people outside. When it was "all over but the shouting, boys," cheers and revolver shots resounded outside. When it developed that the woman's husband had no money, everyone wanted to chip in. About a year later the husband came driving into town, slicked and prosperous. He had hit a rich vein on his property and was ready to clear all debts and report that his wife was no longer the shy retiring recluse the wen had made her and was her old gay self again.

Abe Brown had the best four-mule span of any of the freighters who carted ore from the nearby mines through town. Big cream-colored beasts they were that could out-pull anything else on hoofs. But one of them contracted an enormous tumor on one shoulder and could no longer be used in harness. Abe called on the Doc. Another community operation. A good crowd had assembled by time Dr. Gardiner came out wearing a rubber apron and carrying his impromptu tools, a well-sharpened butcher knife and a big sail needle used for sewing canvas and some stout codfish line saved from fishing days. Straw was heaped in the middle of a corral and the mule led to it and thrown on its side and tied firmly fore and aft. Dr. Gardiner had once worked on a man whose skull had been crushed by a mule's hoof and was taking no chances. The only way he could get at the tumor was to sit astride the mule's body. Cutting through the skin was like cutting through the sole of a shoe. He hit an artery and blood spurted in his face and splattered him thoroughly before that was under control. Out came the tumor and was tossed on the ground. Sewing up was the hardest of all — and as he pulled the last stitch through, several Meeker dogs scented the tumor and started fighting over it. Abe left his post at the mule's head and swung at the dogs and slipped and hit the Doc instead and off the mule's body he went into the bloody mud beside it. Men jumped down from the grandstand of the corral rails and joined in grabbing at the dogs and a right lively scramble took place. Various Meekerites were still laughing half an hour afterwards. Ludicrous as the whole business was, **Dr. Gardiner** had the satisfaction two weeks later of looking out his office window and seeing his patient, in harness again with the other three, proudly pulling a great wagon piled high with rich ore.

A cowboy came larruping in one winter day on a lathered horse to report an interesting situation at young Jack Good's place eighteen miles away. Jack had left early that morning to spend two days in the mountains cutting cedar posts. Young Mrs. Good was in the cabin alone, with labor pains starting a month ahead of time. Ten minutes later Dr. Gardiner was aboard the handiest bronc larruping in his turn out of town. The temperature was falling fast and by time he reached the cabin a real blizzard, western Colorado style, was beating at him. Mrs. Good was a frontier gal from a frontier family and knew first things came first. "See about the stock," was her greeting from the bed. He fought his way to the corral, turned his horse in with the other animals there, forked out a good supply of hay — and by then the storm was so bad he was chilled through and could see only a few feet in any direction. The cabin was lost completely in the swirling snow. But Jack Good was a frontier young man from a frontier family and he had things rigged right. A rope was tied from a corral post to the cabin and Dr. Gardiner went hand over hand along that. He was badly frostbitten by time he staggered inside. While wind shook the building and snow piled against the windows, he built up the fire in the big cookstove and heated water. Mrs. Good was having a hard struggle but the hours passed and there was no result. By midnight it was obvious this would have to be an instrument delivery. He put cotton in the bottom of a tumbler and dripped chloroform on it and Mrs. Good held the tumbler upside down over her own nose and mouth until she was unconscious and he worked as rapidly as he could in the dim light of candles set well away from the chloroform fumes and the fire sank low and the subzero cold outside crept in — and at last there was a new young Good yipping in the night and it was a boy, too. He built up the fire again and put on one of Mrs. Good's aprons and held the yipping infant on his lap and washed him thoroughly and wrapped him in a blanket and tucked him in the bed by his now-conscious mother. Suddenly the little Doc himself was all in, close to fainting, and he slumped down on the floor to rest. Mrs. Good was indignant and insisted he get up off the cold boards and into the warm bed. That was the way Jack Good, who had made a snug camp in the timber to wait out the storm and had been roused by a strange feeling his Annie needed him and had battled his way through the blizzard, found the three of them when he burst in through the doorway in early morning. He roared with relief and laughter and pride in his firstborn son and began to rehearse the tale he would tell of finding the Doc in bed with his wife. Mrs. Good lit into him in fresh indignation, then burst into mingled tears and laughter and in a brief while they were all laughing together and eating a hearty breakfast of Jack Good's finest flapjacks. Just another routine item to go into a game little doctor's logbook. Just another baby saved for a healthy boyhood in the high country of the West.

It was not all the saving of lives and the curing of crippling ailments. There were such things as being tangled in the nasty business of a lynching party, postmortems on rotting bodies, coroner's inquests that generated bitterness and animosities. A doctor had frequent contact with the seamier side of existence anywhere and particularly in the opening days of the West. But through it all ran the strong bright unbroken thread of the feeling of being vitally alive, of individual achievement in a region where that was the common rule, of being an accepted affectionately joshed one among men who, with the inevitable sorry exceptions and despite their crude and often coarse barbaric ways, were strong in loyalty and friendship — "men in the rough, simple and true and unafraid."

The Meeker area was growing, with more settlers and more small settlements. It was no longer so dependent on one lone little doctor covering the long miles. His profession was progressing rapidly too, with new knowledge and new methods, and he ought to progress with it. He had become particularly interested in the treatment of tuberculosis and its arrest or cure in the high climate of the West. He had a son (he would soon have a daughter too) and felt that the family should be in some larger town where better schooling would be available.

He moved back across the mountains to Colorado Springs in Colorado's El Paso County.

Colorado Springs was no Meeker, not by a long sight. It was, for the West of the period anyway, a quiet and dignified town. General Palmer and his Denver & Rio Grande Western Railroad had founded it to be just that, had discouraged the development there of factories and other businesses which might afflict it with noise and dirt. For many years all property deeds contained a clause prohibiting the manufacture or sale of intoxicating liquors on the premises. It was the kind of place to which men who had scrabbled fortunes out of mines and mills and smelters and railroad shops elsewhere would retire for leisurely respectability. It was also, by climate and position in the foothills of the Front Range of the Rockies with Pike's Peak rising behind it, an excellent location for health resorts.

Here his daughter was born. Here too at times he regretted the decision to leave Meeker. In the second year after his daughter's birth his Daisy died of tuberculosis contracted while nursing her sister who had come to the Springs. If he had stayed at Meeker, living the rougher harsher but healthier life there, he might not have lost the companionship that had meant so much to him. But he was here, at the Springs, moving forward in his profession, well established. He stayed. And a few years later he married again, Miss Fanny Anderson of St. Louis. A good life for a man into his forties, a respected doctor in a growing dignified and respectable community. But often and often he looked back to those wilder, freer, happier years at Meeker. Echoes of them occurred now and then when some sun-and-wind-tanned man from the western slopes would come up to him on the street saying, I couldn't pay you back then, Doc, but I've hit it rich these days, and would shove a roll of bills into his hand.

Here, at Colorado Springs, he was definitely Dr. Gardiner, not just the Doc. But the man himself was unchanged, active as ever, ready as ever to answer any emergency call. People like General Palmer were among his patients — but so too were any and all of the poor folk struggling to get started in the country around and into the hills beyond. During the first years he still got about on horseback to make good time. Once, racing to answer an emergency summons, he broke a leg when his horse slipped on ice and went down. Then and there, alone and unaided, he himself set and splinted the broken bone.

A few more years and he was a familiar sight throughout the area, dashing about in a two-wheeled two-horse gig that could take the miles at a fast pace. A few more and he was doing the same in an air-cooled Franklin automobile. He wrote and published in the East the article about the Springs and its possibilities which really launched the town on its health resort career. He contributed articles to the national medical journals. Twice he went back to his old medical school in New York for postgraduate courses in the new knowledge. He invented the Gardiner Tent for tubercular patients to get them out of and keep them out of stuffy overheated houses. He went to Philadelphia as a delegate to the American Medical Association meeting there and on to Washington to read a paper on his specialty before the Congress of American Physicians and Surgeons. He was charter member and president of the El Paso Medical Society and active in the state medical association and the Colorado College Scientific Society. He was president of the local Red Cross. He even found time to help launch the Cheyenne Mountain Country Club and be a member of others in the region and to take up wood carving as a hobby.

He was on the first staff of the Glockner Hospital, established by the Sisters of Charity, and became more and more annoyed that the nurses were dressed in black. Not precisely a color encouraging to the patients they treated. He was told it was against Church rules for them to wear anything but black. Promptly he organized the other doctors and announced that on and after such and such a date it would be against their rules to operate unless the nurses wore white. There was a row that shook the institution — but on the day, white uniforms were in use.

That feeling of being vitally alive found at Crested Butte and at Meeker was with him always. There are old-timers who were youngsters in those days who still remember him as a slight, quick-moving, twinkle-eyed, smiling man, known to them as "Daddy" Gardiner, inspiring confidence and friendliness in everyone he met. "Few men," remarked the *Colorado Springs Gazette,* nominating him the town's No. 1 citizen, "get as much fun out of life as Dr. Gardiner . . . Few here," it added, "do as much for others."

More years passed and he was the dean of the town's many doctors. In 1936, seventy-nine years old, he retired from active practice. Thinking back over more than fifty years as a doctor in the West, he remembered vividly those years at Crested Butte and at Meeker. Prosperity and prestige and mild renown in his profession had come with the later years. But those early ones had had the vitality and the flavor and the special human warmth to remain more firmly in memory. He began to write about them. On his eighty-first birthday the Caxton Press published one of the finest, freshest, most readable books ever to come out of the Colorado mountains, *Doctor at Timberline.*

Into the mid-1940's and "Daddy" Gardiner, the little Doc, eighty-five years old, was still dashing about, in an up-to-date fast modern car. His family and friends thought he should be kept from behind the wheel, should have someone to drive for him. They asked the police to persuade him he was too old to renew his license. The next day the License Bureau called his daughter to tell her that he had been in, had passed the driver's test with a 100 percent score, had been given a renewal — and was safer to have on the highways than most of the young ones anyway!

He went right on dashing about. He had things to do. Every day he visited each of the three hospitals in town and made his rounds, calling on the old and the lonely and the sick who had few or no other visitors, taking them flowers, magazines, books.

At last the day came, in his ninetieth year, when the little Doc could not make his calls. A month later he died quietly at his home.

Elfego Baca

FEBRUARY 27, 1865 — AUGUST 23, 1945

PEOPLE in New Mexico felt strongly about Elfego
Baca, for and against, while he was alive. They still
feel strongly about him, for and against, twenty years
after his death at the age of eighty. The tales about him
are many and they often can be picked up in pairs, both
of each pair about the same happening, one for and one
against. But they all always agree on one thing. Here was
a man who lived his whole life with gusto and flair and a
fine disdain for fear in any form.

Who would grasp the full flavor of the flavorous Elfego must remember that he was what some people still
call a Mexican, others more polite a Spanish-American — that is, one of the southwestern American citizens
who happened to be of Spanish and Mexican ancestry
and actually had a stronger claim to the label American
than those who insisted upon calling them Mexicans.
The ancestors of most of them had explored and settled
the southwestern part of what is now the United States
centuries ago, many of them long before the landings at

Jamestown and Plymouth Rock. And Elfego lived and operated right in the middle of that big slice of central and southern New Mexico into which Texans were moving, after the Civil War, with their remember-the-Alamo hatred of "Mexicans," killing them on any excuse or without any, bullying them, dispossessing them, asserting supposed Anglo-Saxon superiority with the usual Texan exuberance.

Elfego was born in 1865 in Socorro, that town on the upper Rio Grande where the invading Texans rode high. His birth, being somewhat unusual, might have been a portent of things to come. He was born on a softball field — where just a few moments before his mother had been one of the players! The family, Francisco and Juanita Baca and small son Abdenago and now smaller son Elfego, had a cattle ranch near town. That was a rather precarious business with Texan cattlemen taking over the territory. Soon after Elfego was born, father Francisco moved his family to Topeka, Kansas, for a safer environment and better schools. Thus Elfego had a chance at a better education than he would have acquired in the New Mexico of the period and an equal chance to pummel his way through a healthy boyhood among gringos who, whatever else their faults, were not afflicted with race prejudice — and who, as a matter of fact, were inclined to look down their noses at Texans. A particular Kansan friend was a boy named Charlie Curtis who would later become Republican leader of the United States Senate.

For fourteen years Francisco Baca did well enough as a small-time contractor in and about Topeka. Then Juanita, the restraining influence, died and he decided to move back to New Mexico. Kansas was becoming too settled and tamed and domesticated for the male members of the family anyway. Elfego and Abdenago went on ahead to visit an uncle in Socorro while their father remained in Topeka to wind up his business.

Young Elfego, fifteen years old, was back in his native territory, footloose and fancy free. He wandered about considerably — there were plenty of Baca cousins to visit here and there. He was experienced in the ways of gringos and spoke better English than Spanish. He would have to catch up on his Spanish. But meanwhile no one would rag him about it. He was already quite capable of resenting quite effectively any slur on his capabilities. About this time, according to some of the tales, he made the acquaintance of a young man four or five years older, the Henry McCarty who assumed the name of William Bonney and became Billy the Kid. There are even a few tales of supposedly hilarious doings together and these probably derive from the itch of tale-tellers to couple the names of two young men, both expert in the use of Samuel Colt's hardware, who happened to be in the same general area (a tremendously vast area) at approximately the same time. If there were any acquaintance, it was very brief and very casual. When Elfego returned to New Mexico, Billy was already near the end of his rope, only months away from Pat Garrett's bullet. And Elfego was of a different breed entirely.

He had a better example to follow. His father had soon settled affairs in Topeka and come home to New Mexico and had taken the job of marshal of the small town of Belen upriver from Socorro.

Quite a father, Francisco Baca. He had the temerity to let a horse of his win a race from one belonging to an important citizen of the town of Los Lunas and when this important citizen raised a rumpus, to administer a thorough licking with hard-flying fists. Then he had the further temerity to eliminate in a rousing gun battle two cowboys from over Los Lunas way who made the mistake of trying to shoot up Belen. Such a combination of circumstances had the interesting result that when the chance offered, he was nabbed by some Los Lunas stalwarts, tried before a Los Lunas court, and sentenced to a long jail term.

Quite a son, Elfego Baca, quite ready to do something about this. He was seventeen now and already had his growth, and not merely of the body. He and a young friend named Chávez ambled quietly to Los Lunas during the night of a saint's feast day when the inhabitants were sleeping off the effects of festivity, found a ladder, used it to climb into the second-floor courtroom directly over the jail, sawed a hole in the floor, and hoisted Francisco and two other prisoners who happened to be there too up through the hole. They politely replaced the ladder where they had found it and the whole party, now five, adjourned to a field of high grass across the road from the jail building. All the next day they lay hidden in the tall grass, munching on food thoughtfully brought along by Elfego, and watched posses ride off to scour the surrounding country and ride back in disgust. When night came again with the possemen sleeping the sleep of the indignantly weary, the two extra prisoners departed northward toward Albuquerque and the two Bacas and Chávez departed southward toward country full of Baca cousins. Francisco kept right on southward and joined a brother who had a store safely outside New Mexico near El Paso, where he could remain in reasonable security. The whole affair was a typical Elfego Baca maneuver in

a land where the law at the time was whatever the dominant group in any particular area wanted to make it and
the right and wrong of actions depended upon personal
points of view.

That was Elfego at seventeen. At nineteen he made
the play that established his reputation.

In those days Socorro County was larger than some eastern states and extended all the way west to the Arizona
border. Socorro itself, county seat, was a rough tough
town well accustomed to gunplay and bloodshed. But the
worst place for trouble in the whole county was the strag-
gling town of Francisco (now known as Reserve and seat
of Catron County) over near the Arizona line. It was a
onetime sleepy Spanish settlement consisting of three
scattered plazas, Upper and Middle and Lower, far out
in the midst of seemingly endless miles of range country
which was being invaded now by Anglo ranchers in general and Texan in particular. They made their own rules
and their cowboys enjoyed themselves taking over Frisco
and thinking up means of amusement usually at the expense of the property and hides and even the lives of the
native inhabitants. The basic conflicts of the time and
territory, Americanos versus Mejicanos, Texans versus
New Mexicans, cattlemen versus farmers, cowboys versus
townsmen, all contributing to bitter political rivalries
too, came to a focus at that little town more than one
hundred and thirty miles distant from the nearest other
town of any consequence.

Elfego was living in Socorro, working for a merchant
there named José Baca, getting room and board and $20
a month for services unspecified. Probably they included
protection of the store and its proprietor. Elfego was al-

ready known as a young man with a startling ability to make a gun appear in his hand and a remarkable efficiency in its use.

Into the Baca store in Socorro one day in October of 1884 came a Pedro Sarracino who ran a store of his own in Frisco and was very unhappy about his experiences as deputy sheriff in the far-off town. He was afraid to make any arrests there for fear of his own life. He told tales to justify his fear. Recently a bunch of cowboys, in his own store too, had seized a native known as El Burro, stretched him out on a counter, and (as Elfego delicately put it later) "right then and there poor Burro was alterated in the presence of everybody." Another native named Martinez had objected — and had been taken out and tied to a tree and used as a target for pistol practice.

When Sarracino drove his buckboard back to Frisco with supplies for his store, Elfego Baca rode with him. Elfego wore a Prince Albert coat and two capable Colts made bulges under it. In his pocket was a badge of the mail-order variety. Perhaps, as he himself later insisted, he was already determined to act as a self-appointed deputy, a substitute for the frightened Sarracino. More likely, though ready for whatever might develop, his primary interest was electioneering for his party. An election was coming up and he had political ambitions for the future.

What is certain is that he was in Frisco, staying at the Sarracino house in the Lower Plaza, and more precisely happened to be in the Upper or Milligan's Plaza on the day and at the time when a cowboy named McCarty from the famous Slaughter outfit camped nearby, after absorbing a quantity of the fierce liquid dispensed in Milligan's saloon, began shooting up the town. There was nothing unusual in that. The cowboys, just for the hell of it, often delighted in shooting Frisco dogs and cats and chickens. The Frisco natives were following their custom of staying discreetly indoors and behind safely solid objects. The unusual ingredient was the presence of Elfego Baca.

He sought out the alcalde, one López, the native justice of the peace, and asked why this McCarty was permitted to upset normal business and jeopardize lives in such high-handed manner. He was told that any attempt to arrest McCarty would bring a real invasion of Texans hot for revenge. Better just to lie quiet. Elfego argued that the more the Texans were allowed to get away with this sort of thing, the bolder they would become. It was a sound argument — but not as impressive as the Frisco respect for Texan guns. All right. He, Elfego Baca, would handle this affair.

Sided by one Francisquito Naranjo, the only Friscoan who would stick with him, he went after McCarty and "arrested" him — took him right from among some of his companions, who immediately scattered to spread word of this startling and unprecedented action. The alcalde, afraid of repercussions, refused to hear the case. All right, said Elfego again. He would take his prisoner to Socorro, would leave with him in the morning. He marched his prisoner down to the Lower Plaza and to the Sarracino house and settled down for the night.

Meantime the word had reached the Slaughter outfit and a batch of the boys, headed by the foreman himself, rode into town and demanded instant release of the prisoner. Elfego stepped out and informed them that he would count three and thereafter, if they lingered and still insisted, he would take it for granted that gunfire

was in order. They were so startled that a mere greaser
dared even to talk back that they were not quite sure
what was happening until they heard Elfego calmly
count — and open fire. There is no indication that as yet
he was shooting to kill. He nipped one cowboy in the leg
and wounded the foreman's horse. Unfortunately the
horse reared over backwards and fell on its rider, crushing him badly. The others scattered fast — but a Texan
was dying. Riders dashed off to the other trail outfits and
the ranches in the area shouting that a Mexican uprising
was under way.

By morning Frisco was swarming with indignant
Texans, most of them astonished to discover that the rebellion by bloodthirsty "Mexicans" said to be determined to wipe out all "Americans" in the area consisted
of one young man at the moment quietly sleeping with
his prisoner in the Lower Plaza. Milligan's was open
early and doing fine business. A few cool heads temporarily prevailed and arranged for a trial of McCarty that
would not offend his Texan dignity — that is, they located an "American" justice of the peace. They sent
word to Elfego to produce his prisoner, which he
promptly did. McCarty was fined five dollars and that
was that. Or should have been.

Some of the crowd was already drifting away. Not the
hotter-heads. Elfego knew, the very smell of it was in the
air, what he was up against when he stepped out of the
building in which the trial was being held and was
greeted with epithets and a gun was fired. With all these
Texans about no one in Frisco, not even Naranjo, would
side him. He could count only on himself and his guns
and he would be very lucky to get out of Frisco alive. He
slipped around a corner of the building and away to a

small jacal, a small house made of upright posts with the
cracks between chinked with mud. Not exactly a solid
fortress, since much of that mud had dropped from the
cracks and would stop no bullets anyway, but with the
advantage that he could see out in all directions much
better than anyone could see into the dim interior. A
woman and two boys were there and he told them to get
away fast.

A group of the hotter-heads, led by a Jim Herne, were
determined to lynch this upstart greaser. They advanced
on the jacal. Rifle in hand, Herne battered on the door,
shouting that he would drag the "dirty little Mexican"
out of there. Elfego had not the slightest intention of letting the Texans get hold of him. What Herne dragged
out of there was a pair of bullets that dropped him, mor-
tally wounded, into the arms of a companion who carried him away.

Even now, except for the two shots at the man attempting to break in the door, Elfego was not shooting to kill.
He did not drop the man carrying Herne away, as he
could easily have done. What he did do in the next few
minutes was some neat hat-popping to drive the others
back and warn them to stay well away. But by now the
crowd, or mob, was gathering again, taking supposedly
safe positions wherever possible around the jacal. Pistol
and rifle bullets began to whip through the flimsy little
building. The battle was on in earnest.

It is almost beyond belief, but all the rest of that day,
on through the night and most of the next day, about
thirty-six hours in all, young Elfego held off eighty and
more gun-handy Texans intent on his life. From their
positions around they poured hundreds upon hundreds
of bullets into the building. A later count showed three

hundred bullet holes in the door alone. Just about every object inside was riddled or splintered or scarred. Not Elfego. He set his hat on a large plaster saint in one corner and drew considerable fire toward that vaguely seen figure while he was in the opposite corner. The floor inside was dug about a foot lower than the ground outside and when the firing grew particularly hot, he lay flat, rising to reply when it slackened. He was shooting to kill now all right. He killed two more Texans and wounded at least a half dozen who were incautious enough to expose some portion of anatomy to his watchful eye.

There were eighty and more of them. Why did they not rush him and overwhelm him? For that an Elfego Baca would have been needed to lead in the rushing. And the only Elfego Baca in that part of the country at that time was inside that jacal, ready and waiting, wasting no ammunition, nipping flesh with almost every shot, a man who could — and did — put a part in the scalp of a Texan who tried creeping up behind an iron stove-front and made the mistake of letting the top of his head show for an instant.

They tried to set fire to the jacal, threw burning brands on the roof. The roof was covered with a foot or more of dirt and refused to catch fire. During the night they got hold of some dynamite, attached a fuse, lit it, and tossed the package close in by the jacal. It went off with a wonderful roar and collapsed in one whole portion of the little building. Even then they were wary of approaching near enough to find out what had happened inside. They waited until morning light and then they knew.

This was the final, the perfect touch. They saw smoke

rising from the dilapidated chimney. Elfego was cooking breakfast!

It was a good breakfast. He had found some beef in there for a stew. And some coffee. He even made himself some tortillas.

As the second day dragged on with sporadic bursts of firing, the excitement began to subside. No one had any new ideas, certainly none in any way connected with a close approach to the jacal. Some of the Texans wandered off to the funeral of Herne. Others drifted away, tired of what was usually a sport to them and in this case had backfired, a few of them claiming that Elfego had a charm which made him immune to bullets. One of them later solemnly testified in court his belief that if a loaded .45 were aimed point-blank at Elfego and fired until empty, it would have no effect on him whatever.

Once again by late afternoon a few cool heads prevailed. A deputy sheriff named Ross whom Elfego had known in Socorro had arrived. Francisquito Naranjo was persuaded to act as spokesman. Elfego would let him approach for a parley. Shouted talk back and forth offered Elfego the assurance that if he would come out and surrender into the custody of deputy Ross, his protection would be guaranteed. His reply to that was that if they would all stand well out in the open where he could watch them, he would come out — but under no circumstances would he give up his guns. Agreed. He came out, not through the door as expected, but with a quick leap through a window, guns ready in hands. There was a tense moment as native Friscoans, assembled at a distance, shouted to him to make a run for it. But he knew that was just what the remaining Texans, now that he was out in the open, would want him to do. He stepped in close by the cool heads who had arranged the truce and kept his guns trained on them while they, not so cool now and sweating, talked all others out of any renewed action.

The next morning deputy Ross and his "prisoner" headed for Socorro in a buckboard. It was the "prisoner" who was calling the tune. The escort of six cowboys rode in advance, well out ahead and in plain sight. Deputy Ross was on the driving seat and behind him sat Elfego, both guns still ready to hands, where he could go into his kind of action at the slightest indication of trouble.

There was none. There had been talk of attempts at lynching him on the way. But it was obvious that any attempt would result in the instant death of deputy Ross, not to mention perhaps a few others. At Socorro Elfego readily surrendered himself and guns and was put into the new jail being built on the very field on which his birth had once interrupted a softball game. He was its first prisoner and while there watched with interest the roof being put on. A man of his capabilities could easily have managed a break. He had no such intention. He wanted this Frisco fracas settled finally and completely. After four months he was taken to Albuquerque for trial. This was no local court making its own law. This was a federal court under a judge appointed from Washington. Able Anglos handled the prosecution. Equally able Anglos undertook the defense. He was tried not once, but twice, and those trials have their own New Mexican fame. Both times he was acquitted. The Frisco fracas was over.

While sojourning in the Socorro jail and later during the trials, Elfego had plenty of time to decide what, in the light of his experiences to date, he wanted to do. As he explained it years later, he decided he wanted "to be an A No. 1 peace officer, likewise a criminal lawyer." He summed his ambition neatly: "I wanted the outlaws to hear my steps a block away from me."

Not long after the Frisco affair Elfego made another play which proved that his reputation was well established and helped his later political career.

At the mining town called Kelly about fifteen miles into the hills out of Socorro a Baca cousin named Conrado with an Anglo partner had a combination store and saloon. The business might have been profitable if the miners and cowboys of the immediate area had not been such jolly fun-loving characters. They quickly discovered that the partners lacked backbones. It was fine sport to demand and obtain free drinks, to bounce bullets off pans on the shelves with resultant ear-tickling clatter, and in general to treat the place as if it were the local shooting gallery. After one particularly festive evening during which Conrado's hat was popped off his head and there was talk of trying to nip the buttons off his vest, the partners abandoned the field and fled to Socorro. Would cousin Elfego go to Kelly and see what could be done about this situation?

Cousin Elfego would. But would the partners go with him? No. They preferred to stay behind in Socorro until a report was made.

Elfego rode out to Kelly with the same two capable Colts or adequate duplicates with him. It was evening when he arrived. He found the establishment in the possession of a batch of the miners and cowboys doing their best to exhaust the liquor supply. He stepped in and demanded to know what they thought they were doing. The various motions in the directions of side arms suddenly ceased when by some magic two guns appeared in Elfego's hands. "Who the hell are you?" asked one of the men who, like the rest, had hands properly upraised.

"I am Elfego Baca."

The effect was more than satisfactory. Professions of friendship filled the air. Why, shucks, they were not doing much of anything, just taking care of the place until the owners came back. Another drink around and they would gladly turn it over to Elfego if he wanted it. Which they did. And departed considerably sobered despite that last drink.

Then again the final, the perfect touch, typical of the incurably romantic free-wheeling Elfego.

He was annoyed that cousin Conrado and partner had not come with him. If they did not have the gumption to fight, even just to help fight, for their business, did they deserve to have a business? He sent word to the native population all around and the next morning began handing out the merchandise from the shelves to all comers free of charge. Definitely a red-letter day in Kelly.

He returned to Socorro to report.

Any complaints, cousin Conrado?

No-o-o-o-o. Not to you, Elfego.

It was at this stage, at the ripe age of twenty, that Elfego married Miss Francisquita Pohmer — a marriage which produced in good time a son and five daughters. But he was a true Spanish-American of the Southwest in this: he kept his private and his public life separate and apart. Insofar as the record shows, the one never intruded on the other. Talk and tales about Elfego himself rang through all New Mexico — but none about his family. The children grew up and married and scattered through the West, to various places in California and to the state of Washington. His family had no part in his own public legend.

With energy enough for three men and a zest for living enough for half a dozen, he was usually involved in a variety of different enterprises at one and the same time. But he moved rather steadily toward his ambition. During the next years, among many other activities, he was a deputy sheriff with a badge not of the mail-order type, then a deputy United States marshal. On occasion more shots were fired at him and he replied with his now customary efficiency. He acquired a collection of knife-cut scars and once an icepick almost did what no bullet ever did. He recovered and went on with his work. Tales of his exploits were becoming standard conversational fare through much of New Mexico. He was the man, for example, who arrested the outlaw José Chávez y Chávez who had long defied the officials of San Miguel County then made the mistake of invading Elfego's territory. He was the man who, when others had failed, went after the notorious José García. As his own latest exploit, García had killed a man in Belen and carried off the man's wife and then, tiring of her, had cut her into quarters and hung these from a tree limb like butcher's meat. Feeling ran high about him. Elfego stuck to his trail and at last plucked him from out of his own stronghold in the hills, took him to the nearest town, and serenely held off a lynch mob until the next train came along and he could transport his prisoner to jail. He was coming close to being an A No. 1 peace officer.

Along about 1890 he started toward the other part of his ambition, began to read law in the office of a Socorro judge. In 1894 he was admitted to the New Mexican bar and could begin to use his free-wheeling tactics in the courts. He was as effective a champion of his people there as ever he was in tight spots with his guns. Innumerable were the poor "Mexicans" who, when in trouble with Anglo law, hurried to find Elfego. He was as adept as any Anglo (there were some mighty adept ones on hand in those wild scrambling territorial days) at picking the right juries and at locating witnesses who might not really have seen what had happened but could be persuaded to think that they had. When he stood up, cold of eye and stubborn of jaw, convinced that whatever were the legal niceties involved his client deserved decent treatment, he had an uncanny but understandable knack of convincing jurors that it would be to their own best interests to dispose of the case in the proper manner.

Court etiquette meant little to Elfego when he was aroused. Indignant at some ruling from the bench, he might talk back to the judge and become eloquent in expressing a personal opinion of his honor and his honor's mental processes. About the time the judge would be bellowing for a bailiff, a sheriff, a deputy, anyone to clear this impudent scoundrel out of the room and throw him in jail for contempt of court, it would be discovered that all such officers recently on hand had quietly departed on sudden errands elsewhere. Trying to remove Elfego from a place where he had personal intentions of staying was a task none of them cared to undertake. It would blow over soon anyway. Elfego might be short-fused on matters of proper procedure, but he had a basic respect for the law itself (when it did not tread too hard and too arrogantly on his toes and those of his clients) and his heart was in the right place. Very likely in a brief while he and the judge would have patched up their quarrel and the judge would be chuckling at one of Elfego's dry drawled stories and eventually the trial would be under way again.

One time it did not blow over — and Elfego's outspoken estimate of that judge as "corrupt and personally immoral" turned out to be correct and the judge was removed from office.

There were some judges who enjoyed having Elfego liven their courtrooms. Other lawyers grumbled that Federal Judge Neblett in Albuquerque, usually meticulous and stern about procedure, would let Elfego "get away with anything" in his court — with things for which they might be slapped down. But the difference was in the manner of doing. They were self-conscious, lacked Elfego's simple almost elemental spontaneity. It could be a pleasure for an understanding judge, weary of the routine dull details of most trials, to observe in action a man so warmly human in all his responses and so completely his own independent unique self.

The New Mexican bar too was divided in its opinion of Elfego, for and against. Among those for was Judge Freeman, who had recently served a term as a highly respected associate justice of the territorial Supreme Court. Not long after Elfego was admitted to the bar, a new law firm opened offices in Socorro: Freeman & Baca. Not many young lawyers could claim with such promptness such a partnership accolade.

To be of Spanish extraction in New Mexico Territory and to be a lawyer and to have considerable personal prestige was automatically to be in politics. Most of the Texans who had been invading the territory for years were Democrats; naturally most of the native inhabitants were Republicans. By natural process Elfego was a staunch Republican. He enjoyed the political game and was a vigorous campaigner, more vigorous than he needed to be. He could not be Elfego and do otherwise. But all he really had to do in his own county to be elected to office was to run for it. He was mayor of Socorro. He was county school superintendent. He was county clerk. He was assistant district attorney. He was district attorney. He was so many things at one time and another and engaged in so many sideline activities that he himself, in later years, lost count and track of them all.

Eugene Manlove Rhodes, busy concocting his flavorous fables of his highly personalized Southwest, of little world waddies and trusty knaves and hired men on horseback, was at first one of those against. Viewing Elfego strictly from the perspective of a confirmed Anglo, Rhodes tucked him into one of his early novelettes, *Hit the Line Hard,* as one Octaviano Baca, a district attorney of not exactly admirable qualities except perhaps those of sheer effrontery and courage. Elfego is said to have remarked that Rhodes had better stay out of his way. Rhodes himself claimed that Elfego "swore for years he would kill me." Nonsense. If Elfego had done any such swearing, Rhodes's career would have been cut short and

New Mexico would have had another memorable trial. As a matter of fact, Elfego developed a fondness for the Rhodes fables and later Rhodes became one of those for and wrote some very nice things about Elfego for local newspapers. After reading one of them Elfego dispatched a letter to Rhodes in his best flowery epistolary style, closing with the flourish: "remember that at any time I can be of any service to you, all you have to do is to command me."

When old Mexico plunged into another of its revolutionary periods in 1910, it was all but inevitable that Elfego would have some connection with what was happening not far away, just below the international border.

He was already acquainted with one of the prominent performers, a swarthy-skinned tough hombre known as Pancho Jaime. A few years before, Elfego, in one of his official capacities, had gone into Mexico on the trail of a cattle rustler for whom a big reward had been offered. Elfego never had any aversion to any rewards that could be picked up in the line of duty. But word followed him that the reward had been canceled and the man was not wanted so badly after all. There was not much point in further action in the matter. Meantime he had met Pancho Jaime and Pancho Jaime had taken a liking to him. Not many men faced Pancho Jaime with the serenity and fearless eye of this gringo from above the border. The two of them even tried a brief mining venture together. As they rode to their diggings in a Model T Ford in the mornings they absorbed quantities of Mexican beer and tossed the empty bottles along the side of the road. As they rode back in the early evenings they spiced the time with shooting at the bottles. That Pancho, Elfego remarked later, was a very good shot. He never missed a bottle. It was not necessary for him to add that the same could be said of Pancho's companion.

Now in 1910–11 the Madero revolution was ousting the old president, Porfirio Diaz, and the last-ditch fighting of the old regime was in the neighborhood of Juárez just across the Rio Grande from El Paso. Among the revolutionists was a notorious bandit known as Pancho Villa with a motley horde of tough hombres as followers. Could this Pancho Villa be the Pancho Jaime of a few years before? Elfego went to El Paso and across the river to find out.

It was. During the next days Elfego was rather in the midst of happenings below the border, renewing his acquaintance with Villa and meeting most of the leaders of the revolution. Madero himself, and Generals Carranza and Huerta and Orozco and Salazar — he became acquainted with them all. He was on hand during the battle of Juárez and during the bitter quarrels which developed among the revolutionists themselves after their victory. It was anyone's guess how all the bloodshed and turmoil in Mexico would turn out. But these contacts with the revolutionary leaders might prove to be valuable.

They did. The various "generals" scattered with their "armies" and fought one another and continued to fight, each holding what territory he could and trying to name his own president. Along in 1913–14, when General Huerta emerged briefly as dominant among them and as briefly held the title of president, it was Elfego Baca. attorney, of Socorro, New Mexico, who was named by Huerta as his American representative. And when General Salazar, now a Huerta man, was defeated in a battle

and fled across the United States border and was seized
by American authorities and charged with violation of
American neutrality, it was Elfego Baca who was named
to defend him.

Elfego now had business back and forth across the border. The fact that such jaunts were dangerous bothered
him not at all. Pancho Villa, leading his own revolutionary movement now which was, in effect, simply an
excuse for widespread banditry, was operating along the
Rio Grande and annoying the United States with raids
across it that would lead to General Pershing's expedition against him. He was very angry at his onetime min-
ing-partner for being a Huerta man and had sworn to kill
him. His anger was not eased when Elfego arranged a
pleasant coup which resulted in Elfego's obtaining one
of the four custom-made Mauser rifles Villa had imported from Germany. Villa offered $30,000 (American
money too) to anyone who would return the rifle to him
— plus Elfego's hide. Elfego's response was to plan another coup by which he hoped to obtain the $30,000 for
himself — plus Villa's hide. But American troops were
soon chasing the same latter item and Elfego had no
chance to try his plan. Aficionados of the gun duel and
the well-directed bullet were disappointed that those two
never met again face to face.

Meantime there was the case of General Salazar. He
was being held incommunicado at Fort Wingate. Elfego
bluffed and wangled his way through military red tape
and managed to talk to his client. Then he went to Washington to besiege the War Department and the State Department for the general's release. But by now some
American marines had been arrested at Tampico and in
retaliation American troops had occupied Veracruz and

Huerta had broken off diplomatic relations with the
United States. There was no official disposition to look
kindly on one of Huerta's generals who happened to be
in American custody. Elfego could make no progress at
all.

While he was in Washington he followed the directions given him about collecting a fee for his services in
behalf of Huerta and Salazar. He went to the proper
bank, identified himself. Quite right. Huerta funds were
there and with them instructions he should be paid.
What was his fee? Into Elfego's mind popped the $30,000
valuation Villa had put on him. He did not know it, but
in matters of this kind he was out of his league in Washington. After he had the $30,000, he was told he could
just as easily have made it $100,000.

While he was in Washington, too, a Congressional
committee summoned him to testify in regard to Villa
and conditions along the border. As so often in a courtroom, he managed to liven the session and bring chuck-
les to the committee members.

What, asked a member in a typical exchange, was
Villa's normal occupation?

"He had a horse and cattle ranch," said Elfego.

"Where did he buy his horses and cattle?" asked the
chairman.

"Where did he buy them?" replied Elfego. "He didn't.
He just sold them."

The Salazar business dragged on, month after month.
Elfego was back in New Mexico, in his own league again.
It was a sad situation. The United States was not treating
Salazar as a general of a neighboring country should be

treated. What had he done that was such a serious offense? He had simply stepped across the border to rest and recuperate before going back to fight some more for his president. And the United States was keeping him locked up without even a formal hearing on the charges against him. American authorities had so confused and tangled him with frequent tricky interrogations that they now had a perjury charge against him too. It looked very much as if they were trying to find some way of keeping him locked up without ever facing the original flimsy charge. That was not a neighborly way to behave.

Elfego went before the federal court in Santa Fe and obtained a writ of habeas corpus. But before that could be put into effect, orders came from Washington to quash the writ and keep Salazar in military custody. That was really going too far.

Rumors began to circulate of plots for a sudden assault across the border from Mexico to snatch the general from his military guardians. He was moved further north for safer keeping and to be on hand if or when the perjury case came to trial. To the Bernalillo County jail in Albuquerque. Well, well. Right into the home territory of his attorney, Elfego Baca.

Not many evenings later, when only the jailer and one guard were on duty at the jail, a telephone call came from a woman in distress. A burglar was trying to break into her house. Without bothering to wonder why she had called the jail instead of the police, the guard gallantly dashed off. He hunted for the address given quite a while before he realized it was fictitious. Meanwhile the jailer was left alone in the guardroom. Not for long. Two masked men joined him, guns in hands, tied him to a chair, and relieved him of his keys. Shortly thereafter they departed and General Salazar went with them. When next heard of, the general was residing again in Mexico.

Argument can still be stirred in Albuquerque over that affair. There is little doubt that the two masked men were temporary visitors from below the border (one of them very likely the redoubtable General Orozco) and that the two men become three took the night train to El Paso and were well on their way by time the escape was discovered. But what keeps argument alive is the interesting coincidence that at almost the precise moment the two were breaking into the jail, Elfego Baca was in a downtown bar asking several respected local citizens the time so he could set his watch which he said had stopped. That turned out to be very helpful when a charge of participation in the break was cited against him.

Sometime later, when Elfego happened to be in El Paso on business, he was accosted by a Celestino Otero, who said he had some private matter to discuss and insisted on a meeting at a certain small café. Elfego drove there in the car and company of a friend named Dr. Romero. When they stopped by the café, they saw Otero and several companions a short distance away coming toward them. As Elfego stepped out of the car and went around it to confront them, Otero whipped out a gun and fired. He was, understandably perhaps, a bit flustered at what he was doing and his bullet only nipped Elfego slightly in the groin. He failed to fire a second and more effective shot for the sufficient reason that by a magic as potent as ever a gun had appeared in Elfego's

hand and two bullets were whipping through Otero's
heart. The companions scattered and Elfego jumped
back in the car. Dr. Romero drove him to the home of a
lawyer friend and checked his wound and Elfego himself
telephoned to the chief of police. He was somewhat annoyed by his wound and the whole business. "Come your-
self," he said. "If you send some cop who tries to get
rough with me, you know what'll happen to him." The
chief came.

Once again Elfego was on trial for a killing. That
someone, for himself or for hire, should shoot at Elfego
was not in itself surprising. It had happened often
before. Quite a few people carried real or fancied griev-
ances against him, dating particularly from the times he
had worn a badge. But this case had an interesting angle.
Those who had long been hoping to see him collide with
the law in some final form had a fine time convicting
him of sinister doings in their conversations.

One of the rumors following the Salazar affair had
been that the runaway trio had hid out after the break at
the so-called ranch of this same Celestino Otero. Was it
not obvious now that Elfego had engineered the whole
thing, then had quarreled with Otero over payment for
his part in it, and had framed this killing to prevent
Otero from talking?

But when the evidence was all in, the El Paso jury
promptly acquitted him.

Oh, well, ran a postscript to the tale, no one in his
right mind would ever expect Elfego Baca to be convicted of anything by one of those "Mexican" juries.

But the final postscript is that there was not a "Mexican" among the jurors. They were all Anglos. They lis-

tened to the evidence and were out less than five
minutes, just long enough to take a single oral poll.

Elfego was into his fifties now, mustachioed, plump,
even portly, somewhat more deliberate in manner, but
not slowed in any of the essentials in any way in the
slightest. He had not forgotten his early ambition. In 1919
he ran for sheriff, the most important position in Socorro
County. Naturally he was elected.

One of his first moves was to assemble all outstanding
warrants in the sheriff's office and those just recently
handed down by the grand jury and dispatch notes to the
men wanted telling them to come in and give themselves
up or he, Elfego Baca, would suspect intentions of resisting arrest and go after them with his own intention of
shooting on sight. The virtually unanimous response,
even from men who had carefully nurtured reputations
for toughness and nose-thumbing at the law, surprised
some people — but not Elfego himself. He knew, as did
the recipients of the notes, that he meant precisely what
he wrote. They came in, one after another, usually
shuffle-footed and shamefaced and grinning. *Hello, Elfego; I got your note and here I am.* One man sent a
return missive, very impolite, inviting him to make good
on his threat and be at a certain place at a certain time.
Elfego buckled on a gun and went to the place at the
time. The man was not there. When Elfego returned to
the office, the man was waiting for him. *Shucks, Elfego,
that was just a joke, just whisky talking in me.*

Once, to his disgust, there was a break from his own

jail. One of a pair of young hardcases who had been shar-
ing a cell while waiting trial, got himself promoted by
the jailer, while Elfego was away for a few days, to temporary cook — and took the opportunity to ease out the
kitchen door and away. Elfego pondered the problem for
a while. To go after the escapee would take time and be
a nuisance and to bring him back a corpse as could very
well happen would not properly balance the fact of escape. He was only a young one anyway, not yet convicted
of anything, only charged.

Elfego summoned the other young hardcase from the
cell, took him out to a good dinner, gave him a deputy's
badge, a gun, a pair of handcuffs, and seventy-five dollars
in cash. Go find your friend, he said, who will think you
got away too and not take to shooting and if you slap
these handcuffs on him and bring him back, it will help
you with the judge at the trial.

Days passed and Elfego began to worry. He was being
kidded by his friends in Socorro, told he had developed
softening of the brain. What if the two young men had
simply joined forces and skipped off together? He, Elfego
Baca, would be laughed at and have to take it because he
would deserve it and he would have to go after the two
and bring them back, alive or dead, and then do the only
decent thing, resign as sheriff. But at the end of a long
week he received a long telegram, collect, which cost him
$8.75 to obtain and read. It told in fulsome detail how
the second young hardcase had found the first and
achieved the feat of getting the handcuffs on him and
now would like to know what to do with him.

Elfego sat down and composed his own telegram, using exactly the ten words the minimum rate would

cover: "Kiss him twice and bring him in you damn fool."

This was the same Elfego who, as county clerk, had known what a difficult time many of his own people had scraping up the money for the filing fees on deeds and mortgages and bills of sale and even though his own pay was contingent upon those fees had regularly declared January and February as special months during which no fees would be charged. Now, as sheriff, he was annoyed at a new law enacted by the legislature imposing jail sentences on debtors until their debts were paid. Here was his jail cluttered up with poor people whose crimes consisted of failure to pay some paltry amounts. And how was a man to pay a debt while cooped up in a jail? He unlocked the doors and shooed the debtors out and told them to get busy and earn some money and pay their debts. When the district attorney objected, he patiently explained that they ate too much and ran up the county bills — and, anyway, if any of them were brought back he would not let them in his jail. The law was repealed at the next session of the legislature.

On the other hand, when the county wanted to build, say, a new garage, Elfego could show uncanny ability at rounding up lawbreakers who happened to have some skill as bricklayers, carpenters, mechanics. It did them no harm to be working for the county for nothing for a while. They got room and board. They kept in practice at their trades. And they saved the taxpayers money.

That is the way those for him liked and still like best to remember Elfego Baca, as sheriff of Socorro County, a plump, still stalwart jovial man of fifty-five, full of zest for living, still quite ready to walk into any situation and talk with tongue or fists or guns as need might be. He had achieved the ambition worked out for himself while waiting trial for the Frisco affair. Though there were people who might say the accent should be on the adjective instead of the noun, he was a criminal lawyer all right, well known to the New Mexican courts. Though his methods and procedures were unorthodox, he was an A No. 1 peace officer. And there was no doubt whatsoever that outlaws heard his steps a block away from him. Considerably more than a block. They could hear them in words on pieces of paper carried across many miles.

He was of an age now when he could have been expected to slow down, to coast along on past exploits and present reputation. Not Elfego. He did not know how to slow down. He always operated under a full head of steam. He went right on providing material for more tales, for and against.

When Albert B. Fall, whose own career in New Mexican politics was and remains a subject for controversy, became Secretary of the Interior in the Harding administration, he found on his desk in Washington continuing complaints that the Piute Indians of southern Utah had an apparently incurable habit of running off stock from nearby ranches and then of being very inhospitable to officers who tried to pursue them. There seemed to be no Federal officers left in the region who cared to tackle the problem. Secretary Fall considered it briefly, remembered a plump now-approaching-sixty "Mexican" back in his home state, asked him to take the matter in hand, and went on to other matters serenely confident he could forget that one. He could. Elfego hooked an old familiar badge of a deputy United States marshal to his left sus-

pender, dropped a pair of old familiar guns into a small
bag, and headed into southern Utah. Soon there was
peace in the Piute country . . .

When the New Mexican Cattle Growers' Association
held its convention in the town of Magdalena, smack in
the middle of that same cattle country in which Elfego
years before had interesting experiences at Frisco and at
Kelly, he was invited to be one of the speakers. He never
missed a chance to make a speech. He spoke and his au-
dience as usual enjoyed his drawling tone and dry
humor. At the close of the convention the town gave a
grand ball in honor of the assembled guests. Dancing was
not one of Elfego's accomplishments, but he had been
invited and he attended as a spectator. Interesting things
began to happen. A young cowboy, nerved to it by liquor, tried to pick a quarrel with him and went for his
gun. He was just a young one; Elfego simply beat him to
the draw, not with a gun, but with a fist to the jaw. Then
an older man of the Texan variety known to New Mexicans as Texicans, that is to say as men who worked at
being Texans, this one named Saunders and with three
supposed notches on his gun, tried the same thing. He
was suddenly discouraged when, his own gun half drawn,
the barrel of Elfego's was being poked in his ribs. Elfego
disarmed him, whirled him about, and sent him sprawling with a vigorous kick. Then, in disgust at such rude
happenings on what should be a festive occasion, Elfego
retired to his hotel room.

The proprietor soon brought news that Saunders was
armed again and he and companions were at a nearby
bar, vowing vengeance. By now Elfego was convinced
there was a plot afoot to take advantage of his presence
in Magdalena and try to kill him.

If there was one rule running through the whole of Elfego Baca's life, it was this: when trouble is looking for you, don't wait for it; go find it — and finish it. He buckled on both guns (out of politeness he had simply had one in his belt at the dance) and went straight to the saloon where Saunders and companions were absorbing liquid courage. He stepped in and faced them down without even drawing a gun. And then again the final, the perfect touch.

He ordered drinks for everyone in the place. He drew a gun and laid it on the end of the bar and stood by it, fingering it with amiable carelessness, watching to see that acceptance of the drinks was unanimous. While they were being gulped, he talked with amiable sarcasm. He was a wild Texas cowboy, he was. None of those "damned Mexicans" for him. No. Nothing but fine Texas cowboys like himself. And now, how about another round? He was a wild Texas cowboy, he was, wild and woolly and full of fleas and he liked to see all those like him drink good liquor. And surely, now that the second round of drinks had been downed, the bartender didn't expect a rooting tooting Texas cowboy like him to pay for them? They were on the house, weren't they? The bartender thought this over and decided that yes, he thought they were. Elfego marched out and to the next saloon and repeated the performance. And to the next and until he had covered all in town. . . .

When the once famous Tivoli was at the height of its fame just across the Rio Grande in Juárez, Elfego was for a time what he himself cheerfully called its chief bouncer. Despite the informality of the title, the position was quite in keeping with his dignity and reputation. The Tivoli, with Mexican clientele right at hand and with American clientele coming regularly in droves across the international bridge, was the largest and most popular gambling casino of the period in all of North America. Elfego had fourteen men on his "police" force and the protection of the place and its customers under his care. His personal duties were light. He kept an eye on the dealers to see that they had proper respect for the money passing through their hands and he superintended the daily payoff of all employees. He was paid a princely salary plus room and board and an automobile with a chauffeur was at his disposal.

His duties were light. But he was not being paid for them. He was being paid simply for being there.

The Tivoli operation was a big one with large sums of money involved. With discouraging regularity a prominent citizen of the Juárez underworld known as Numero Ocho had been leading his gang in raids at the height of gambling activities and making off with much of that money. The consistent failure of the regular Juárez police to do anything effective about this had led to the suspicion they were either in league with him or afraid of him. The owners of the Tivoli had sent for Elfego Baca.

Here again Elfego applied his rule with typical promptness. He strapped on those old familiar guns and went forth and hunted through the worst haunts of Juárez until he located Numero Ocho and some of his gang in their cellar hangout. He walked straight in and invited Numero Ocho to try to make good on his reported threats of what he would do to this fat old has-been of an ex-sheriff from up Socorro way. When it was obvious that Numero Ocho, like so many others before him, had no real desire to test whether the Baca magic with guns was as potent as ever, Elfego stepped up to him and with open palms started to slap him silly. As Numero Ocho scrambled for a back exit, Elfego assisted him on his way with impetus from a hefty boot sole. Elfego spoke a few words to the others remaining and returned to his light duties at the Tivoli.

There were no raids, not even attempted raids, while he was chief bouncer.

There were occasions when disappointed customers became noisy and/or obstreperous and had to be escorted outside. The Tivoli was proud of its quiet restrained atmosphere and disapproved of upsetting uproar. There were pleasant incidents too. When the Chicago Grand Opera Company was playing in El Paso, the famous Mary Garden and others of the company came across the bridge to the Tivoli. Mary Garden had luck at one of the tables and squealed in operatic appreciation and her party became somewhat noisy. Elfego had to warn her that winning was all right but excessive noise was not.

"I am Mary Garden," said the opera star with confidence in the power of the name.

"I am Elfego Baca," said Elfego with equal confidence.

Very likely neither of them had ever heard of the other before, but they were in some respects two of a kind. The result was that Elfego was Mary Garden's escort all the rest of the day and took her riding in his chauffeured car to show her the sights of Juárez. In return she gave him a ticket to *Carmen*. He went, but he did not like it much. "All that hollering around," he said. "I like the Mexican string bands better."

There were no raids on the Tivoli while Elfego was there. But one evening a young man raised a rumpus and Elfego promptly jugged him. The young man hap-

pened to be the son of the Juárez chief of police. In the
very nature of things in such a community Elfego's use-
fulness in Juárez was ended. He resigned and returned
to New Mexico. But his personal record was intact. . . .

In the later years as the frontier and frontier conditions faded even in New Mexico and humdrum business
began to replace more colorful and more romantic activities, Elfego moved to Albuquerque. He was even more
portly than before and his jowels were settling down by
his chin to give him the look of an elderly bulldog, but
his eyes were as bright and keen as ever. He promptly
acquired a political job to help on finances while he established his law business in new quarters.

Not long after the move he became annoyed at the
rough manner in which an Albuquerque policeman was
arresting a native acquaintance of his and he whopped
the policeman over the head with the big silver watch on
one end of the chain that usually adorned his vest. That
was bad for the watch and just as bad for the policeman
and Elfego had to put in an appearance at the Albuquerque night court, which was located in the newer more
respectable part of town. Ten dollars and costs, said the
judge, or thirty days in jail. With unprecedented meek-
ness Elfego said he would take the thirty days. A constable
was pulled out of a poker game to escort him to the jail
in the Old Town section and he was turned over to a
rather astonished guard there. It just so happened that
Elfego's new job, unknown to the judge and the constable, was that of jailer. As soon as the constable had
hurried away to get back to his poker game, Elfego took
charge, dutifully entered his own name as a prisoner,
then released himself on his own recognizance. For the

next thirty days he went about as usual — and collected the daily stipend allowed him as jailer for himself as prisoner. The amount neatly covered the cost of a new watch. A change of locale had not changed Elfego Baca.

One day he stopped a fellow lawyer on the street to ask him if such and such procedure in a certain case would be ethical for an attorney. No. Not at all. But could a private detective do it? Well, yes, it might be all right for a detective. Elfego produced his card. On one side it read: *Elfego Baca, Attorney at Law.* On the other: *Elfego Baca, Private Detective.* He moved on, triumphant. He would follow the procedure, but not in his capacity as a lawyer, in his capacity as a detective.

Nothing would ever change Elfego Baca.

As the years wore on there were people who were proud that nothing could change him. He was something indestructible out of the past with the flavor of the old days always with him. He was still as ready to swing a solid fist at a man who irritated him as to kiss a buxom woman who pleased him. He still expressed his opinion of what he regarded as an unjust decision at a prize fight by climbing through the ropes and bopping the referee on the nose. He drove a car exactly as he did everything else. Other cars scattered when his came in sight. Once, roaring up to Santa Fe, he careened off what was generously known as the highway and the car spun over three times and came to rest on its top and he was seen to climb out unhurt and give it a good kick and shake his fist at it.

He owned a small building in Albuquerque, given him by Senator Bronson Cutting, on the corner of Sixth and Gold Streets and conducted his law business from an office on the second floor. He was well into his seventies,

but he could still upset the courts, injecting sudden human warmth into cold legal proceedings. He still handled a few important cases for Anglo clients and many
important-to-them cases for the poor of his own people.
He could still, when a Rio Grande water bill, vital to
New Mexico, was stalled in the Senate, go to Washington
and breeze past the battery of secretaries who were keeping everyone else unofficial away from the august majority
leader himself, Senator Curtis, and talk of the old days in
Kansas — and put across the necessity of knocking that
bill loose and pushing it through.

Bernalillo County was not Socorro County. When he
wanted to run for district judge of Bernalillo County, his
own party rebuffed him. Too old. Too old-fashioned.
That was no way to treat Elfego Baca. He ran anyway as
an independent and staged a last-minute campaign with
echoes of the oldtime vigor and did precisely what he
intended to do — split the party and let the Democrats
win.

In 1940 came the Coronado Cuarto Centennial celebrating the four hundredth anniversary of the conquista-
dor's historic march into New Mexico. At the big ban-
quet in Albuquerque commemorating the event learned
scholars and historians spoke as they usually speak and
the evening droned on in dullness. Then Elfego Baca
rose to speak. Big old head of a bulldog wagging, eyes
beaming through glasses, face wrinkles crinkling with humor, dry drawling tone twisting his shaggy mustache, he
told tale after tale out of the old days — and the evening
livened into memorable enjoyment and there were those
who said they saw the stern face of Coronado himself in
the portrait on the wall soften in proud approval.

*

A man who should have known better was making a nuisance of himself claiming that Elfego owed him $500, a supposed debt which Elfego did not regard as legitimate. The man came up to him on the street one day and asked pointblank what he, Elfego Baca, would do if someone owed him money and refused to pay. "I'd sue the son of a gun," said old Elfego promptly and cheerfully. A few days later he was served notice of a suit against him for $500. He sat down at his desk and wrote out a bill and dropped around to serve it on the man in person. $500 for legal advice given and taken.

Nothing but death would ever stop him.

In the summer of 1945 an era in New Mexico ended. The first atomic bomb was successfully tested in that portion of the Tularosa Desert appropriately known as La Jornada del Muerto. And in August the Albuquerque *Tribune* carried a two-column head:

ELFEGO BACA, OLD FRONTIER LINK,
GUN FIGHT HERO, DIES HERE AT 80